Better Homes and Gardens®

fresh grilling

200 DELICIOUS GOOD-FOR-YOU SEASONAL RECIPES

SALINE DISTRICT LIBRARY
555 N. Maple Road
Saline, MI 48176

HOUGHTON MIFFLIN HARCOURT
BOSTON ○ NEW YORK ○ 2014

Better Homes and Gardens® *Fresh Grilling*

Editor: Jan Miller

Project Editor: Tricia Bergman, Waterbury Publications, Inc.

Project Writer: Lisa Kingsley, Waterbury Publications, Inc.

Recipe Testing: Better Homes and Gardens® Test Kitchen

Better Homes and Gardens® Test Kitchen Product Supervisor: Juliana Hale

Contributing Photographers: Karla Conrad, Jason Donnelly

Contributing Stylists: Main Dish Media, Sue Mitchell, Jennifer Peterson, Charles Worthington

Houghton Mifflin Harcourt

Publisher: Natalie Chapman

Editorial Director: Cindy Kitchel

Executive Editor: Anne Ficklen

Senior Editor: Adam Kowit

Editorial Assistant: Molly Aronica

Managing Editor: Marina Padakis

Production Editor: Jacqueline Beach

Production Director: Tom Hyland

Design Director: Ken Carlson, Waterbury Publications, Inc.

Associate Design Director: Doug Samuelson, Waterbury Publications, Inc.

Production Assistant: Mindy Samuelson, Waterbury Publications, Inc.

Our seal assures you that every recipe in *Better Homes and Gardens® Fresh Grilling* has been tested in the Better Homes and Gardens® Test Kitchen. This means that each recipe is practical and reliable and meets our high standards of taste appeal. We guarantee your satisfaction with this book for as long as you own it.

For information about permission to reproduce selections from this book, write to Permissions, Houghton Mifflin Harcourt Publishing Company, 215 Park Avenue South, New York, New York 10003

www.hmhco.com

Library of Congress Cataloging-in-Publication Data
Fresh grilling : 200 delicious good-for-you seasonal recipes / Better Homes and Gardens.
pages cm
Includes index.
ISBN 978-0-544-24219-7 (paperback); ISBN 978-0-544-24544-0 (ebk)
1. Barbecuing. I. Better Homes and Gardens.
TX840.B3F745 2014
641.7'6—dc23
2013045023

Book design by Waterbury Publications, Inc., Des Moines, Iowa.
Cover Photograph: Grilled Flank Steak Salad, page 66

DOW 10 9 8 7 6 5 4 3 2 1

4500464838

Printed in the United States of America

contents

garden-fresh grilling

IT'S THE EVOLUTION OF GRILLING: WHAT STARTED AS THE ANCIENT PRACTICE OF COOKING A PIECE OF MEAT, FISH OR GAME OVER A FLAME GETS FAR MORE INTERESTING WITH THE ADDITION OF A FRESH ELEMENT—SEASONAL FRUITS AND VEGETABLES THAT BRING FRESHNESS, FLAVOR, AND NUTRITION TO THIS POPULAR COOKING METHOD.

More and more, it seems, we want to eat our vegetables. The proliferation of home gardens, farmer's markets and CSAs (Community Supported Agriculture) both supports and is proof of a growing interest in the healthfulness and variety of the foods we eat. No longer relegated to side-dish status, fresh vegetables and fruits now more readily take center stage or are given equal weight to the meats, poultry and fish on our plates. The days of steaming or boiling being the only options for cooking fresh vegetables are long past. Flame-kissed fruits and veggies are extraordinarily flavorful—and beautiful too.

Every recipe in Better Homes and Gardens® *Fresh Grilling* features fresh produce in some form—and in a variety of preparations, from classic American (Southern Spiced Flat Iron Steaks with Grilled Green Tomatoes, page 59) to flavors from around the world (Piri Piri Scallops with Spinach-Pineapple Salad, page 117). There are recipes for any occasion, from a quick fork-free weeknight dinner (Muenster, Cabbage, and Apple Sandwiches, page 158) to elegant appetizers (Grilled Artichoke Hearts with Grilled Sweet Onion and Lemon Aïoli, page 40) and desserts (Grilled Strawberries with Sweet Corn Shortcakes and Limoncello Whipped Cream, page 250) perfect for entertaining.

Special features of *Fresh Grilling* include a Grilling Basics section (starts on page 9) that covers equipment needs and grilling methods. On-page tips included with recipes provide information on ingredients, preparation, and grilling timings and methods. A series called 6 Fresh Ideas inspires with quick-hit uses for some of the most popular and prolific produce, including tomatoes, zucchini and summer squash, strawberries, and sweet peppers. And before you even start cooking, check out the Produce Guide that starts on page 269 for information on choosing, storing and preparing fresh fruits and vegetables, from Apples to Zucchini.

With a grill and some gorgeous fresh produce, a delicious dinner is just a few flame-licks away. Enjoy!

at a glance

The recipes in this book feature icons to help you find something healthy or quick—or both.

The following icons indicate a recipe meets the following criteria:

LOW CALORIE Appetizers 200 calories or less per serving; Main Dishes 500 calories or less per serving; Salads and Sides 150 calories or less per serving; Desserts 300 calories or less per serving.

WEEKDAY FRIENDLY Recipe is 30 minutes or less from start to finish.

grilling basics

COOKING FOOD OVER AN OPEN FLAME MAY BE THE MOST PRIMITIVE WAY TO MAKE DINNER, BUT THERE ARE A FEW THINGS YOU NEED TO KNOW ABOUT MODERN GRILLING BEFORE YOU EMBARK ON IT. HERE ARE THE FUNDAMENTALS OF EQUIPMENT, FUEL, AND COOKING TECHNIQUES.

grill types

THE KIND OF GRILL YOU BUY WILL DEPEND ON YOUR PERSONALITY, YOUR LIFESTYLE, AND YOUR COOKING STYLE—WHETHER YOUR DAYS ARE RELAXED OR BUSY, AND WHETHER YOU WANT EVERYTHING AS STREAMLINED AS POSSIBLE OR IF YOU DON'T MIND SOME EXTRA STEPS. HERE'S A QUICK LOOK AT THE TWO BASIC TYPES OF GRILL.

CHARCOAL GRILLS

The fuel for this most basic type of grill is charcoal. They generally have a round or square box construction with a charcoal grate that holds hot coals on the bottom and a grill rack above. Most models feature vents on the bottom and the lid to control temperature.

The most common type of charcoal grill is the kettle grill, which features a deep, rounded bowl and lid that is ideal for barbecuing and smoking. The temperature is controlled by

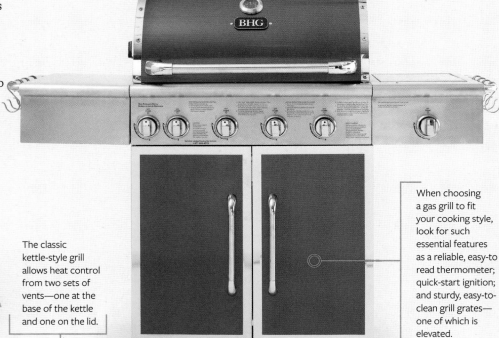

The classic kettle-style grill allows heat control from two sets of vents—one at the base of the kettle and one on the lid.

When choosing a gas grill to fit your cooking style, look for such essential features as a reliable, easy-to-read thermometer; quick-start ignition; and sturdy, easy-to-clean grill grates—one of which is elevated.

manipulating vents on the top and bottom. For a portable option, consider a hibachi. This grill consists of a small firebox with one or two grill racks. Use it for direct-cooking small cuts of meat.

GAS GRILLS

Fueled by propane tanks or a natural-gas hookup, this type of grill is a convenient alternative to a charcoal grill. Gas grills have a metal box lined with liquid-propane burners on the bottom. The burners are topped by a heating surface of metal bars, lava rocks, or ceramic briquettes that disperse heat throughout the grill. The smoky aroma and flavor of grilling is generated as drippings from food fall onto the hot bars or stones.

KEEP IT CLEAN

Retain your new grill's sparkly clean exterior and keep it ready to use by investing in an inexpensive grill cover. Put the cover on the grill as soon as the grill has cooled after each time you use it.

THERE'S MORE THAN ONE WAY TO MAKE A FIRE. FIND THE FUEL THAT BURNS BEST FOR YOU.

NATURAL BRIQUETTES

These are made from pulverized lump charcoal held together with natural starches instead of the synthetic binders used in composition briquettes.

COMPOSITION BRIQUETTES

Made from burned wood and scraps, coal dust, camphor, and paraffin or petroleum binders, these briquettes can give food an unpleasant taste. Use a quality brand if you do use them; inexpensive brands can give you less-than-satisfactory results.

CHARWOOD OR LUMP CHARCOAL

The fuel choice of chefs and professional grillers, lump charcoal is formed from hardwoods such as maple, oak, and hickory that have been burned down at very high temperatures. It lights more quickly and burns cleaner and hotter than briquettes. It does not contain additives or petroleum and imparts some natural flavor to foods. Downsides include occasional sparking, limited availability, and a higher cost than alternatives.

WOOD

The first fire built by humans was fueled by natural wood, and it continues to be the best choice for delivering intense heat, a long burn, and producing great smoky flavor. Natural woods, such as hickory, oak, and fruit-tree wood, are available in chips and chunks.

CHIMNEY STARTER

This method of lighting coals involves placing charcoal or wood chunks on a grate in the middle of a cylindrical steel pipe. Crumpled newspapers or paraffin starters are placed in the bottom and lit.

temperature control

THERE ARE TWO METHODS OF COOKING ON A GRILL: USING DIRECT HEAT OR INDIRECT HEAT. WHICHEVER YOU USE, THE GRILL TEMPERATURE HAS TO BE MONITORED FOR BEST RESULTS. THAT MAY BE SIMPLER ON A GAS GRILL—JUST CHECK THE THERMOMETER AND TEMPERATURE GAUGE—BUT IT CAN BE DONE ON A CHARCOAL GRILL AS WELL.

DIRECT AND INDIRECT GRILLING

Direct grilling is the method of placing food on the grill rack directly over the heat source. This can be done with the lid on or off—check the manufacturer's directions to be sure. Direct grilling is the best method for tender, thin, or smaller quick-cooking foods that generally cook in less than 30 minutes. This includes burgers, steaks, chops, chicken pieces, and vegetables. For even cooking, you usually need to turn the food just once during grilling time.

To set up a two-burner gas grill for direct grilling, set one burner on high for searing, and one burner on medium for finishing grilling. To set up a three- or four-burner gas grill, set one burner on high and one or two burners on medium. Leave the remaining burner off.

Indirect grilling is ideal for larger foods, such as roasts or turkeys, that take longer to cook. This low, slow grilling method positions food on the rack away from, or to the side of, the heat source with the grill cover closed. It allows them to cook through without burning. Similar to roasting in an oven, heat inside the grill reflects off the interior surfaces, cooking the food from all sides. There is no need to turn the food.

To set up a two-burner gas grill for indirect grilling, set one burner on high and cook the food over the unlit burner. For a three-burner grill, turn on the front and rear or outside burners and cook the food in the center. For a four-burner, turn on the outside burners.

ADJUST THE COALS

To lower the temperature in the grill, spread the coals farther apart. To make the fire more intense, gently tap the coals with long-handled tongs to remove loose ash and pile them closer together.

ADJUST THE VENTS

The flow of oxygen inside the grill determines the temperature—the more air, the higher the heat, and vice versa. To increase the heat, open the vents. To decrease it, partially close them.

ADJUST THE RACK HEIGHT

Some grills have adjustable grill racks. Use low levels to sear food and high levels for slow cooking. For medium heat, place the grate about 4 inches from the fire.

HAND CHECK

Coals are ready for cooking when they are covered with ash. To check the temperature, use a built-in or separate flat grill thermometer. Or, you can use the method many chefs use: Place the palm of your hand 2 to 3 inches above the grill rack and count the number of seconds you can hold it there. The chart below will help you determine the temperature.

HAND-CHECK METHOD

TIME	THERMOMETER	TEMPERATURE
2 seconds	400°F to 450°F	Hot (high)
3 seconds	375°F to 400°F	Medium-high
4 seconds	350°F to 375°F	Medium
5 seconds	325°F to 350°F	Medium-low
6 seconds	300°F to 325°F	Low

DIRECT AND INDIRECT GRILLING SETUPS FOR A CHARCOAL GRILL

To set up a charcoal grill for the direct grilling method, spread the hot coals evenly over the bottom of the charcoal grate. No matter where the food is placed on the cooking grate, it will be directly above the heat source. The most common way to set up a charcoal grill for indirect grilling is to set the coals to the side next to a drip pan over which to place the food (below, left). You can also set up a ring of fire and place the food in the center (below, middle). The reverse is the bull's-eye, which creates a small area of direct heat in the center, with a perimeter of indirect heat (below, right).

grilled vegetables & fruits

THE RECIPES IN THIS BOOK INCLUDE INSTRUCTIONS FOR GRILLING THE FEATURED FRUIT OR VEGETABLE, BUT FOR QUICK REFERENCE OR FOR USE IN OTHER RECIPES—OR SIMPLY AS A QUICK SIDE DISH—HERE'S HOW TO GRILL SOME OF THE MOST COMMON FRUITS AND VEGETABLES. TO COOK THEM EVENLY WITHOUT CHARRING, KEEP THE HEAT AT MEDIUM—YOU'LL BE ABLE TO HOLD YOUR HAND ABOVE THE HEAT FOR 4 SECONDS BEFORE PULLING AWAY.

ASPARAGUS
PREP: Snap off and discard tough, woody base from the stems.
PRECOOK: No
GRILL DIRECTLY: 7 to 10 minutes over medium heat or until tender. Grill perpendicular to grill rack so they do not fall through or use a grill basket.

CHERRY TOMATOES
PREP: Thread tomatoes on wooden skewers that have been soaked, leaving a ¼-inch space between pieces.
PRECOOK: No
GRILL DIRECTLY: 3 to 5 minutes over medium or until tomatoes have softened, turning once.

EGGPLANT
PREP: Cut off tops. If smaller size, cut lengthwise; if larger cut crosswise into 1-inch slices.
PRECOOK: No
GRILL DIRECTLY: 8 to 10 minutes over medium heat or until tender.

FENNEL
PREP: Remove fronds. Trim and quarter fennel bulb.
PRECOOK: No
GRILL DIRECTLY: 11 to 14 minutes or until tender.

MANGOES
PREP: Halve, seed, and peel mango.
PRECOOK: No
GRILL DIRECTLY: 6 to 8 minutes over medium heat or until tender, turning once.

NEW POTATOES
PREP: Halve potatoes.
PRECOOK: Bring water to boiling in a saucepan; add potatoes. Simmer, covered, for 10 minutes or until nearly tender. Drain well.
GRILL DIRECTLY: 10 to 12 minutes over medium heat on grill rack or until tender, or use a grill basket.

CORN

PREP: Peel back husks and remove silks. Replace husks around corn. Place corn with husks in a bowl or pan. Cover with water. Soak for 1 hour; drain. Tie husks at the top with strips of husks or 100-percent cotton kitchen string. Remove husk strip or string and pull husks down to serve.

PRECOOK: No

GRILL DIRECTLY: 25 to 30 minutes over medium heat.

DRIP PAN

GRILL BASKET

Grill baskets and woks come in handy when you don't want to risk losing one precious piece through the grates of your grill. Perforated baskets with low sides are available in various sizes and shapes, making it easy to flip and turn ingredients. Before cooking in the grill basket, toss veggies in oil. Grill veggies, covered, checking for doneness every 5 minutes.

GREEN BEANS

PREP: Trim green beans.
PRECOOK: Bring water to boiling in a saucepan. Add green beans; blanch for 3 minutes. Transfer to a bowl of ice water to cool for 5 minutes. Dry on paper towels
GRILL DIRECTLY: Preheat grill basket for 5 minutes over medium heat. Toss beans with olive oil; add to basket and grill 8 minutes or until tender.

ONION
PREP: Peel and cut crosswise into 1-inch slices.
PRECOOK: No
GRILL DIRECTLY: 10 minutes over medium heat or until tender.

PEACHES
PREP: Halve and pit ripe peaches.
PRECOOK: No
GRILL DIRECTLY: 8 to 10 minutes or until tender.

PINEAPPLE
PREP: Cut ½-inch slices of fresh pineapple.
PRECOOK: No
GRILL DIRECTLY: 6 to 8 minutes over medium heat or until lightly browned, turning once.

RADISHES
PREP: Scrub and trim radishes. Brush with olive oil.
PRECOOK: No
GRILL DIRECTLY: Preheat grill basket 5 minutes over medium heat. Add radishes; grill 8 to 10 minutes or until tender and lightly browned, turning once.

ROMAINE LETTUCE
PREP: Wash lettuce and dry as much as possible. Cut lettuce in half lengthwise.
PRECOOK: No
GRILL DIRECTLY: 2 to 4 minutes over medium heat until tender and grill marks appear.

STRAWBERRIES
PREP: Hull strawberries. Thread on soaked wooden skewers, leaving a ¼-inch space between pieces.
PRECOOK: No
GRILL DIRECTLY: 3 to 5 minutes over medium heat or until lightly browned, turning once.

ZUCCHINI AND SUMMER SQUASH
PREP: Wash and slice lengthwise.
PRECOOK: No
GRILL DIRECTLY: 5 to 6 minutes over medium heat or until tender.

BABY SWEET PEPPERS
PREP: None
PRECOOK: No
GRILL DIRECTLY: 6 to 8 minutes over medium heat or until tender.

TOMATILLOS
PREP: Husks removed and rinsed.
PRECOOK: No
GRILL DIRECTLY: 8 to 10 minutes or until softened.

Grilled Cucumber Salsa, *recipe page 23*

sauces, salsas, marinades & rubs

THE FLAVOR IMPARTED TO FOODS BY THE SMOKE AND FIRE OF THE GRILL GETS A BOOST FROM THESE MARVELOUS MÉLANGES THAT COME IN BOTH LIQUID AND DRY FORM.

Grilled Sweet Cherry Tare Sauce

sauces

mango-mustard sauce

MAKES: 2 CUPS (ABOUT SIXTEEN 2-TABLE-SPOON SERVINGS)

- 1 slice bacon, finely chopped
- 1 tablespoon vegetable oil
- 1 cup chopped onion (1 large)
- 1 large fresh jalapeño chile pepper, stemmed, seeded, and finely chopped (see tip, right)
- 1 cup mango chutney
- 1 cup white wine vinegar
- ⅔ cup coarse ground mustard
- ⅓ cup cold strong brewed coffee
- ½ teaspoon salt
- ½ teaspoon ground black pepper

1. In a large skillet cook bacon in hot oil for 3 minutes. Add onion and chile pepper. Cook and stir about 5 minutes or until bacon is crisp and onion is soft and tender.

2. Snip large pieces of chutney. Stir chutney, vinegar, mustard, coffee, salt, and black pepper into bacon mixture. Bring to boiling; reduce heat. Simmer, uncovered, for 10 minutes or until thickened. Serve with pork or poultry.

grilled pineapple tare sauce

MAKES: ⅔ CUP (ABOUT TEN 1-TABLESPOON SERVINGS

- 4 ½-inch slices fresh pineapple
- 1 cup sweet rice wine (mirin)
- ½ cup reduced-sodium soy sauce
- 2 medium shallots, minced
- 2 tablespoons packed brown sugar
- 2 tablespoons peeled and grated fresh ginger
- 2 cloves garlic, smashed
- ½ teaspoon crushed red pepper

1. For a gas or charcoal grill, place the pineapple slices on a grill rack directly over medium heat. Cover and grill 4 to 6 minutes or until heated through and lightly browned, turning once.

2. When cool enough to handle, core and coarsely chop pineapple. Place pineapple in a food processor or blender; cover and process or blend until nearly smooth.

3. In a small saucepan combine pineapple puree, mirin, soy sauce, shallots, brown sugar, ginger, garlic, and crushed red pepper. Bring to boiling; reduce heat. Simmer, uncovered, for 25 to 30 minutes or until reduced by half. Strain sauce through a fine-mesh sieve; discard solids. Serve with beef, pork, poultry, fish, or shellfish.

grilled sweet cherry tare sauce

MAKES: ¾ CUP (ABOUT SIX 2-TABLESPOON SERVINGS

- 1 pound fresh dark sweet cherries, stemmed and pitted
- ½ cup ruby port
- 1 tablespoon orange juice
- ¼ cup reduced-sodium soy sauce
- ¼ cup chopped green onions
- 1 tablespoon sugar
- ½ teaspoon finely shredded orange peel
- 1 tablespoon peeled and grated fresh ginger
- 2 cloves garlic, smashed
- ¼ teaspoon ground black pepper

1. Thread cherries on skewers (see tip, page 30), leaving ¼ inch between pieces. For a gas or charcoal grill, place skewers on a grill rack directly over medium heat. Cover and grill 5 to 8 minutes or until cherries have softened, turning occasionally.

2. Cool cherries slightly. Place in a food processor or blender. Add the port and orange juice to the cherries. Cover and process or blend until nearly smooth. Strain mixture through a fine-mesh sieve, pressing out liquid from cherry pulp. Discard pulp.

3. In a small saucepan combine strained cherry juice mixture, soy sauce, green onions, sugar, orange peel, ginger, garlic, and pepper. Bring to boiling; reduce heat. Simmer, uncovered, for 20 to 25 minutes or until reduced to 1 cup, stirring occasionally. Strain sauce through a fine-mesh sieve; discard solids. Serve with poultry or pork.

HOT TIP

Because chile peppers contain volatile oils that can burn your skin and eyes, avoid direct contact with them as much as possible. When working with chile peppers, wear plastic or rubber gloves. If your bare hands do touch the peppers, wash your hands and nails well with soap and warm water.

Grilled Plum Salsa

salsas

grilled cucumber salsa
MAKES: 3 CUPS (ABOUT TWELVE ¼-CUP SERVINGS)

- 2 medium cucumbers, halved lengthwise and seeded (12 ounces each)
- 1 medium fresh jalapeño chile pepper, halved and seeded (see tip, page 21)
- 1 roma tomato, seeded and chopped (¼ cup)
- 2 tablespoons chopped green onions
- 1 tablespoon snipped fresh cilantro
- ½ teaspoon finely shredded lime peel
- 1 tablespoon lime juice
- 1 clove garlic, minced
- ¼ teaspoon ground cumin
- ¼ teaspoon salt

1. For a gas or charcoal grill, place cucumbers and jalapeño on the rack of a grill directly over medium heat. Cover and grill 6 to 8 minutes for the cucumber and 3 to 4 minutes for the jalapeño or until just lightly charred, turning once.

2. When cool enough to handle, chop cucumbers and jalapeño. In a medium bowl combine cucumber, jalapeño, tomato, green onions, cilantro, lime peel, lime juice, garlic, cumin, and salt. Serve with pork, poultry, fish, or shellfish.

salsa verde
MAKES: 2 CUPS (ABOUT EIGHT ¼-CUP SERVINGS)

- 12 ounces fresh tomatillos, husked (see tip, page 277), or one 13-ounce can tomatillos, rinsed and drained
- ¼ cup snipped fresh cilantro or Italian (flat-leaf) parsley
- 2 tablespoons finely chopped red onion
- 1 fresh serrano or jalapeño chile pepper, seeded and finely chopped (see tip, page 21)
- ¼ teaspoon salt
- ¼ teaspoon sugar

1. Finely chop tomatillos. In a small bowl stir together chopped tomatillos, cilantro, onion, jalapeño, salt, and sugar. Cover; chill for 4 hours to 3 days before serving, stirring occasionally.

2. Serve with pork, poultry, fish, or shellfish.

grilled plum salsa
MAKES: 2¼ CUPS (ABOUT TWELVE 3-TABLESPOON SERVINGS)

- 4 medium plums, (1 to 1¼ pounds) halved and pitted
- 1 ½-inch slice red onion
- 1 tablespoon sesame oil
- ½ teaspoon finely shredded orange peel
- 1 tablespoon orange juice
- 2 teaspoons snipped fresh mint
- 2 teaspoons peeled and grated fresh ginger
- 1 teaspoon honey
- ¼ teaspoon salt
- ⅛ teaspoon ground black pepper

1. Brush plums and onion with oil. For a gas or charcoal grill, place plum halves, cut sides down, on the rack of a grill directly over medium heat. Cover and grill onion for 8 to 10 minutes or until tender and lightly charred, turning once. Grill plums for 4 to 5 minutes or until tender and heated through, turning once.

2. When cool enough to handle, chop plums and onion. In a medium bowl combine plums, onion, orange peel, orange juice, mint, ginger, honey, salt and pepper. Serve with beef, lamb, pork, or poultry.

savory strawberry salsa
MAKES: 3 CUPS (ABOUT TWELVE ¼-CUP SERVINGS)

- 2 cups strawberries, coarsely chopped
- 1 medium avocado, halved, seeded, peeled, chopped
- ½ cup seeded and coarsely chopped cucumber
- 2 tablespoons honey
- 1 teaspoon finely shredded lime peel
- 2 tablespoons lime juice
- 1 to 2 fresh jalapeño chile peppers, seeded and finely chopped (see tip, page 21)
- ¼ teaspoon cracked black pepper

1. In a large bowl combine strawberries, avocados, cucumber, honey, lime peel, lime juice, jalapeño, and black pepper. Cover and chill for 1 hour. Serve with pork, poultry, or fish.

Chipotle-Honey Marinade

marinades

chipotle-honey marinade

MAKES: 1½ CUPS (ENOUGH FOR 3 POUNDS MEAT)

- 1 pound roma tomatoes, halved and seeds removed
  Vegetable oil
- ¼ cup canned chipotle peppers in adobo sauce, undrained
- 2 tablespoons snipped fresh oregano
- 6 cloves garlic, minced
- ¾ cup honey
- ¼ cup molasses
- ¼ cup apple cider vinegar
- 1 tablespoon toasted sesame oil
- 1½ teaspoons ground cumin
- 1 teaspoon salt

1. For a charcoal or gas grill, place tomato halves, cut sides down, on a lightly oiled grill rack directly over medium heat. Cover and grill for 5 to 7 minutes or until skins are charred. Cool until easy to handle. Peel and discard skins.

2. Place undrained chipotle peppers in a food processor or blender. Cover and process until smooth. Add tomatoes, oregano, and garlic. Cover and process until smooth. In a large bowl stir together tomato pureed mixture, honey, molasses, vinegar, sesame oil, cumin, and salt.

3. To use, pour marinade over meat in a resealable plastic bag set in a shallow dish; seal bag. Turn to coat meat. Marinate in the refrigerator for 2 to 6 hours, turning bag occasionally. Drain meat, discarding marinade. Grill as desired.

sage-orange marinade

MAKES: ⅓ CUP (ENOUGH FOR 12 OUNCES PORK, POULTRY, OR FISH)

- 1 teaspoon finely shredded orange peel
- ⅓ cup orange juice
- 2 teaspoons olive oil or vegetable oil
- ¾ teaspoon snipped fresh rosemary or ¼ teaspoon dried rosemary, crushed
- ¾ teaspoon snipped fresh sage or ¼ teaspoon dried sage, crushed
- 1 clove garlic, minced
- ¼ teaspoon salt
- ¼ teaspoon ground black pepper

1. In a small bowl stir together orange peel, orange juice, oil, rosemary, sage, garlic, salt, and pepper.

2. To use, pour marinade over pork, poultry, or fish in a resealable plastic bag set in a shallow dish; seal bag. Turn to coat meat, poultry, or fish. Marinate in refrigerator for 6 to 12 hours, turning once. Drain pork, poultry, or fish, discarding marinade. Grill as desired.

curry-lime marinade

MAKES: ¾ CUP (ENOUGH FOR 1 POUND MEAT OR POULTRY)

- ½ cup plain yogurt
- ¼ cup snipped fresh cilantro
- 1 teaspoon finely shredded lime peel
- 2 tablespoons lime juice
- 2 tablespoons olive oil or vegetable oil
- 1 tablespoon honey
- 1 tablespoon Dijon-style mustard
- 2 cloves garlic, minced
- ½ teaspoon curry powder
- ¼ teaspoon salt
- ¼ teaspoon ground black pepper

1. In small bowl stir together yogurt, cilantro, lime peel, lime juice, oil, honey, mustard, garlic, curry powder, salt, and pepper.

2. To use, pour marinade over lamb, pork, or chicken, in a resealable plastic bag set in a shallow dish; seal bag. Turn to coat meat. Marinate in the refrigerator for 4 to 24 hours, turning bag occasionally. Drain meat or poultry, discarding marinade. Grill as desired.

cilantro-pesto marinade

MAKES: ⅔ CUP (ENOUGH FOR 1 POUND MEAT, POULTRY, OR FISH)

- ½ cup firmly packed fresh cilantro leaves
- ½ small red onion, cut up
- 1 teaspoon finely shredded lime peel
- 2 tablespoons lime juice
- 2 teaspoons Worcestershire sauce
- ¼ teaspoon ground cumin
- ¼ teaspoon dried oregano, crushed

1. In blender or food processor combine cilantro, onion, lime peel, lime juice, Worcestershire sauce, cumin, and oregano. Cover and blend or process with a few pulses just until coarsely chopped.

2. To use, pour marinade over meat, poultry, or fish in a resealable plastic bag set in a shallow dish; seal bag. Turn to coat meat, poultry, or fish. Marinate in refrigerator for 1 hour, turning once. Drain meat, poultry, or fish, discarding marinade. Grill as desired.

Asian Rub

rubs

asian rub

MAKES: ¼ CUP (USE 1-TABLESPOON PER POUND MEAT, POULTRY, OR FISH)

- 1 tablespoon onion powder
- 1½ teaspoons cracked black pepper
- 1½ teaspoons garlic powder
- 1 teaspoon salt
- 1 tablespoon dry mustard
- 1 teaspoon ground ginger
- 1 tablespoon five-spice powder
- 1 tablespoon sesame seeds
- 1 teaspoon crushed red pepper

1. In a small bowl stir together onion powder, black pepper, garlic powder, salt, mustard, ginger, five-spice powder, sesame seeds, and crushed red pepper. To use, spread rub evenly over meat, poultry, or fish. Grill as desired.

smoke and fire rub

MAKES: ¼ CUP (USE 1-TABLESPOON PER POUND MEAT OR POULTRY)

- 1 tablespoon smoked paprika
- 1 tablespoon onion powder
- 1 tablespoon finely snipped dried tomatoes
- 1½ teaspoons cracked black pepper
- 1½ teaspoons garlic powder
- 1 teaspoon salt
- 1 teaspoon chipotle chili flakes or crushed red pepper
  Fresh lime juice

1. In a small bowl combine dry ingredients. To use, spread rub evenly over meat or poultry. Drizzle with a little lime juice. Place poultry in a resealable plastic bag. Refrigerate for 8 hours. Grill as desired.

chicago steakhouse rub

MAKES: ¼ CUP (USE 1-TABLESPOON PER POUND MEAT)

- 1 tablespoon dry mustard
- 2 teaspoons granulated garlic
- 2 teaspoons coarsely ground black pepper
- 1 teaspoon sweet smoked Spanish paprika
- ½ teaspoon dried thyme
- ½ teaspoon cayenne pepper

1. In a small bowl stir together the dry mustard, granulated garlic, black pepper, paprika, dried thyme, and cayenne pepper. To use, salt meat to taste; spread rub evenly over meat. Let stand for 30 minutes at room temperature. Grill as desired.

indian spice rub

MAKES: 9 TABLESPOONS (USE 1-TABLE-SPOON PER POUND MEAT OR POULTRY)

- 1 tablespoon cumin seeds
- 1 tablespoon coriander seeds
- 1 teaspoon mustard seeds
- 1 teaspoon whole black peppercorns
- ½ teaspoon whole cloves
- ¼ teaspoon crushed red pepper or red pepper flakes
- 1 tablespoon ground turmeric
- ½ teaspoon salt

1. Heat a dry medium skillet over medium heat. Add cumin seeds, coriander seeds, mustard seeds, peppercorns, cloves, and crushed red pepper. Toast for 1 to 2 minutes or until the mixture is fragrant, lightly toasted, and starting to crackle, stirring

occasionally. Remove from skillet and let cool for 5 minutes.

2. Transfer spice mixture to a clean spice or coffee grinder. Cover and grind to a powder. In a small bowl combine ground spice mixture, turmeric, and salt. To use, spread rub evenly on meat or poultry. Grill as desired.

herbed pecan rub

MAKES: ½ CUP (USE ABOUT 2½-TABLE-SPOONS PER POUND POULTRY OR FISH)

- ½ cup broken pecans
- ½ cup fresh oregano leaves
- ½ cup fresh thyme leaves
- 3 cloves garlic, cut up
- ½ teaspoon ground black pepper
- ½ teaspoon finely shredded lemon peel
- ¼ teaspoon salt
- ¼ cup cooking oil

1. In blender or food processor combine pecans, oregano, thyme, garlic, pepper, lemon peel, and salt. Cover and blend with several on-off turns until a paste forms, stopping several times to scrape down the sides.

2. With the machine running, gradually add oil through hole in lid, blending until mixture forms a paste. To use, spread rub evenly over poultry or fish. Grill as desired.

Cantaloupe-Grapefruit Agua Fresca, *recipe on page 48*

appetizers & beverages

WHETHER YOU'RE STANDING GRILLSIDE, WORKING IN THE KITCHEN, OR SITTING IN A PATIO CHAIR WITH YOUR FEET UP, THESE TASTY BITES AND REFRESHING DRINKS WILL GET THE EVENING STARTED ON THE RIGHT FOOT.

serrano ham and grilled tomato toasts

SERRANO HAM IS A DRY-CURED HAM THAT WAS TRADITIONALLY PRODUCED IN THE MOUNTAINS OR HIGHLANDS OF SPAIN. LIKE ITALIAN PROSCIUTTO, IT IS SERVED IN PAPER-THIN SLICES. IF YOU CAN'T FIND IT, PROSCIUTTO MAKES A PERFECTLY ACCEPTABLE SUBSTITUTE.

8	ounces cherry tomatoes
1	small red onion, cut into 1-inch-thick wedges
3	tablespoons olive oil
¼	teaspoon salt
⅛	teaspoon ground black pepper
8	1-inch-thick slices baguette-style French bread
	Salt (optional)
	Ground black pepper (optional)
2	cloves garlic, halved
3	ounces Serrano ham or proscuitto di Parma
1	tablespoon finely snipped fresh flat-leaf parsley
1	tablespoon finely snipped fresh chives

1. On an 8- to 10-inch skewer (see tip, right), thread tomatoes, leaving ¼ inch between pieces. On another 8- to 10-inch skewer, thread red onion wedges, leaving ¼ inch between pieces. Brush tomatoes and onion with 1 tablespoon of the oil. Sprinkle with the ¼ teaspoon salt and the ⅛ teaspoon pepper.

2. For a charcoal grill or gas grill, place tomato and onion kabobs on a grill rack directly over medium heat. Grill onion, uncovered, for 10 to 12 minutes or until tender, turning once. Grill tomatoes about 5 minutes or just until skins start to char, turning occasionally to brown evenly. Add bread directly to the grill rack for 2 to 4 minutes or until toasted, turning once halfway through grilling.

3. Finely chop tomatoes and onion. Transfer vegetables to a bowl. If desired, season to taste with additional salt and pepper.

4. Rub one side of each toasted bread slice with garlic; brush slices with the remaining 2 tablespoons oil. Generously spread tomato mixture over bread slices. Top with ham and sprinkle with parsley and chives.

PER SERVING: *165 cal., 7 g fat (1 g sat. fat), 6 mg chol., 422 mg sodium, 21 g carb., 1 g fiber, 8 g pro.*

SOAK YOUR SKEWERS

If using wooden skewers, before grilling, soak them in enough water to cover for 30 minutes. Drain before using.

PREP: 20 MINUTES **GRILL:** 10 MINUTES **MAKES:** 8 SERVINGS

chicken pinchos

ENJOYED AT TAPAS BARS IN SPAIN AND IN PUERTO RICO AND THE CARIBBEAN, PINCHOS ARE SMALL FLAVORFUL SKEWERS OF CHICKEN OR PORK—SOMETHING SUBSTANTIAL TO NIBBLE WITH A GLASS OF WINE.

1¼ pounds skinless, boneless chicken breast halves
½ cup olive oil
⅓ cup sherry vinegar or red wine vinegar
2 tablespoons snipped fresh mint
1 teaspoon ground cumin
½ teaspoon garlic pepper seasoning
Small fresh mushroom caps; frozen small whole onions, thawed; red or yellow cherry or grape tomatoes; and/ or whole pitted green olives
1 recipe Pimentón Pepper Sauce (optional)

1. Cut chicken lengthwise into 12 strips. Place chicken in a resealable plastic bag set in a shallow dish. For marinade, in a small bowl combine oil, vinegar, mint, cumin, and garlic pepper seasoning. Pour marinade over chicken; seal bag. Turn to coat chicken. Marinate in the refrigerator for 2 to 8 hours, turning bag occasionally. Drain chicken, discarding marinade.

2. Thread chicken accordion-style on twelve 8-inch skewers (see tip, page 30). If using mushrooms and/or onions, thread one onto the end of each chicken skewer.

3. For a charcoal or gas grill, place chicken skewers on the rack of a covered grill directly over medium heat. Grill for 8 to 10 minutes or until chicken is no longer pink (170°F), turning once halfway through grilling. If using tomatoes and/or olives, thread one onto the end of each skewer for the last 2 minutes of grilling.

4. If desired, serve chicken and vegetables with Pimentón Pepper Sauce for dipping.

PER SERVING: *116 cal., 8 g fat (2 g sat. fat), 30 mg chol., 36 mg sodium, 1 g carb., 11 g pro.*

PIMENTÓN PEPPER SAUCE In a medium saucepan cook ½ cup chopped onion and 2 cloves minced garlic in 2 teaspoons oil over medium heat for 5 minutes or until very tender. Transfer to a food processor. Add one 12-ounce jar roasted red sweet peppers; cover and process until nearly smooth. Wipe out saucepan and return pepper mixture to pan. Stir in 1 tablespoon sherry or balsamic vinegar, 1 teaspoon smoked paprika, and a dash of sugar. Cook and stir until heated through. Season to taste with salt and ground black pepper. Serve warm or at room temperature.

PREP: 25 MINUTES **MARINATE:** 2 HOURS **GRILL:** 8 MINUTES **MAKES:** 12 SERVINGS

skewered scallops with honey-grapefruit drizzle

8 fresh or frozen sea scallops (about 12 ounces total)
⅛ teaspoon salt
⅛ teaspoon ground black pepper
¼ cup fresh grapefruit juice
1 to 2 tablespoons honey
1 tablespoon snipped fresh mint
½ teaspoon peeled and grated fresh ginger
Nonstick cooking spray
2 cups fresh baby arugula or sliced fresh baby spinach
1 cup fresh grapefruit sections, coarsely chopped

1. Thaw scallops, if frozen. Rinse scallops and pat dry with paper towels. On two 10- to 12-inch skewers (see tip, page 30) that are parallel to each other thread four of the scallops, leaving a ¼-inch space between each scallop. Repeat with remaining scallops to make two sets of skewered scallops. Lightly brush scallops with oil; sprinkle with the salt and pepper; set aside.

2. In a small bowl stir together grapefruit juice, honey, mint, and ginger; set aside. For a charcoal or gas grill, place skewers on a rack directly over medium-high heat. Cover and cook for 11 to 14 minutes or until scallops are opaque, turning once halfway through grilling.

SECTIONING CITRUS

To get neat sections of grapefruit without any bitter white pith, cut a thin slice off of the top and bottom of the grapefruit. Cut the peel off in strips, moving from the top to the bottom of the fruit. Using a small sharp knife, cut down toward the center of the fruit on either side of each section and pop it out. Work over a bowl to catch the juices. (See page 272.)

3. To serve, arrange arugula on a platter. Top with coarsely chopped grapefruit and the scallops. Stir the honey-grapefruit mixture and drizzle over the scallops.

PER SERVING: *54 cal., 10 mg chol., 205 mg sodium, 8 g carb., 1 g fiber, 6 g pro.*

PREP: 20 MINUTES **COOK:** 11 MINUTES **GRILL:** 11 MINUTES **MAKES:** 8 SERVINGS

grilled radish crostini

NOT SO LONG AGO, RADISHES WERE ONLY EATEN RAW, ON A SALAD OR AS A CRUNCHY CRUDITÉ. ALL KINDS OF CREATIVE WAYS HAVE BEEN DISCOVERED TO COAX OUT THEIR NATURALLY SWEET FLAVOR WITH HEAT BY ROASTING, BRAISING—AND NOW GRILLING.

1 pound radishes, cleaned and halved
3 tablespoons olive oil
  Salt and ground black pepper
½ 12-inch whole grain baguette-style French bread (split horizontally)
8 slices Gruyère cheese (4 ounces)
2 tablespoons lemon juice
1 tablespoon shallot, minced
1 teaspoon honey
½ teaspoon Dijon-style mustard
1 cup shredded fresh baby spinach

1. In a medium bowl toss radishes with 1 tablespoon of the oil. Sprinkle with salt and pepper. Place radishes in a grill basket.

2. For a gas or charcoal grill, place grill basket on grill rack directly over medium heat. Cover and grill 8 to 10 minutes or until tender and lightly browned, turning radishes in the basket once or twice.

3. Add bread directly to the grill rack, cut side down, and grill 1 to 2 minutes over medium heat, or until toasted. Turn and top toasted side of bread slices with cheese. Cover and grill 1 to 2 minutes more or until melted. Remove from grill; cover and keep warm.

4. Chop or slice radishes; set aside. In a medium bowl combine remaining 2 tablespoons oil, the lemon juice, shallot, honey, and mustard. Season to taste with salt and pepper. Add spinach and radishes and toss to coat; place on top of crostini. Cut crosswise and serve immediately.

PER SERVING: *229 cal., 11 g fat (4 g sat. fat), 16 mg chol., 424 mg sodium, 26 g carb., 4 g fiber, 8 g pro.*

PREP: 30 MINUTES **GRILL:** 10 MINUTES **MAKES:** 8 SERVINGS

grilled onion flatbread with bacon and arugula

4   small red onions
1   tablespoon olive oil
    Kosher salt
    Ground black pepper
6   ounces cream cheese, softened
¼   cup strong dark ale
2   teaspoons Worcestershire sauce
    Pinch cayenne pepper
2   10-inch packaged soft flatbreads
1½ cups torn arugula
1   cup cherry tomatoes, halved or
    quartered
6   slices crisp-cooked bacon, crumbled

1. Peel and halve onions. Brush with oil, then sprinkle with salt and black pepper.

2. Grill onions on the rack of a covered charcoal or gas grill directly over medium-high heat for 6 to 8 minutes, just until charred and slightly softened, turning once halfway through grilling. Cool.

3. In a medium bowl whisk together cream cheese, ale, Worcestershire sauce, and cayenne pepper until smooth. Chop two of the grilled onions; stir into cream cheese spread. Season to taste with salt and black pepper. Quarter the remaining two onions; set aside.

4. Grill flatbreads on the rack of a covered grill directly over medium-high heat for 2 to 4 minutes or until crisp, turning once halfway through grilling. Transfer to a cutting board. Spread half the cream cheese spread on each flatbread. Top with arugula, tomatoes, bacon, and quartered onions. Slice and serve.

PER SERVING: *230 cal., 13 g fat (6 g sat. fat), 32 mg chol., 589 mg sodium, 20 g carb., 1 g fiber, 7 g pro.*

PREP: 10 MINUTES   **GRILL:** 8 MINUTES   **MAKES:** 8 SERVINGS

plank-smoked camembert with lambic peach-cherry chutney

LAMBIC BEER IS A SPECIALTY OF BELGIUM, WHERE IT IS MADE IN OPEN VATS TO CAPTURE THE NATURALLY OCCURRING YEAST IN THE AIR. IT IS OFTEN INFUSED WITH FRUIT SUCH AS RASPBERRIES, PEACHES, OR CHERRIES. IT HAS A SLIGHTLY SWEET, ROUND FLAVOR.

⅔ cup lambic beer or hard cider
½ cup sugar
1 large peach, pitted and chopped
½ cup dried tart or sweet cherries
½ teaspoon ground ginger
½ teaspoon finely shredded lemon peel
  Dash salt
1 15×7×½-inch cherrywood or cedar grill plank
8 ounces baguette-style French bread, cut diagonally into ½-inch slices
1 8-ounce round Camembert cheese

1. For chutney, in a small saucepan combine beer and sugar. Cook and stir over medium heat until sugar dissolves. Stir in peach, dried cherries, ginger, lemon peel, and salt. Bring to boiling; reduce heat. Simmer, uncovered, for 15 to 20 minutes or until mixture is thickened. Transfer to a small bowl. Cover and chill for at least 4 hours (chutney will thicken slightly as it chills).

2. For at least 1 hour before grilling, soak grill plank in enough water to cover. Weight down plank to keep it submerged during soaking. Drain plank before using.

3. For a charcoal or gas grill, place the plank on a rack directly over medium heat. Heat plank, uncovered, for 3 to 5 minutes or until it starts to char and pop. While plank is heating, add bread slices to grill. Grill for 2 to 4 minutes or until toasted, turning once. Turn plank over. Place cheese on charred side of plank. Cover and grill for 10 to 12 minutes or until cheese is softened and side is starting to droop.

4. Serve cheese on plank with some of the chutney spooned on top. Serve with toasted bread slices and the remaining chutney.

PER SERVING: *359 cal., 10 g fat (6 g sat. fat), 27 mg chol., 595 mg sodium, 55 g carb., 2 g fiber, 12 g pro.*

PREP: 25 MINUTES **COOK:** 15 MINUTES **CHILL:** 4 HOURS **SOAK:** 1 HOUR **GRILL:** 13 MINUTES **MAKES:** 6 SERVINGS

smoky pineapple guacamole

Nonstick cooking spray
2 ripe avocados, halved, seeded, and peeled (see page 272)
2 slices fresh pineapple (see page 276)
2 tablespoons sour cream
1 tablespoon snipped fresh cilantro
1 tablespoon lime juice
1 teaspoon finely chopped canned chipotle pepper in adobo sauce
¼ teaspoon salt
Tortilla chips or assorted vegetables

1. For a charcoal or gas grill, place avocado halves and pineapple slices on a grill rack directly over medium heat. Cover and grill for 5 to 6 minutes or until heated through and golden grill marks appear, turning once. Finely chop pineapple.

2. In a heavy resealable plastic bag place avocados, pineapple, sour cream, cilantro, lime juice, chipotle pepper, and salt; seal bag. Knead bag with your hands to combine ingredients.

3. Cover and chill for 1 hour and up to 8 hours. Serve guacamole with tortilla chips or assorted vegetables.

PER SERVING: *172 cal., 10 g fat (1 g sat. fat), 1 mg chol., 160 mg sodium, 21 g carb., 3 g fiber, 3 g pro.*

AVOCADO PERFECTION

To keep your avocados creamy-smooth and blemish-free, buy the fruit when it is green, hard, and not yet ripe. It requires a little advance planning because you have to let the avocados ripen on your countertop for a few days before using, but they won't bruise as easily in the store or on the way home.

PREP: 20 MINUTES **GRILL:** 5 MINUTES **CHILL:** 1 HOUR **MAKES:** 16 SERVINGS

grilled artichoke hearts with grilled sweet onion and lemon aïoli

6   fresh artichokes (see page 270)
3   tablespoons lemon juice
1   tablespoon olive oil
    Salt and ground black pepper
½   small sweet onion, cut into ½-inch slices
⅔   cup mayonnaise
2   tablespoons finely shredded Parmesan cheese
½   teaspoon finely shredded lemon peel
2   tablespoons lemon juice
1   tablespoon snipped fresh flat-leaf parsley
¼   teaspoon ground black pepper
    Lemon wedges (optional)

1. In a large Dutch oven bring a large amount of lightly salted water to boiling. Wash artichokes; trim stems and remove dark outer leaves, leaving the pale green and yellow leaves exposed. Cut through the artichoke crosswise, cutting off the pale green and yellow leaves above the base. Using a spoon, scoop out the choke. Cut each artichoke heart in half lengthwise through the stem. Using a vegetable peeler, trim any rough edges from the outside of the artichoke hearts or stems.

2. Place prepared artichoke hearts in a large bowl containing water and the 3 tablespoons lemon juice while preparing the remaining artichokes. Drain and add prepared artichoke hearts to the Dutch oven. Return to a boil. Cover and simmer 10 to 12 minutes or until tender; drain. Toss artichoke hearts with oil and sprinkle with salt and pepper.

3. For a gas or charcoal grill, place onion slices and artichoke hearts on the rack of a grill directly over medium heat. Cover and grill artichoke hearts 4 to 6 minutes or until lightly charred, turning once or twice. Grill the onion slices 8 to 12 minutes or until tender and lightly charred, turning once or twice. Chop the onion.

4. For the grilled sweet onion and lemon aïoli, in a medium bowl combine onion, mayonnaise, cheese, lemon peel, the 2 tablespoons lemon juice, parsley, and the ¼ teaspoon pepper. Serve aïoli with artichoke hearts and lemon wedges, if desired.

PER SERVING: *257 cal., 21 g fat (4 g sat. fat), 12 mg chol., 402 mg sodium, 14 g carb., 7 g fiber, 5 g pro.*

PREP: 45 MINUTES   **COOK:** 10 MINUTES   **GRILL:** 8 MINUTES   **MAKES:** 6 SERVINGS

grilled stuffed green chiles

ANAHEIM CHILES ARE ONE OF TWO TYPES OF CHILES (THE OTHER IS THE POBLANO) COMMONLY USED TO MAKE BATTER-FRIED AND CHEESE-STUFFED CHILES RELLENOS. THESE GRILLED STUFFED CHILES ARE A BIT LIKE A LIGHTER VERSION OF THAT CLASSIC DISH.

4   large fresh Anaheim chile peppers (see tip, page 21)

3   ounces soft goat cheese (chèvre) or cream cheese, softened

1   cup shredded Colby cheese or Colby and Monterey Jack cheese (4 ounces)
    Dash cayenne pepper
    Vegetable oil

1   recipe Fresh Tomato Salsa

1. Rinse the chile peppers; pat dry. Carefully cut a lengthwise slit down one side of each pepper. Using a small, sharp knife, gently scrape out as many seeds and as much membrane as possible without tearing the pepper. Leave stems attached.

2. For a charcoal grill or gas grill, place chile peppers on a rack directly over medium-high heat. Cover and grill for 10 to 12 minutes or until skin turns dark and blisters, turning often.

3. Wrap chile peppers in foil; let stand for 20 minutes. When cool enough to handle, hold peppers under cold running water, carefully peeling away blackened skin. Be careful not to tear peppers.

4. In a small bowl stir together goat cheese, Colby cheese, and cayenne pepper. Spoon 2 to 3 tablespoons of the cheese stuffing into each of the whole chile peppers. Do not overstuff. Pinch edges together with cheese to seal.

5. Lightly brush stuffed peppers with oil. If desired, place peppers in a grill basket. For a charcoal or gas grill, place peppers on a grill rack directly over medium-high heat (or place grill basket on rack directly over medium-hot heat). Cover and grill for 3 to 4 minutes or just until cheese melts. Do not turn. Serve warm with Fresh Tomato Salsa.

FRESH TOMATO SALSA In a medium bowl combine 2 cups coarsely chopped tomatoes, ¼ cup finely chopped sweet onion, 1 to 2 small fresh serrano or jalapeño chile peppers (see tip, page 21), 1 teaspoon sugar, and ½ teaspoon salt. Cover and chill for 1 hour.

PER SERVING: *278 cal., 21 g fat (10 g sat. fat), 36 mg chol., 550 mg sodium, 12 g carb., 2 g fiber, 13 g pro.*

PREP: 20 MINUTES   **GRILL:** 13 MINUTES   **STAND:** 20 MINUTES   **MAKES:** 4 SERVINGS

baba ghanoush

THIS MIDDLE EASTERN DIP HAS ALWAYS HAD A FABULOUS FIRE-ROASTED FLAVOR BECAUSE IT'S MADE FROM EGGPLANT COOKED OVER AN OPEN FLAME. THE SMOKINESS OF THIS VERSION IS ENHANCED WITH A SPRINKLE OF SMOKED PAPRIKA RIGHT BEFORE SERVING.

1 large eggplant, halved lengthwise
2 tablespoons olive oil
3 tablespoons lemon juice
2 tablespoons tahini (sesame seed paste)
3 cloves garlic
¼ teaspoon salt
¼ teaspoon ground cumin
¼ teaspoon ground black pepper
1 tablespoon snipped fresh flat-leaf parsley
⅛ teaspoon smoked paprika
8 whole wheat pita bread rounds

1. Prick eggplant with a fork several times. Brush eggplant with 1 tablespoon of the oil.

2. For a charcoal or gas grill, place eggplant on a grill rack directly over medium heat. Cover and grill for 16 to 20 minutes or until tender and browned, turning once.

3. Allow eggplant to cool slightly. When cool enough to handle, peel eggplant or scoop out flesh from peel using a spoon. For dip, transfer eggplant flesh to a food processor. Add the remaining

1 tablespoon oil, the lemon juice, tahini, garlic, salt, cumin, and pepper. Cover and process until nearly smooth.

4. Transfer to a serving dish. Sprinkle with parsley and paprika. If desired, warm the pita bread rounds. Cut each pita bread round into 6 to 8 wedges. Serve dip with the pita wedges.

PER SERVING: 124 cal., 4 g fat (1 g sat. fat), 0 g chol., 180 mg sodium, 21 g carb., 4 g fiber, 4 g pro.

PREP: 10 MINUTES   GRILL: 16 MINUTES   MAKES: 16 SERVINGS

grilled onion salad with grape tomatoes and cabrales cheese

3 tablespoons olive oil
1 tablespoon sherry vinegar
¼ teaspoon salt
¼ teaspoon ground cumin
⅛ teaspoon paprika
⅛ teaspoon freshly ground black pepper
6 red boiling onions, quartered lengthwise, or 2 medium red onions, cut into ½-inch slices
1 tablespoon olive oil
1½ cups grape tomatoes or cherry tomatoes
6 cups torn fresh watercress, arugula, or spinach
½ cup crumbled Cabrales cheese or other blue cheese (2 ounces)

1. For dressing, in a screw-top jar combine the 3 tablespoons oil, vinegar, salt, cumin, paprika, and pepper. Cover and shake well; set aside.

2. Brush onions with the 1 tablespoon oil. For a charcoal or gas grill, place onions on a rack of an uncovered grill directly over medium heat about 10 minutes or until onion is softened and slightly charred, turning once. Thread tomatoes onto skewers, leaving ¼ inch between pieces. Grill with onion about 5 minutes or until skins start to char, turning occasionally to brown evenly. Remove onions and tomatoes from grill rack. Cool slightly.

3. Separate onion slices into rings. In a large bowl combine onions, tomatoes, and watercress. Shake dressing. Drizzle over watercress mixture; toss gently to coat. Arrange watercress on a large serving platter. Sprinkle with cheese.

PER SERVING: *115 cal., 9 g fat (3 g sat. fat), 6 mg chol., 204 mg sodium, 6 g carb., 1 g fiber, 4 g pro.*

PREP: 25 MINUTES **GRILL:** 10 MINUTES **MAKES:** 8 SERVINGS

Cantaloupe-Grapefruit Agua Fresca, *recipe on page 48*

cantaloupe-grapefruit agua fresca *pictured on page 46*

AGUA FRESCA MEANS "FRESH WATER" IN SPANISH, AND THE MAGICAL COMBINATION OF FRESH FRUIT, WATER, SUGAR, AND LIME REFRESHES LIKE NOTHING ELSE. MADE WITH A VARIETY OF FRUITS SUCH AS WATERMELON, MANGO, GUAVA, AND PASSIONFRUIT, AGUA FRESCA IS THE PERFECT ALCOHOL-FREE PARTY DRINK.

1 medium cantaloupe
2 ruby-red grapefruits, juiced
3 cups cold water
2 tablespoons lime juice
2 tablespoons honey
1 tablespoon snipped fresh basil
  Ice
  Small basil sprigs (optional)

1. Cut the rind from the cantaloupe; discard rind. Cut cantaloupe into cubes; you should have about 6 cups.

2. In a blender combine cantaloupe, grapefruit juice, and 1 cup of the water. Cover and blend until smooth (blend half of the melon at a time, if needed). Strain through a fine-mesh sieve into a pitcher; discard solids.

3. Stir in remaining water, lime juice, honey, and basil. Chill until ready to serve. Strain to remove snipped basil, if desired. Serve in glasses over ice and, if desired, garnish with small basil sprigs.

PER SERVING: *97 cal., 0 g fat, 0 g chol., 26 mg sodium, 24 g carb., 2 g fiber, 2 g pro.*

FRESH SQUEEZED

How much juice can you squeeze from a fresh grapefruit? According to the Florida Department of Citrus, a medium grapefruit will yield about 8 ounces of juice. To maximize the amount of juice you get, have the fruit at room temperature. Gently roll the grapefruit on the countertop, pressing down gently, before juicing it.

START TO FINISH: 25 MINUTES **MAKES:** 6 SERVINGS

ginger-peach margaritas

1 tablespoon coarse sugar
1 tablespoon crystallized ginger, very finely chopped
1 lime
2 medium fresh peaches (6 to 8 ounces each), unpeeled, pitted, and cut up
1 recipe Ginger Syrup
½ cup tequila
⅓ cup Cointreau or Triple Sec
⅓ cup lime juice
2½ cups ice

1. In a shallow dish combine the sugar and crystallized ginger; set aside. Cut a thick slice of lime; cut slice in half. Rub halves around rims of 5 or 6 glasses. Dip rims into the sugar mixture to coat; set glasses aside. Slice remaining lime into 5 or 6 slices; set aside for garnish.

2. In a blender combine peaches, Ginger Syrup, tequila, Cointreau, and lime juice. Cover and blend until smooth. Gradually add ice, blending until smooth (blender will be full). Pour into glasses. Garnish with the reserved lime slices.

GINGER SYRUP In a small saucepan combine ¼ cup sugar, ¼ cup water, and one 1-inch piece fresh ginger, cut into thin slices. Bring to boiling, stirring constantly until the sugar has dissolved. Boil gently, uncovered, for 4 minutes or until thickened. Remove from heat; let cool. Remove and discard the ginger. Makes ¼ cup.

PER SERVING: *183 cal., 0 g fat., 0 g chol., 2 mg sodium, 29 g carb., 1 g fiber, 1 g pro.*

START TO FINISH: 15 MINUTES **MAKES:** 5 SERVINGS

watermelon–basil lemonade

¼ cup fresh basil leaves
1 cup lemon juice (juice from 4 lemons), rinds reserved
½ to ¾ cup sugar
4 cups boiling water
3 cups pureed watermelon
Fresh basil leaves
Ice

1. In a 4-quart bowl or heatproof pitcher, use the back of a wooden spoon to bruise ¼ cup fresh basil leaves. Add lemon juice. Mix juice with sugar. Pour boiling water over juice mixture, stir to dissolve sugar. Add lemon rinds and watermelon. Cover and refrigerate for 2 to 3 hours. Remove and discard rinds. Strain through a fine-mesh sieve into a pitcher. Add watermelon wedges and additional fresh basil leaves. Stir before serving. Serve lemonade over ice.

PER SERVING: *94 cal., 0 g fat, 0 g chol., 4 mg sodium, 25 g carb., 0 g fiber, 1 g pro.*

MUDDLING THROUGH

Fresh herbs such as basil contain aromatic oils that are released when the fibers in the leaves are broken down. That's why the basil leaves in this recipe are bruised with a wooden spoon (also called "muddling")—so they infuse the lemonade with wonderful flavor and aroma. Mint is another herb that is commonly muddled to add flavor to a drink—in both Mint Juleps and Mojitos, for instance.

PREP: 15 MINUTES **CHILL:** 2 HOURS **MAKES:** 6 SERVINGS

Warm Salad with Lamb Chops and Mediterranean Dressing, *recipe page 72*

main dishes

NO MATTER WHAT YOU'RE EATING—BEEF, PORK, LAMB, CHICKEN, TURKEY, FISH, OR SHELLFISH—EVERYTHING TASTES BETTER WHEN IT'S COOKED OVER AN OPEN FLAME. YOU'LL FIND EVERY KIND OF DISH ON THESE PAGES—FROM QUICK WEEKNIGHT MEALS TO ELEGANT ENTRÉES TO SHARE WITH FRIENDS.

beef short ribs with fennel gremolata and potato planks

GREMOLATA IS AN AROMATIC GARNISH OF LEMON ZEST, GARLIC, AND PARSLEY THAT IS TRADITIONALLY SPRINKLED OVER OSSO BUCO—BRAISED VEAL SHANKS—TO ADD A TOUCH OF FRESH FLAVOR AND COLOR. THIS VERSION ADDS SNIPPED FRESH FENNEL FRONDS TO THE MIX.

2 pounds beef short ribs
Salt and ground black pepper
1 bulb fennel (see page 273)
1 large onion, cut into ½-inch slices
1 32-ounce carton reduced-sodium beef broth
1 recipe Fennel Gremolata
1 pound russet potatoes, scrubbed and cut lengthwise into ½-inch slices
2 tablespoons olive oil

1. Sprinkle short ribs with salt and pepper. Save and chop fennel fronds. Trim and quarter fennel bulb.

2. For a charcoal grill, arrange medium-hot coals on one side of the grill. Test for medium heat above the empty side of the grill. Place short ribs, fennel quarters, and onion slices on the rack of a grill directly over medium-high heat. Cover and grill 8 to 10 minutes or until vegetables and ribs are just browned, turning once halfway through grilling. When cool enough to handle, coarsely chop the fennel and onion. (For a gas grill, preheat grill. Reduce heat to medium. Adjust for indirect cooking. Grill as above.)

3. Place a 13½×9½×3-inch disposable foil pan on the grill rack above the empty side of the charcoal or gas grill. Add beef broth, chopped fennel, and onion. Bring to boiling. Add ribs to pan, meaty side down. Cover pan tightly with foil. Cover and cook over indirect heat for 1 hour. Remove foil from pan, cover grill and continue to simmer 45 to 60 minutes or until ribs are tender, adding more coals as needed to maintain heat.

4. Remove ribs from the pan. Remove fennel mixture with a slotted spoon; keep warm.

5. Brush potatoes with 1 tablespoon of the oil and season with salt and pepper. Place on a grill rack directly over medium heat. Cover and grill 8 to 10 minutes or until golden brown and tender, turning once or twice. Drizzle with remaining 1 tablespoon oil.

6. Sprinkle Fennel Gremolata over ribs. Serve with potato planks.

FENNEL GREMOLATA In a small bowl combine 1 tablespoon of the fennel fronds, 1 tablespoon snipped fresh flat-leaf parsley, 4 cloves minced garlic, 2 teaspoons finely shredded lemon peel, and ½ teaspoon cracked black pepper.

PER SERVING: *487 cal., 24 g fat (9 g sat. fat), 128 mg chol., 850 mg sodium, 31 g carb., 4 g fiber, 40 g pro.*

PREP: 25 MINUTES **GRILL:** 2 HOURS **MAKES:** 4 SERVINGS

spicy skirt steak with avocado dipping sauce

SKIRT STEAK GETS ITS NAME FROM ITS SOURCE—THE LOWER MIDSECTION OF THE BEEF ANIMAL, ABOUT WHERE A SKIRT WOULD FALL. IT'S THE TRADITIONAL MEAT FOR FAJITAS. BECAUSE IT IS A LESS TENDER CUT OF MEAT, IT IS SLICED THINLY FOR EATING.

1 English cucumber
1 medium avocado, peeled and pitted
¼ cup sour cream
¼ cup roughly chopped fresh dillweed
2 tablespoons lime juice
2 teaspoons minced fresh jalapeño chile pepper (see tip, page 21)
1 teaspoon minced garlic
½ teaspoon kosher salt
2 teaspoons kosher salt
1 teaspoon dry mustard
1 teaspoon chipotle chile powder
½ teaspoon ground black pepper
½ teaspoon ground coriander
½ teaspoon ground cumin
2 pounds skirt steak, trimmed of fat
  Olive oil
1 recipe Cucumber Salad

1. For the avocado dipping sauce, cut about 3 inches from the cucumber and coarsely chop (reserve remaining cucumber for Cucumber Salad). Place chopped cucumber in a food processor or blender. Add avocado, sour cream, dillweed, lime juice, jalapeño, garlic, and the ½ teaspoon salt. Puree until smooth. Pour into a bowl; cover and chill until ready to use.

2. For the rub, in a small bowl combine the 2 teaspoons salt, the dry mustard, chipotle chile powder, black pepper, coriander, and cumin; set aside. Lightly brush steaks with oil; season with rub. Let stand at room temperature for 30 minutes.

3. For a charcoal or gas grill, place steak on a grill rack directly over high heat. Cover and grill for 4 to 6 minutes for medium rare (145°F), turning once. Remove steak from grill; let rest for 5 minutes. Thinly slice steak. Serve with avocado dipping sauce and Cucumber Salad.

CUCUMBER SALAD In a medium bowl combine reserved cucumber, sliced; 1 miniature yellow sweet pepper, sliced; 1 small shallot, sliced; ¼ cup chopped red sweet pepper; 2 tablespoons lime juice; 1 tablespoon oil; 1 tablespoon chopped fresh dillweed. Season to taste with salt and ground black pepper.

PER SERVING: *363 cal., 22 g fat (7 g sat. fat), 90 mg chol., 695 mg sodium, 7 g carb., 2 g fiber, 33 g pro.*

PREP: 30 MINUTES **GRILL:** 4 MINUTES **STAND:** 35 MINUTES **MAKES:** 6 SERVINGS

garlic-lime skirt steak with grilled tomato-pepper chutney

MARINATING THE MEAT FOR UP TO 24 HOURS NOT ONLY GIVES IT GREAT FLAVOR, BUT TENDERIZES IT TOO.

2   pounds beef skirt or flank steak,
    cut ½ to ¾ inch thick
2   tablespoons lime juice
2   tablespoons balsamic vinegar
2   tablespoons minced garlic (12 cloves)
1   tablespoon vegetable oil
1   teaspoon kosher salt
½   teaspoon ground black pepper
⅓   cup finely snipped fresh cilantro
8   to 10 miniature red, yellow, and/or
    green sweet peppers
1   recipe Grilled Tomato-Yellow Pepper
    Chutney

1. Trim fat from steak. Place steak in a large resealable plastic bag set in a shallow dish. In a small bowl whisk together lime juice, vinegar, garlic, oil, salt, and black pepper. Stir in cilantro. Pour marinade over steak; seal bag. Turn to coat meat. Marinate in the refrigerator 2 to 24 hours, turning bag occasionally. Drain steak from marinade; discarding marinade. Let steak stand at room temperature 30 minutes.

2. For a charcoal or gas grill, place steak on the grill rack directly over medium-high heat. Cover and grill for 10 to 12 minutes for medium rare (145°F), turning once halfway through grilling. Let steak stand 5 minutes. Thinly slice steak.

3. While steak stands, place sweet peppers on the grill rack. Cover and grill directly over medium heat about 5 minutes or until lightly charred, turning frequently. Serve sliced steak with the grilled peppers and Grilled Tomato-Yellow Pepper Chutney.

GRILLED TOMATO-YELLOW PEPPER CHUTNEY For a charcoal or gas grill, place 1 large yellow sweet pepper on the grill rack directly over medium heat. Cover and grill for 10 to 12 minutes or until blistered and charred, turning occasionally. Wrap pepper in foil, folding edges together to enclose peppers; let stand 15 minutes. Using a sharp knife, loosen edges of skins; gently pull off skin in strips and discard. Chop pepper, discarding stems, seeds, and

membranes; set aside. In a 9-inch foil pan combine 2 medium tomatoes, seeded and chopped; ½ cup chopped onion; ½ teaspoon salt; and ¼ teaspoon crushed red pepper. Cover tightly with foil. Place pan directly on the grill rack over medium heat. Cover and grill for 20 minutes; remove foil. Stir in the reserved chopped sweet pepper, 2 tablespoons finely snipped fresh cilantro, and 1 tablespoon honey. Grill for 5 minutes or until most of the liquid has evaporated. Transfer to a serving bowl. Cool for about 30 minutes before serving or until chutney is at room temperature.

PER SERVING: *245 cal., 11 g fat (4 g sat. fat), 74 mg chol., 473 mg sodium, 10 g carb., 2 g fiber, 25 g pro.*

PREP: 45 MINUTES **MARINATE:** 2 HOURS **STAND:** 35 MINUTES **GRILL:** 45 MINUTES **MAKES:** 8 SERVINGS

southern spiced flat iron steaks with grilled green tomatoes

FLAT IRON STEAK (ALSO CALLED TOP BLADE STEAK) IS A RELATIVELY NEW CUT OF BEEF THAT HAS BECOME VERY POPULAR IN THE LAST FEW YEARS FOR ITS REASONABLE PRICE COMPARED TO ITS FLAVOR, LEANNESS, AND TENDERNESS. FLAT IRON IS CUT FROM THE SHOULDER OF THE ANIMAL.

2 green tomatoes, sliced ½ inch thick
¼ cup olive oil
¼ cup white balsamic vinegar or apple cider vinegar
1 tablespoon packed brown sugar
3 cloves garlic, minced
¼ cup sour cream
¼ cup mayonnaise
1 chopped green onion
1 recipe Barbecue Spice Rub
Milk (optional)
4 6-ounce boneless beef chuck top blade (flat iron) steaks

1. Place tomatoes in a large resealable plastic bag set in a shallow dish. Add oil, vinegar, brown sugar, and garlic; seal bag. Turn to coat tomatoes. Marinate for 30 to 60 minutes. Drain tomatoes from marinade, discarding marinade.

2. For barbecue dip, in a small bowl whisk together sour cream, mayonnaise, green onion, and half of the Barbecue Spice Rub. Thin with milk to desired consistency. Cover and chill until ready to serve.

3. Sprinkle remaining Barbecue Spice Rub on the steaks. Rub in with your fingers.

4. For a charcoal or gas or grill, place steaks and tomato slices on the rack of a grill directly over medium heat. Cover and grill steaks 10 to 12 minutes for medium rare (145°F) or 12 to 15 minutes for medium (160°F), turning once. Grill tomato slices 3 to 4 minutes or until lightly charred, turning once halfway through grilling.

5. Serve steaks and tomatoes with barbecue dip.

BARBECUE SPICE RUB In a small bowl combine ¾ teaspoon kosher salt; ¾ teaspoon ground pasilla, New Mexico or Hatch chile pepper; ¾ teaspoon packed brown sugar; ¾ teaspoon onion powder; ¾ teaspoon paprika; ½ teaspoon celery seed, crushed; ½ teaspoon ground cumin; ½ teaspoon dry mustard, and ¼ teaspoon ground black pepper.

PER SERVING: *590 cal., 43 g fat (11 g sat. fat), 122 mg chol., 585 mg sodium, 17 g carb., 1 g fiber, 34 g pro.*

PREP: 20 MINUTES **MARINATE:** 30 MINUTES **GRILL:** 10 MINUTES **MAKES:** 4 SERVINGS

teriyaki-glazed grilled steak with broccoli rabe

THE SWEET TERIYAKI GLAZE ON THE STEAK NICELY COMPLEMENTS THE PLEASANT BITTERNESS OF THE BROCCOLI RABE. GET THE YOUNGEST, TENDEREST BROCCOLI RABE YOU CAN FIND TO AVOID HAVING IT BE OVERLY BITTER.

3 tablespoons soy sauce

5 tablespoons sweet rice wine (mirin)

1 tablespoon honey

1 teaspoon peeled and grated fresh ginger

2 cloves garlic, minced

1 tablespoon sesame oil

1 pound broccoli rabe or broccolini, trimmed

4 beef chuck eye steaks (about 1¾ pounds total)
Salt and ground black pepper

2 large shallots, halved lengthwise

1 teaspoon sesame seeds, toasted (see tip, page 77)

1. In a small saucepan combine soy sauce, mirin, honey, ginger, and garlic. Bring to boiling; reduce heat. Simmer, uncovered, about 10 minutes or until reduced to ¼ cup. Remove from heat; set aside.

2. Blanch broccoli rabe in boiling water for 2 minutes; drain well. Drizzle broccoli rabe with sesame oil. Sprinkle steaks with salt and pepper.

3. For a charcoal or gas grill, place steaks, broccoli rabe, and shallots on a grill rack directly over medium heat. Cover and grill 10 to 12 minutes for medium rare (145°F) or 12 to 15 minutes for medium (160°F). Grill broccoli rabe 4 minutes and shallots 6 to 8 minutes or until tender and lightly charred, turning once halfway through grilling. The last 3 minutes of grilling time, brush steaks with teriyaki glaze.

4. When cool enough to handle, slice shallots. Sprinkle broccoli rabe with sliced shallots and sesame seeds. Season to taste with salt and pepper. Serve with steak.

PER SERVING: *579 cal., 37 g fat (14 g sat. fat), 135 mg chol., 1250 mg sodium, 24 g carb., 3 g fiber, 42 g pro.*

PREP: 30 MINUTES **GRILL:** 10 MINUTES **MAKES:** 4 SERVINGS

beef and asparagus with caramelized onion aïoli

TARE IS A JAPANESE SAUCE WHOSE BASIC ELEMENTS ARE SOY SAUCE, SWEET RICE WINE, AND SUGAR—THOUGH THERE ARE COUNTLESS VARIATIONS. IT IS USED AS BOTH A DIPPING SAUCE FOR COOKED FOODS AND A BASTING SAUCE FOR YAKITORI—SKEWERS OF GRILLED CHICKEN.

1 **pound beef flank steak**
1 **recipe Tare Sauce**
1 **tablespoon olive oil**
½ **cup chopped onion (1 medium)**
⅓ **cup mayonnaise**
2 **tablespoons lime juice**
1 **tablespoon snipped fresh Italian (flat-leaf) parsley**
1 **tablespoon grated Parmesan cheese**
¼ **teaspoon ground black pepper**
1 **pound fresh asparagus spears, trimmed (see page 270)**
1 **tablespoon vegetable oil**
  Snipped fresh flat-leaf parsley
  Toasted sesame seeds (see tip, page 77)

1. Trim fat from steak. Thinly slice steak across the grain into long strips. Place steak in a large resealable plastic bag set in a shallow dish. Add ½ cup of the Tare Sauce; seal bag. Turn to coat steak. Marinate in the refrigerator for 1 to 12 hours, turning bag occasionally. Cover and chill the remaining Tare Sauce until needed.

2. Meanwhile, for aïoli, in a medium skillet heat oil over medium-low heat. Add onion. Cook, covered, for 13 to 15 minutes or until onion is tender, stirring occasionally. Cook, uncovered, over medium-high heat for 3 to 5 minutes or until onion is golden, stirring frequently. Transfer to a small bowl; cool. Stir in mayonnaise, lime juice, the 1 tablespoon parsley, cheese, and pepper. Cover and chill until ready to serve.

3. Drain steak, discarding marinade. On eight 10- to 12-inch skewers (see tip, page 30) thread meat accordion-style, leaving ¼ inch between pieces.

4. Place asparagus in a shallow dish. Drizzle with 1 tablespoon of the remaining Tare Sauce and the vegetable oil; toss to coat.

5. For a charcoal or gas grill, place asparagus perpendicular to grate of the rack directly over medium heat. Cover and grill about 7 minutes or until asparagus is crisp-tender, turning occasionally. Remove from grill; cover to keep warm. Place steak skewers on grill rack. Cover and grill for 5 to 6 minutes or until steak is slightly pink in center, turning and brushing once with the remaining Tare Sauce halfway through grilling.

6. Sprinkle steak, asparagus, and aïoli with additional parsley and sesame seeds. Serve steak and asparagus with aïoli.

TARE SAUCE: In a small saucepan combine 1 cup beef broth, ½ cup sweet rice wine (mirin), ¼ cup soy sauce, 3 tablespoons sugar, 1 tablespoon peeled and grated ginger, 1 tablespoon minced garlic, 1 teaspoon fish sauce, and ½ teaspoon ground black pepper. Bring to boiling; reduce heat. Simmer, uncovered, for 25 to 30 minutes or until reduced to 1 cup; cool. Strain sauce through a fine-mesh sieve; discard solids.

PER SERVING: *461 cal., 30 g fat (7 g sat. fat), 61 mg chol., 800 mg sodium, 20 g carb., 3 g fiber, 29 g pro.*

PREP: 1 HOUR **MARINATE:** 1 TO 12 HOURS **GRILL:** 12 MINUTES **MAKES:** 4 SERVINGS

tandoori-spiced sirloin with summer couscous

LIKE TANDOORI CHICKEN, THIS STEAK IS MARINATED IN CURRY-SPICED YOGURT BEFORE COOKING.

4   6-ounce boneless beef top loin steaks, about 1-inch thick
½   cup plain low-fat yogurt
¼   cup snipped fresh mint
3   tablespoons lemon juice
6   cloves garlic, minced
2   teaspoons packed brown sugar
2   teaspoons curry powder
2   teaspoons paprika
1   teaspoon kosher salt
1   recipe Summer Couscous

1. Place steaks in a large resealable plastic bag set in a shallow dish. In a small bowl combine yogurt, mint, lemon juice, garlic, brown sugar, curry powder, paprika, and salt. Pour marinade over steaks; seal bag. Turn to coat steaks. Chill for 1 to 4 hours.

2. Remove steaks from marinade (some marinade should be clinging to the steaks). Discard marinade. For a charcoal or gas grill, place steaks on a greased grill rack directly over medium heat. Cover and grill for 10 to 12 minutes for medium rare (145°F) and 12 to 15 minutes for medium

(160°F), turning once halfway through grilling. Thinly slice steaks and serve with Summer Couscous.

SUMMER COUSCOUS In a small saucepan bring ½ cup water to boiling. Stir in ½ cup couscous. Remove from heat; cover and let stand for 5 minutes. Fluff with a fork. In a medium bowl combine couscous, ⅔ cup seeded and chopped tomato, ⅔ cup chopped cucumber, ⅔ cup chopped summer squash, ½ cup snipped fresh flat-leaf parsley, ½ cup rinsed and drained chickpeas (garbanzo beans), ½ cup crumbled feta cheese, 2 tablespoons oil, 2 tablespoons lemon juice, and ½ teaspoon cumin. Season to taste with salt and pepper. Cover and chill until ready to serve.

PER SERVING: *665 cal., 41 g fat (16 g sat. fat), 127 mg chol., 979 mg sodium, 33 g carb., 4 g fiber, 41 g pro.*

PREP: 15 MINUTES **CHILL:** 1 HOUR **STAND:** 5 MINUTES **GRILL:** 10 MINUTES **MAKES:** 4 SERVINGS

grilled tomatoes

IN SUMMER, WHEN JUICY, RIPE TOMATOES OF ALL SIZES, COLORS, AND SHAPES ARE POPPING UP IN THE PRODUCE SECTION AND FARMERS' MARKETS, GIVE ONE (OR MORE) OF THESE TASTY DISHES A TRY.

1. GRILLED BALSAMIC CHERRY TOMATOES In a 13½×9½×3-inch disposable foil baking pan combine 2 pints red and/or yellow cherry tomatoes, halved; 1 tablespoon oil; 2 to 4 cloves garlic, minced; 2 teaspoons balsamic vinegar; and 1 teaspoon snipped fresh oregano. Place pan on grill rack directly over medium heat. Cover and grill 15 minutes or until tomatoes are wilted, stirring occasionally. Serve over hot cooked pasta, or with grilled meat, or fish. Makes about 4 cups.

2. STEAKS WITH GRILLED TOMATOES AND GORGONZOLA BUTTER In a bowl stir together 2 tablespoons crumbled Gorgonzola cheese and 2 tablespoons cream cheese with onion and garlic, 2 tablespoons softened butter, and 1 tablespoon toasted pine nuts, chopped (see tip, page 77). Shape into 1-inch diameter log. Wrap in plastic wrap and chill until firm; slice into 8 slices. Serve grilled cherry tomatoes (see page 14) and Gorgonzola butter on top of 4 grilled steaks. Makes 4 servings.

3. GRILLED TOMATO AND GARLIC PIZZA Brush a 12-inch Italian bread shell with oil. Generously rub crust with garlic. Arrange grilled cherry tomatoes (see page 14) and pitted black olives on bread shell. Sprinkle with crumbled goat cheese. Place pizza directly on grill rack over medium heat. Cover and grill for 3 to 5 minutes or until cheese melts. Sprinkle with snipped fresh basil. Makes 6 to 8 side-dish servings.

4. MELTED TOMATO SALAD Place 4 cups halved cherry tomatoes in a 13½×9½×3-inch disposable foil baking pan. Drizzle with 3 tablespoons oil. Add ¼ cup snipped fresh basil, ¼ teaspoon salt, and ¼ teaspoon ground black pepper. Place pan on grill directly over medium heat. Cover and grill 15 minutes. Place 6 cups fresh spinach on a serving platter. Spoon tomatoes and pan juices on top of spinach. Makes 6 side-dish servings.

5. ROASTED TOMATO-BREAD TOSS Place 6 cups red and/or yellow cherry tomatoes in a disposable foil baking pan. Place 6 cups torn baguette in a large bowl; drizzle with 3 tablespoons oil and toss to combine. Add bread to tomatoes. Place pan on grill rack directly over medium heat. Cover and grill for 15 minutes. Makes 8 side-dish servings.

6. GRILLED TOMATO AND PANCETTA SANDWICHES In a bowl combine 2 cups halved grilled cherry tomatoes (see page 14) and 2 tablespoons chopped fresh flat-leaf parsley. Preheat broiler. Cut 4 ounces thinly sliced pancetta into thirds. Place on broiler pan and broil 3 to 4 inches from heat 2 to 3 minutes or until crisp, turning once. Cut ciabatta loaf in half lengthwise. Drizzle cut sides with oil. Cut each half crosswise into 8 slices. Top with tomatoes and pancetta. Makes 16 appetizer servings.

grilled flank steak salad *pictured on cover*

THIS COMBINATION OF GRILLED SWEET PEPPERS, CORN, GREENS, AND TOMATOES IS SUMMER IN A SALAD BOWL.

1 recipe Cilantro Dressing
8 ounces beef flank steak
2 small yellow and/or red sweet peppers, seeded and halved
1 ear of fresh sweet corn, husked and silks removed
2 green onions, trimmed
   Vegetable oil
2 cups arugula or mixed greens
4 cherry tomatoes, halved

1. Prepare Cilantro Dressing. Reserve half of dressing.

2. Trim fat from steak. Score both sides of steak in a diamond pattern by making shallow diagonal cuts at 1-inch intervals. Place steak in a resealable plastic bag set in a shallow dish. Pour half of the Cilantro Dressing over steak; seal bag. Turn to coat steak. Set remaining dressing portion aside. Marinate in the refrigerator for 30 minutes. Drain steak from marinade, discarding marinade.

3. Lightly brush sweet peppers, corn, and green onions with oil.

4. For a charcoal or gas grill, place steak and corn on the grill rack directly over medium heat. Cover and grill for 17 to 21 minutes for medium (160°F) and until corn is tender, turning steak once and turning corn occasionally. Add sweet pepper halves to the grill the last 8 minutes of grilling and green onions the last 4 minutes grilling, turning frequently. Let steak stand 5 minutes.

5. Thinly slice steak. Coarsely chop sweet peppers and green onions; cut corn from cob.

6. Divide arugula between two bowls. Place sliced steak, grilled vegetables, and tomatoes on arugula. Drizzle salads with the reserved half of the Cilantro Dressing.

CILANTRO DRESSING In a blender or small food processor combine 3 tablespoons lime juice, 2 tablespoons chopped shallot, 2 tablespoons snipped fresh cilantro, 1 tablespoon oil, 1 tablespoon water, 2 teaspoons honey, 1 large clove garlic, peeled and quartered, ½ teaspoon chili powder, ¼ teaspoon salt, and ¼ teaspoon ground cumin. Cover and blend or process until combined.

PER SERVING: *357 cal., 15 g fat (4 g sat. fat), 47 mg chol., 376 mg sodium, 31 g carb., 5 g fiber, 29 g pro.*

PREP: 30 MINUTES **MARINATE:** 30 MINUTES **GRILL:** 17 MINUTES **STAND:** 5 MINUTES **MAKES:** 2 SERVINGS

lebanese beef and tabbouleh salad

SPICES SUCH AS CINNAMON, NUTMEG, AND ALLSPICE ARE COMMONLY USED IN SAVORY DISHES IN MIDDLE EASTERN COOKING TO IMPART JUST THE SLIGHTEST TOUCH OF SWEETNESS.

2	cups boiling water
1	cup bulgur
¼	cup lemon juice
2	tablespoons olive oil
¼	teaspoon salt
2	medium tomatoes, seeded and chopped (1 cup)
1	cup snipped fresh flat-leaf parsley
½	cup chopped green onions (4)
1	teaspoon ground cumin
½	teaspoon paprika
½	teaspoon ground black pepper
¼	teaspoon ground cinnamon
⅛	teaspoon ground nutmeg
⅛	teaspoon ground allspice
1½	pounds beef flank steak

1. In a large bowl combine boiling water and bulgur. Cover and let stand for 1 hour. Meanwhile, for dressing, in a small bowl whisk together lemon juice, oil, and salt; set aside.

2. For tabbouleh, drain bulgur; return to bowl. Add tomatoes, parsley, and green onions. Whisk dressing, then add to bulgur mixture. Toss to combine; set aside.

3. In a small bowl combine cumin, paprika, pepper, cinnamon, nutmeg, and allspice. Sprinkle spice mixture over steak; rub in with your fingers.

4. For a charcoal or gas grill, place steak on the grill rack directly over medium heat. Cover and grill for 17 to 21 minutes or until medium (160°F), turning once halfway through grilling.

5. Transfer steak to a cutting board. Cover with foil; let stand for 10 minutes. Thinly slice steak across the grain. To serve, spread tabbouleh on a serving platter; arrange steak over tabbouleh.

PER SERVING: *304 cal., 12 g fat (3 g sat. fat), 47 mg chol., 178 mg sodium, 22 g carb., 6 g fiber, 28 g pro.*

PREP: 25 MINUTES **GRILL:** 17 MINUTES **STAND:** 10 MINUTES **MAKES:** 6 SERVINGS

port-glazed grilled porterhouse salad

1 pound tiny Yukon gold potatoes
1 pound fresh asparagus spears, trimmed (see page 270)
1 tablespoon olive oil
¼ teaspoon garlic powder
¼ teaspoon ground black pepper
2 beef porterhouse steaks, cut 1 inch thick (2 to 2½ pounds total)
2 to 3 teaspoons cracked black pepper
1 teaspoon kosher salt
1 recipe Port Glaze and Vinaigrette
½ cup crumbled blue cheese (2 ounces)
1 5-ounce package mesclun mix

1. In a covered Dutch oven cook potatoes in boiling salted water about 10 minutes or until almost tender. Remove with a slotted spoon. Add asparagus to boiling water. Cook about 2 minutes or just until tender; drain. Immediately place asparagus in a bowl of ice water to stop cooking; drain. Drizzle potatoes and asparagus with oil; sprinkle with garlic powder and ¼ teaspoon ground pepper. Place potatoes and asparagus in a grill basket; set aside.

2. Trim fat from steaks. Sprinkle steaks with the cracked black pepper and kosher salt; rub in with your fingers.

3. For a charcoal or gas grill, place steaks on the rack of a grill directly over medium heat. Cover and grill for 10 to 13 minutes for medium rare (145°F) and 12 to 15 minutes for medium (160°F), turning once and brushing with Port Glaze during the last 5 minutes of grilling. Remove steaks from grill; sprinkle with cheese. Meanwhile, place grill basket on grill rack. Grill for 8 to 10 minutes or until golden grill marks appear on potatoes and asparagus, turning basket occasionally.

4. Slice steaks diagonally across the grain. Halve potatoes. Spread mesclun on a large serving platter. Arrange steaks, potatoes, and asparagus on top of mesclun. Drizzle with Port Vinaigrette.

PORT GLAZE AND VINAIGRETTE For the glaze, in a small saucepan heat 1 tablespoon oil over medium heat. Add 1 tablespoon chopped shallot; cook about 3 minutes or until shallot is tender, stirring occasionally. Remove from heat. Carefully add 1 cup ruby port, 2 tablespoons fig jam (large pieces snipped), and ½ teaspoon dried thyme, crushed. Return to heat. Simmer, uncovered, about 8 minutes or until reduced by half. Remove half of the mixture for the glaze. For the vinaigrette, whisk 3 tablespoons red wine vinegar, 3 tablespoons oil, ¼ teaspoon salt, and ⅛ teaspoon ground black pepper into the glaze in the saucepan.

PER SERVING: *436 cal., 28 g fat (9 g sat. fat), 66 mg chol., 477 mg sodium, 19 g carb., 3 g fiber, 20 g pro.*

PREP: 45 MINUTES **GRILL:** 10 MINUTES **MAKES:** 8 SERVINGS

rosemary-garlic grilled steak salad

THE CANDIED ROSEMARY WALNUTS MAKE A TASTY SNACK AS WELL AS A SALAD TOPPING. TO MAKE THEM SPICY AND SWEET, ADD ⅛ TEASPOON GROUND CAYENNE PEPPER TO THE SUGAR-SPICE MIXTURE.

2¼ pounds boneless beef top loin steaks, cut 1 inch thick
1 tablespoon snipped fresh rosemary
6 cloves garlic, minced
1 tablespoon olive oil
½ teaspoon salt
¼ teaspoon ground black pepper
4 4- to 5-ounce fresh portobello mushrooms, stems and gills removed
1 medium red onion, cut into ½-inch slices
8 to 10 cups torn red and/or green leaf lettuce
1½ cups cooked barley
1 cup cherry or grape tomatoes, halved
1 recipe Red Wine Vinaigrette
1 recipe Candied Rosemary Walnuts

1. Trim fat from steaks; set aside. In a small bowl combine rosemary, garlic, oil, salt, and pepper. Sprinkle mixture evenly over steaks; rub in with your fingers.

2. For a charcoal or gas grill, place steaks on a grill rack directly over medium heat. Cover and grill for 10 to 12 minutes for medium rare (145°F) or 12 to 15 minutes for medium (160°F), turning once. Meanwhile, place mushrooms and onion slices on grill rack. Cover and grill for 8 to 10 minutes or until tender and lightly charred, turning once halfway through grilling. Coarsely chop mushrooms and onion.

3. Spread lettuce on a large serving platter. In a large bowl combine mushrooms, onion, barley, and tomatoes. Add half of the Red Wine Vinaigrette; toss to coat. Spoon barley mixture on top of lettuce.

4. Slice steaks. Arrange steak slices on top of salad. Drizzle with the remaining vinaigrette. Top with Candied Rosemary Walnuts.

RED WINE VINAIGRETTE In a screw-top jar combine ⅓ cup red wine vinegar, ⅓ cup oil, 2 teaspoons Dijon-style mustard, 1 teaspoon sugar, 1 teaspoon snipped fresh rosemary, 2 cloves minced garlic, and ½ teaspoon salt. Cover and shake well.

CANDIED ROSEMARY WALNUTS Preheat oven to 325°F. Line a baking sheet with foil. Coat foil with nonstick cooking spray; set aside. In a small bowl stir together 2 tablespoons sugar, 1 teaspoon snipped fresh rosemary, dash salt, and dash ground black pepper; set aside. In a medium bowl combine 1 egg white and 1 tablespoon water. Add 1 cup walnuts; toss to coat. Drain excess liquid. Sprinkle sugar mixture over walnuts; toss to coat. Spread nuts on the prepared baking sheet. Bake for 20 minutes, stirring once. Transfer foil with the nuts to a wire rack; cool. If necessary, break into pieces.

PER SERVING: *408 cal., 25 g fat (4 g sat. fat), 71 mg chol., 423 mg sodium, 19 g carb., 3 g fiber, 28 g pro.*

PREP: 45 MINUTES **BAKE:** 20 MINUTES **GRILL:** 10 MINUTES **MAKES:** 8 SERVINGS

warm salad with lamb chops and mediterranean dressing

⅓ cup olive oil

3 tablespoons red wine vinegar

2 tablespoons finely chopped green onion (1)

1 tablespoon snipped fresh marjoram

2 teaspoons snipped fresh thyme

½ teaspoon salt

¼ teaspoon ground black pepper

8 lamb rib chops, cut 1 inch thick

2 small heads radicchio

1 cup small red and/or yellow cherry or grape tomatoes

6 cups torn romaine, arugula, and/or spinach

4 radishes, coarsely chopped

1. For dressing, in a medium bowl combine oil, vinegar, green onion, marjoram, thyme, salt, and pepper.

2. Place lamb chops in a resealable plastic bag set in a shallow dish. Pour about ¼ cup of the dressing over chops. Cover and set aside remaining dressing. Seal bag; turn to coat chops. Marinate in the refrigerator for 1 to 2 hours. Drain chops from marinade, discarding marinade.

3. Meanwhile, cut each head radicchio through the core into 6 wedges; brush lightly with some of the remaining dressing. Thread tomatoes onto 4 wooden skewers (see tip, page 21). Thread radicchio wedges onto additional skewers, leaving a ¼-inch space between pieces.

4. For a charcoal or gas grill, place chops on a grill rack directly over medium heat. Cover and grill for 12 to 14 minutes for medium rare (145°F) and 15 to 17 minutes for medium (160°F), turning once halfway through grilling. Add radicchio and tomatoes to grill. Cover and grill for 2 to 3 minutes or until radicchio is slightly wilted and tomatoes are beginning to blister, turning once halfway through grilling.

5. Divide greens among four plates. Remove radicchio and tomatoes from skewers. Place lamb chops, radicchio, and tomatoes on greens. Drizzle with remaining dressing; top with radishes.

PER SERVING: *264 cal., 22 g fat (4 g sat. fat), 28 mg chol., 338 mg sodium, 7 g carb., 3 g fiber, 11 g pro.*

PREP: 30 MINUTES **MARINATE:** 1 HOUR **GRILL:** 12 MINUTES **MAKES:** 4 SERVINGS

lamb chops with barley salad and tomato dressing

⅔ cup regular (pearled) barley
1 recipe Tomato Vinaigrette
4 small lamb loin chops, cut 1 inch thick
  Salt and ground black pepper
1 small cucumber, seeded and chopped
½ cup red sweet pepper strips
¼ cup sweet onion, chopped
½ cup snipped fresh flat-leaf parsley or mint
4 oval-shaped flatbreads, toasted
4 cups mixed greens

1. Prepare barley following package directions; drain. Rinse with cold water; drain again. Set aside.

2. Prepare Tomato Vinaigrette; reserve ¼ cup of the vinaigrette.

3. Trim fat from lamb. Brush with reserved vinaigrette. Season with salt and black pepper. For a charcoal or gas grill, place chops on a grill rack directly over medium heat. Cover and grill 12 to 14 minutes for medium rare (145°) and 15 to 17 minutes for medium (160°F); turning once halfway through grilling. Add flatbreads directly to the grill rack over medium heat. Cover and grill 1 to 2 minutes or until lightly toasted on bottom. Turn and grill 1 to 2 minutes. Remove from grill; cover and keep warm.

4. In large bowl combine cooked barley, cucumber, sweet pepper, onion, and parsley. Toss with about ¾ cup of the tomato vinaigrette. Top each flatbread with greens, barley salad, and lamb chop. Pass remaining vinaigrette.

TOMATO VINAIGRETTE In a blender or food processor combine 1 cup coarsely chopped tomatoes, 2 tablespoons red wine vinegar, 2 cloves minced garlic, 1 teaspoon cinnamon, 1 teaspoon ground black pepper, and ½ teaspoon salt. Blend until almost smooth. Add 3 tablespoons oil and blend until combined.

PER SERVING: *580 cal., 21 g fat (7 g sat. fat), 61 mg chol., 674 mg sodium, 71 g carb., 9 g fiber, 28 g pro.*

PREP: 40 MINUTES **COOK:** 45 MINUTES **GRILL:** 12 MINUTES **MAKES:** 4 SERVINGS

grilled peach and pistachio stuffed lamb chops

RESERVE MAKING THIS DISH FOR LATE SUMMER, WHEN PEACHES ARE AT THEIR SWEET AND JUICY PEAK.

- 1 peach or nectarine, halved and pitted (see page 275)
- 2 ½-inch slices red onion
- ¼ cup chopped pistachios
- 1 teaspoon peeled and grated fresh ginger
- 2 cloves garlic, minced
- ½ teaspoon finely shredded lemon peel
- ¼ teaspoon ground allspice
- ¼ teaspoon crushed red pepper
- ¼ teaspoon ground cinnamon
- 4 lamb loin chops, cut 1½ to 2 inches thick (1¾ to 2 pounds)
- ¼ teaspoon salt
- ¼ teaspoon ground black pepper
- 2 peaches or nectarines, halved and pitted (optional)

1. For a gas or charcoal grill, place 2 peach halves and the onion slices on a grill rack directly over medium heat. Cover and grill 8 to 10 minutes or until tender and lightly charred.

2. When cool enough to handle, chop peach halves and onion. In a medium bowl combine peaches, onion, pistachios, ginger, garlic, lemon peel, allspice, and crushed red pepper.

3. Trim fat from chops. Make a pocket in each chop by cutting horizontally from fat side almost to bone. Spoon one-fourth of the filing into each pocket. Secure openings with wooden toothpick. Sprinkle outside of chops with salt and black pepper.

4. For a charcoal grill, arrange medium-hot coals around a drip pan. Test for medium heat above pan. Place chops on grill rack over drip pan. Cover and grill 30 minutes or until done (145°F), turning once halfway through grilling. (For a gas grill, preheat grill. Reduce heat to medium. Adjust for indirect cooking. Grill as above.)

5. Remove meat from grill. Cover with foil and let stand for 15 minutes. (Meat temperature will rise 10°F during standing.) Meanwhile, grill extra peach halves 6 minutes or until slightly charred, turning once; if desired, to serve with lamb chops

PER SERVING: *284 cal., 11 g fat (3 g sat. fat), 105 mg chol., 260 mg sodium, 9 g carb., 2 g fiber, 36 g pro.*

PREP: 25 MINUTES GRILL: 42 MINUTES STAND: 15 MINUTES MAKES: 4 SERVINGS

lamb kefta with grilled apricot couscous

IN MOROCCO, KEFTA MEANS GROUND MEAT—PARTICULARLY GROUND BEEF, LAMB, OR A COMBINATION OF THE TWO. IN THIS COUNTRY, THE TERM MORE COMMONLY REFERS TO WELL-SPICED CHUNKS OF GROUND MEAT FORMED AROUND A SKEWER AND COOKED OVER AN OPEN FLAME.

1 egg, lightly beaten
¼ cup finely chopped onion
1 cup soft bread crumbs
1 tablespoon snipped fresh flat-leaf parsley
1 tablespoon snipped fresh cilantro
2 cloves garlic, minced
½ teaspoon salt
½ teaspoon ground cumin
½ teaspoon ground cinnamon
1 pound ground lamb
3 medium apricots, halved and pitted
1 cup chicken broth
½ cup couscous
½ cup chopped cucumber
¼ cup chopped walnuts, toasted (see tip, right)
½ cup plain Greek yogurt
1 tablespoon snipped fresh mint
¼ teaspoon cayenne pepper

1. In a large bowl combine egg, onion, bread crumbs, parsley, cilantro, garlic, salt, cumin, and cinnamon. Add lamb; mix well. Divide into 4 portions; shape each by forming a 6-inch log. Let meat logs rest for 15 minutes. Slide a metal skewer through each log. Press firmly around each skewer. Chill for 30 minutes before grilling.

2. For a gas or charcoal grill, place kabobs and apricots on the greased grill rack directly over medium heat. Cover and grill kabobs 10 to 12 minutes or until done (160°F), carefully turning once halfway through grilling. Grill apricots 4 to 6 minutes or until heated through and lightly charred, turning once halfway through grilling.

3. When cool enough to handle, chop apricots.

4. For couscous, in a small saucepan bring broth to boiling. Stir in couscous. Remove from heat and let stand 5 minutes. Fluff with a fork. Stir in half of the apricots, the cucumber, and walnuts.

5. In a small bowl combine remaining half of the apricots, yogurt, mint, and cayenne pepper. Serve kefta with couscous and apricot-yogurt sauce.

PER SERVING: *547 cal., 35 g fat (14 g sat. fat), 34 mg chol., 646 mg sodium, 30 g carb., 3 g fiber, 29 g pro.*

TOASTING NUTS

To toast whole nuts or large pieces, spread them in a shallow pan. Bake in a 350°F oven for 5 to 10 minutes, shaking the pan once or twice. Toast coconut in the same way, but watch it closely to avoid burning it. Toast finely chopped or ground nuts or seeds in a dry skillet over medium heat, stirring often.

PREP: 45 MINUTES **CHILL:** 30 MINUTES **GRILL:** 10 MINUTES **MAKES:** 4 SERVINGS

grilled mango-glazed pork chops with watermelon salsa

1   ¾-inch crosswise slice fresh watermelon
1   fresh mango, halved, seeded and peeled (see page 275)
2   ½-inch slices red onion
2   tablespoons olive oil
½   cup chopped cucumber
1   fresh jalapeño chile pepper, seeded and minced (see tip, page 21)
½   teaspoon finely shredded lime peel
2   tablespoons lime juice
4   teaspoons honey
1   tablespoon chopped fresh mint
¼   teaspoon salt
    Pinch cayenne pepper
4   boneless pork top loin chops, ¾ to 1 inch thick (about 1 pound)
    Salt and ground black pepper

1. Brush watermelon, mango, and onion with 1 tablespoon of the oil. For a gas or charcoal grill, place watermelon, mango, and onion on a grill rack directly over medium heat. Cover and grill watermelon 4 to 6 minutes until lightly charred. Grill mango and onion 6 to 8 minutes or until mango is lightly charred and onion is tender, turning once halfway through grilling. Remove from grill as they are each done.

2. Let watermelon, mango, and onion cool. Chop watermelon (you should have about 2 cups) and onion. Set aside one-fourth of the mango and chop remaining mango. In a medium bowl combine watermelon, onion, chopped mango, cucumber, jalapeño, lime peel, 1 tablespoon of the lime juice, 2 teaspoons of the honey, the mint, and salt. Cover and chill until ready to serve

3. In a blender or food processor, combine reserved mango, remaining 1 tablespoon oil, 1 tablespoon lime juice, 2 teaspoons honey, and a pinch of cayenne pepper. Cover and blend or process until smooth. Sprinkle chops with salt and black pepper.

4. Place chops on the grill rack directly over medium heat. Brush with mango sauce. Cover and grill 7 to 9 minutes or until an instant-read thermometer reads 145°F when inserted into the pork, turning once and brushing again with the mango sauce.

PER SERVING: *322 cal., 15 g fat (4 g sat. fat), 76 mg chol., 348 mg sodium, 22 g carb., 2 g fiber, 26 g pro.*

PREP: 25 MINUTES   **GRILL:** 13 MINUTES   **MAKES:** 4 SERVINGS

grilled pork and noodle salad

RICE STICKS ARE THIN NOODLES MADE FROM RICE FLOUR. THEY COME IN A VARIETY OF WIDTHS. THE THINNER ONES ARE BEST FOR SALADS AND SOUPS; THE MEDIUM AND THICK NOODLES ARE BEST FOR STIR-FRIES. IF YOU LIKE, YOU CAN SUBSTITUTE CELLOPHANE NOODLES (MADE FROM MUNG BEAN STARCH) IN THIS SALAD.

3	boneless pork loin chops, cut ½ inch thick
½	cup bottled ginger vinaigrette salad dressing or balsamic vinaigrette salad dressing
¾	teaspoon anise seeds, crushed
1	7-ounce package rice sticks
⅓	cup vegetable oil
2	cups torn romaine lettuce
1½	cups thinly sliced peeled, seeded cucumber
½	cup coarsely snipped fresh mint leaves
½	cup coarsely snipped fresh Thai basil or basil leaves
½	cup shredded carrot (1 medium)
¼	cup coarsely chopped peanuts
	Thinly sliced cucumber
	Fresh cilantro sprigs
	Lime wedges (optional)

1. Trim fat from chops. Place chops in a resealable plastic bag set in a shallow dish. For marinade, in a small bowl combine ¼ cup of the ginger vinaigrette and ¼ teaspoon of the anise seeds. Pour marinade over chops in bag; seal bag. Turn to coat chops. Marinate in the refrigerator for 1 to 4 hours, turning bag occasionally.

2. Cook rice sticks according to package directions; drain in a colander. Rinse with cold water until water runs clear; drain for 20 minutes. Using kitchen scissors, snip rice sticks into 3- to 4-inch lengths. In a medium bowl combine rice sticks, oil, and the remaining ½ teaspoon anise seeds; toss gently to coat. Set aside.

3. Drain chops from marinade, discarding marinade. For a charcoal or gas grill, place chops on a grill rack directly over medium heat. Cover and grill for 4 to 5 minutes or until an instant-read thermometer reads (145°F) when inserted into the pork, turning once halfway through grilling. Remove chops from grill and let stand 3 minutes. Slice diagonally.

4. In another medium bowl combine lettuce, the 1½ cups cucumber, mint, and basil. Pour the remaining ¼ cup ginger vinaigrette over lettuce; toss gently to coat.

5. To serve, divide rice sticks among four shallow bowls or dinner plates. Arrange lettuce and meat on top of rice sticks. Top with carrot, peanuts, additional cucumber, and cilantro. If desired, squeeze juice from lime wedges over salads and garnish with thin cucumber slices.

PER SERVING: 618 cal., 37 g fat (6 g sat. fat), 35 mg chol., 428 mg sodium, 53 g carb., 3 g fiber, 19 g pro.

PREP: 25 MINUTES MARINATE: 1 HOUR GRILL: 5 MINUTES STAND: 3 MINUTES MAKES: 4 SERVINGS

red wine bbq pork with grilled grapes

THE GRAPES ARE BARELY KISSED BY THE FLAME—3 TO 4 MINUTES OVER THE HEAT—JUST ENOUGH TO PLUMP AND WARM THEM AND GIVE THEM SOME BEAUTIFUL CHARRING.

¼ cup balsamic vinegar
¼ cup olive oil
2 to 3 tablespoons dried herbes de Provence
½ teaspoon kosher salt
½ teaspoon ground black pepper
3 1-pound pork tenderloins
1 recipe Red Wine BBQ Sauce
1¼ pounds seedless red grapes with stems

1. In a 3-quart rectangular baking dish combine vinegar, oil, herbes de Provence, salt, and pepper. Add pork tenderloins to baking dish, turning to coat. Cover and chill for 30 minutes or up to 2 hours, turning tenderloins occasionally.

2. For a charcoal grill, arrange hot coals around a drip pan. Test for medium-hot heat above the pan. Place tenderloins on the grill rack over drip pan. Cover and grill for 20 to 30 minutes or until an instant-read thermometer registers 145°F, brushing with half of the Red Wine BBQ Sauce during the last 15 minutes of grilling. (For a gas grill, preheat grill. Reduce heat to medium-high. Adjust for indirect cooking. Grill as above.)

3. Transfer pork tenderloins to a serving plate. Cover with foil; let stand for 15 minutes.

4. Snip grapes into small clusters, keeping grapes on the stems. Grill grapes directly over heat for 3 to 4 minutes or until grill marks are visible and grapes are plump, turning once halfway through grilling. Remove from heat; set aside.

5. To serve, bias-slice pork into ½-inch-thick medallions. Serve with the remaining Red Wine BBQ Sauce and grapes.

RED WINE BBQ SAUCE In a medium saucepan bring 1 cup dry red wine to boiling over high heat. Reduce heat; simmer, uncovered, about 10 minutes or until reduced by half. Add 1 cup beef broth, ¼ cup barbecue sauce, and 1 tablespoon Dijon-style mustard; simmer about 15 minutes or until reduced to 1 cup. Reduce heat to low and slowly whisk in ¼ cup butter, 1 tablespoon at a time, until combined. Season with salt and ground black pepper. Makes 1 cup.

PER SERVING: *411 cal., 19 g fat (7 g sat. fat), 123 mg chol., 569 mg sodium, 19 g carb., 1 g fiber, 35 g pro.*

PREP: 30 MINUTES **CHILL:** 30 MINUTES **GRILL:** 30 MINUTES **STAND:** 15 MINUTES **MAKES:** 8 SERVINGS

chimichurri-stuffed pork loin

1 cup loosely packed fresh flat-leaf parsley leaves
1 cup loosely packed fresh cilantro leaves
1 tablespoon finely shredded lime peel
3 tablespoons olive oil
3 large cloves garlic, minced
1 2½- to 3-pound boneless pork loin roast
¼ teaspoon ground black pepper
1 recipe Grilled Sweet Corn
1 recipe Grilled Pineapple

1. Snip 2 tablespoons each of the parsley and cilantro. In small bowl combine snipped herbs with ½ teaspoon of the lime peel, 1 tablespoon of the oil and 1 clove of the garlic; set aside.

2. Trim fat from meat. Butterfly pork loin.* Brush with the remaining 2 tablespoons oil. Spread remaining minced garlic on surface. Sprinkle with pepper and remaining parsley, cilantro, and lime peel. Roll roast to original shape. Tie at 2-inch intervals with 100-percent cotton kitchen string. Spread snipped herb mixture over outside of roast. Sprinkle with aditional pepper.

3. For charcoal grill, arrange medium-hot coals around a drip pan. Test for medium heat above pan. Place roast on grill rack over pan. Cover and grill 1 to 1¼ hours or until an instant-read thermometer registers 145°F. (For a gas grill, preheat grill. Reduce heat to medium. Adjust for indirect cooking. Grill as above.)

4. Remove roast from grill. Cover with foil; let stand 10 minutes. Remove string. Slice and serve with Grilled Sweet Corn and Grilled Pineapple.

GRILLED SWEET CORN Remove husks from 2 ears of corn. Scrub with a stiff brush to remove silks; rinse. Brush corn with 2 tablespoons melted butter. Sprinkle with salt and pepper. For a charcoal or gas grill, place corn on the grill rack directly over medium heat. Cover and grill for 25 minutes, turning corn occasionally.

GRILLED PINEAPPLE For a charcoal or gas grill, place 4 pineapple slices on the grill rack directly over medium heat. Cover and grill for 6 to 8 minutes or until lightly charred, turning once halfway through grilling.

* To butterfly a pork loin, place loin on cutting board with one end toward you. Using a long sharp knife, make a

lengthwise cut starting 1 inch in from the right side of loin, Cut down to about 1 inch from the bottom of loin. Turn the knife and cut to your left, as if forming a right angle, stopping when you get to about 1 inch from the opposite side of the loin. Open roast nearly flat.

PER SERVING: *385 cal., 15 g fat (6 g sat. fat), 113 mg chol., 283 mg sodium, 30 g carb., 4 g fiber, 35 g pro.*

PREP: 40 MINUTES **GRILL:** 1 HOUR **STAND:** 10 MINUTES **MAKES:** 4 SERVINGS

grilled jerk pineapple pork tenderloin and salsa with plantain chips

TRY TO CHOOSE GREEN PLANTAINS, IF YOU CAN FIND THEM. THEY WILL BE FIRMER AND WILL COOK UP CRISPER THAN THOSE THAT ARE RIPER.

1   green plantain, peeled and thinly bias-sliced (about ⅛ inch) (see page 276)
1   tablespoon olive oil
1   teaspoon Jamaican jerk seasoning
4   ¾-inch crosswise slices fresh pineapple (about 1 lb. 6 oz.)
½   cup chopped red sweet pepper
1   orange, peeled, sectioned, and chopped (see page 272)
¼   cup finely chopped red onion
1   tablespoon chopped fresh cilantro
1   tablespoon lime juice
2   teaspoons peeled and grated fresh ginger
¼   teaspoon salt
1   tablespoon honey
1   1-pound pork tenderloin
     Lime wedges (optional)

1. Preheat oven to 400°F. Line a large baking sheet with parchment paper. In a large bowl combine plantains, oil, and ½ teaspoon of the jerk seasoning. Toss to coat. Spread plantains in a single layer on the prepared baking sheet. Bake 15 to 17 minutes or until crisp, turning once halfway through baking. Watch carefully toward the end of baking so they don't overbrown.

2. For a gas or charcoal grill, place pineapple slices on a grill rack directly over medium heat. Cover and grill 6 to 8 minutes or until lightly charred, turning once halfway through grilling.

3. Chop pineapple (you should have about 1½ cups). Set aside ½ cup of the pineapple. In a medium bowl combine remaining pineapple, the sweet pepper, orange, red onion, cilantro, 1½ teaspoons of the lime juice, ginger, and salt. Toss to combine. Cover and chill until ready to serve.

4. In a blender or small food processor place reserved ½ cup pineapple, remaining 1½ teaspoons lime juice, the honey, and remaining ½ teaspoon Jamaican jerk seasoning. Cover and blend or process until smooth.

5. For a charcoal grill, arrange hot coals around a drip pan. Test for medium-high heat above the drip pan. Place tenderloin on a grill rack over the drip pan. Cover and grill 20 to 30 minutes or until an instant-read thermometer inserted in the center reads 145°F, brushing with the pineapple sauce once or twice. (For a gas grill, preheat grill. Reduce heat to medium-high. Adjust for indirect cooking. Grill as above, except place pork on a rack in a roasting pan.)

6. Serve pork with pineapple salsa, plantain chips, and lime wedges, if desired.

PER SERVING: *329 cal., 6 g fat (1 g sat. fat), 74 mg chol., 286 mg sodium, 45 g carb., 5 g fiber, 26 g pro.*

PREP: 30 MINUTES **GRILL:** 45 MINUTES **MAKES:** 4 SERVINGS

beets, bacon, and cabbage salad

- 1 pound red and/or golden baby beets, scrubbed, trimmed, and halved
- 4 teaspoons olive oil
- 2 ¾-inch crosswise slices red cabbage
- 4 slices bacon
- 3 tablespoons red wine vinegar
- 1 teaspoon packed brown sugar
- 1 teaspoon Dijon-style mustard
- 2 cloves garlic, minced
- ¼ teaspoon salt
- ⅛ teaspoon ground black pepper
- 3 cups torn green or red leaf lettuce
- 1 stalk celery, thinly bias-sliced
- 1 shallot, thinly sliced
- ¼ cup walnut pieces, toasted (see tip, page 77)
- 2 ounces Parmesan cheese, shaved or crumbled goat cheese (chèvre)

1. For a charcoal grill, arrange medium-hot coals around the edge of the grill. Test for medium heat in the center of the grill where the beets will cook. Place beets in a foil pan on the center of the grill rack. Drizzle with 1 teaspoon oil. Cover and grill 55 to 60 minutes or until tender when pierced with a knife, stirring occasionally. Brush the cabbage with the remaining oil and place on the outer edge of the grill rack over the coals for 12 to 15 minutes or until charred and softened, turning once halfway through grilling. (For a gas grill, preheat grill. Reduce heat to medium. Adjust heat for indirect cooking. Grill as above.) Remove beets and cabbage from the grill. Cover foil pan with beets with foil. Let stand until cool enough to handle. If desired, peel beets. Cut into quarters. Chop the cabbage (you should have about 2 cups). Set the beets and cabbage aside.

2. In a large skillet cook bacon until crisp. Drain bacon on paper towels, reserving drippings. Crumble bacon and set aside. Measure 3 tablespoons of the drippings (if there is not enough drippings to make 3 tablespoons, add oil). Whisk together drippings, vinegar, brown sugar, mustard, garlic, salt, and pepper in the skillet. Bring just to boiling; remove from heat.

3. In a large bowl combine cabbage and lettuce. Add vinaigrette and toss to coat. Transfer to a platter. Top with beets, bacon, celery, shallot, walnuts, and Parmesan cheese.

PER SERVING: *362 cal., 26 g fat (8 g sat. fat), 27 mg chol., 693 mg sodium, 22 g carb., 6 g fiber, 13 g pro.*

PREP: 20 MINUTES **GRILL:** 55 MINUTES **COOL:** 1 HOUR **MAKES:** 4 SERVINGS

pork and pineapple kabobs with coconut sauce

1   1-pound pork tenderloin
1   recipe Tare Sauce
1   14-ounce can unsweetened light coconut milk
¼   cup finely chopped shallots (2 medium)
1   tablespoon red curry paste
1   tablespoon peeled and grated fresh ginger
6   cloves garlic, minced
1   tablespoon packed brown sugar
1   teaspoon fish sauce
1   tablespoon cold water
1   teaspoon cornstarch
12 ounces fresh pineapple, cut into 1½-inch pieces (see page 276)
1   large red sweet pepper, seeded and cut into 1½-inch pieces
    Salt
    Ground black pepper
    Coarsely chopped peanuts
    Small fresh basil leaves

1. Trim fat from pork; cut into ½-inch-thick slices. Place pork in a resealable plastic bag set in a shallow dish. Add ½ cup of the Tare Sauce; seal bag. Turn to coat pork. Marinate in the refrigerator for 1 to 24 hours, turning bag occasionally. Cover and chill the remaining Tare Sauce until needed.

2. For coconut sauce, in a medium saucepan combine 2 tablespoons of the coconut milk, the shallots, curry paste, ginger, and garlic. Bring to boiling; reduce heat. Simmer, uncovered, about 5 minutes or until shallots are tender, stirring occasionally. Stir in the remaining coconut milk, brown sugar, and fish sauce. Return to boiling; reduce heat. Simmer, uncovered, for 10 minutes. In a small bowl combine water and cornstarch; stir into coconut mixture. Cook and stir over medium heat until thickened and bubbly. Remove from heat; cover to keep warm.

3. Drain pork from marinade, discarding marinade. Loosely coil each pork slice into a spiral; thread onto four 8- to 10-inch skewers (see tip, page 30), leaving ¼ inch between pieces. On four additional 8- to 10-inch skewers alternately thread pineapple and sweet pepper, leaving ¼ inch between pieces. Sprinkle pork, pineapple, and sweet pepper with salt and black pepper.

4. For a charcoal or gas grill, place kabobs on the grill rack directly over medium heat. Cover and grill for 8 to 12 minutes or until pork is slightly pink in center and sweet peppers are tender, turning and brushing once with remaining Tare Sauce halfway through grilling.

5. Serve kabobs with coconut sauce. Sprinkle with peanuts and basil.

TARE SAUCE In a small saucepan combine 1 cup chicken or beef broth, ½ cup sweet rice wine (mirin), ¼ cup reduced-sodium soy sauce, 3 tablespoons sugar, 1 tablespoon peeled and grated fresh ginger, 1 tablespoon minced garlic, 1 teaspoon fish sauce, and ½ teaspoon ground black pepper. Bring to boiling; reduce heat. Simmer, uncovered, for 25 to 30 minutes or until reduced to 1 cup; cool. Strain sauce through a fine-mesh sieve; discard solids.

PER SERVING: *378 cal., 13 g fat (6 g sat. fat), 74 mg chol., 1186 mg sodium, 38 g carb., 3 g fiber, 29 g pro.*

PREP: 30 MINUTES **MARINATE:** 1 HOUR **GRILL:** 8 MINUTES **MAKES:** 4 SERVINGS

stuffed poblano chiles with chorizo gravy

1 pound tomatoes, coarsely chopped
½ cup chopped onion (1 medium)
½ cup water
2 cloves garlic, minced
6 ounces uncooked bulk chorizo sausage
2 tablespoons all-purpose flour
¼ cup whipping cream
2 ears fresh sweet corn
4 fresh poblanos (see tip, page 21)
1 small zucchini, quartered lengthwise
1 cup shredded Oaxaca cheese or Monterey Jack cheese (4 ounces)
1 teaspoon ground cumin
¼ teaspoon salt
Nonstick cooking spray
Sour cream (optional)

1. For tomato sauce, in a large skillet combine tomatoes, onion, water, and garlic. Bring to boiling; reduce heat. Cover and simmer about 10 minutes or until onion is tender. Remove skillet from heat; cool slightly. Transfer half of the mixture to a food processor or blender. Cover and process or blend until nearly smooth; pour into a bowl. Repeat with remaining tomato mixture. Press through a fine-mesh sieve. Discard seeds and solids. Set tomato sauce aside.

2. For chorizo gravy, in the same skillet cook chorizo over medium heat for 5 to 7 minutes or until browned, stirring to break up meat as it cooks. Drain off fat. Stir flour into sausage. Add whipping cream and the tomato sauce. Cook and stir until thickened and bubbly. Cook for 1 minute more. Remove skillet from heat.

3. Remove husks from the ears of corn. Scrub with a stiff brush to remove silks; rinse.

4. For a charcoal or gas grill, place corn, chile peppers, and zucchini on the grill rack directly over medium heat. Cover and grill for 10 minutes or until chile peppers are charred and corn and zucchini are tender, turning occasionally. Place chile peppers in a bowl; cover and let stand for 10 minutes.

5. For stuffing, cut corn kernels from cobs; place kernels in a large bowl. Cut zucchini into pieces the size of corn kernels. Add zucchini to corn. Stir in half the cheese, the cumin, and salt; set aside.

6. Peel skins away from chile peppers. Discard skins. Cut a lengthwise slit in each pepper. Removes ribs and seeds, leaving stems intact. Spoon stuffing into peppers. Coat a 9×9×2-inch disposable foil pan with cooking spray. Place peppers in pan; sprinkle with the remaining cheese. Place pan on grill rack directly over medium heat. Cover and grill for 5 to 10 minutes or until filling is heated through and cheese is melted.

7. To serve, divide chorizo gravy among four plates. Place a stuffed chile pepper on the gravy. If desired, top with sour cream.

PER SERVING: *472 cal., 30 g fat (10 g sat. fat), 82 mg chol., 700 mg sodium, 30 g carb., 3 g fiber, 24 g pro.*

PREP: 20 MINUTES   COOK: 21 MINUTES   GRILL: 15 MINUTES   STAND: 10 MINUTES   MAKES: 4 SERVINGS

brick chicken with grill-roasted chiles and green beans

1   fresh poblano (see tip, page 21)
1   tablespoon finely shredded lime peel
4   cloves garlic, minced
1¼   teaspoons kosher salt
1   teaspoon paprika
1   teaspoon ground cumin
1   3- to 3½-pound whole roasting chicken
1   pound fresh green beans, trimmed
1   tablespoon olive oil
¼   teaspoon ground black pepper
¼   cup roasted, salted pepitas
     Lime wedges (optional)

1. For a charcoal grill, arrange medium hot coals on one side of the grill. Place a drip pan under the empty side of the grill. Grill chile pepper on the rack of a covered grill directly over medium heat 15 minutes or until chile pepper is charred on all sides, turning occasionally. (For a gas grill, preheat grill. Reduce heat to medium. Adjust for indirect cooking. Grill as above over hot side of the grill.) Immediately wrap chile pepper in foil; set aside. Let stand 10 minutes. Cut chile pepper in half lengthwise; remove stems and seeds. Using a sharp knife, gently peel off skin and discard. Trim each half so it will lay flat.

2. For the lime rub, in a small bowl combine 2 teaspoon of the lime peel, the garlic, 1 teaspoon of the salt, the paprika, and cumin.

3. Remove the neck and giblets from chicken. Place chicken, breast side down, on a cutting board. Using kitchen shears, make a lengthwise cut down one side of the backbone, starting from the neck end. Repeat the lengthwise cut on the opposite side of the backbone. Remove and discard the backbone. Turn chicken skin side up. Press down between the breasts to break the breast bone so the chicken lays flat. Using kitchen shears, remove the wing tips.

4. Starting at the neck on one side of the breast, slip your fingers between skin and meat, loosening skin as you work downward. Free the skin around the thigh. Repeat on the other side. Spread rub all over and under the skin of the chicken with fingers. Lay roasted chile pepper halves under the skin on each breast.

5. Place chicken, breast side down, on grill rack over drip pan. Weight with two foil-wrapped bricks or a large cast-iron skillet. Cover and grill chicken for 30 minutes. Turn chicken bone side down on rack, weighting again with bricks or skillet. Continue to grill, covered, about 20 minutes more or until chicken is no longer pink (180°F in thigh muscle). Remove and let stand 10 minutes. (For a gas grill, place chicken on grill rack away from heat. Grill as above.)

6. Meanwhile, fill a large saucepan about two-thirds full with water. Bring to boiling. Add green beans; blanch for 3 minutes. Using a slotted spoon, transfer green beans to a large bowl of ice water to cool for 5 minutes; drain. Allow to dry on a paper towel–lined tray. Preheat a grill wok directly over medium heat for 5 minutes. Toss green beans with oil, remaining ¼ teaspoon salt, and the black pepper. Add beans to grill wok. Cover and grill 8 minutes, stirring occasionally, or until tender and lightly charred. Sprinkle with pepitas and remaining 1 teaspoon lime peel. Serve with chicken and lime wedges, if desired.

PER SERVING: *359 cal., 16 g fat (3 g sat. fat), 114 mg chol., 762 mg sodium, 15 g carb., 5 g fiber, 42 g pro.*

PREP: 20 MINUTES **GRILL:** 1 HOUR 15 MINUTES **STAND:** 10 MINUTES **MAKES:** 4 SERVINGS

lime-marinated chicken and tomatillo-corn salsa

SO MANY WONDERFUL FLAVORS COME TOGETHER IN THIS SALSA—THE BRIGHT, LEMONY FLAVOR OF TOMATILLOS; THE SWEETNESS OF CORN; AND JUST A SMIDGEN OF HEAT FROM THE POBLANO CHILE PEPPER—ALL INFUSED WITH GREAT, SMOKY FLAVOR FROM THE GRILL.

6 skinless, boneless chicken breasts
¼ cup olive oil
    Juice and peel of 1 lime
1 tablespoon minced garlic (about 6 cloves)
1½ teaspoons kosher salt
½ teaspoon ground black pepper
2 ½-inch-thick slices yellow onion
5 tomatillos, papery skins removed, rinsed (about ½ pound) (see page 277)
1 ear fresh sweet corn, husks and silks removed
1 medium fresh poblano, 3 to 4 inches long (see tip, page 21)
¼ cup tightly packed fresh cilantro leaves
½ teaspoon packed brown sugar
¼ teaspoon salt
½ cup sour cream
1 tablespoon extra virgin olive oil
¼ teaspoon salt
¼ teaspoon ground black pepper
    Fresh lime wedges
    Sliced fresh jalapeño chile peppers (see tip, page 21)
    Cilantro sprigs

1. Remove tenders from underside of each breast if present; save for another use. One at a time, place each breast, smooth side down, between 2 sheets of plastic wrap. Pound to even ½-inch thickness.

2. Place a large resealable plastic bag in a shallow dish. Add ¼ cup oil, 2 tablespoons of the lime juice, the garlic, the 1½ teaspoons kosher salt, and black pepper. Add chicken to the bag; seal bag. Turn to coat chicken. Marinate in the refrigerator for 1 to 2 hours.

3. For the tomatillo-corn salsa, brush onion, tomatillos, corn, and poblano chile pepper with olive oil. For a charcoal or gas grill, place vegetables on a grill rack directly over medium heat. Cover and grill onions 10 minutes or until lightly charred; tomatillos and chile pepper 12 to 5 minutes or until tomatillos soften and begin to collapse and chile pepper is softened and lightly charred; and corn 15 minutes or until tender, turning vegetables once or twice. Place chile pepper in a bowl; cover with plastic wrap; let steam 10 minutes.

4. Peel off skin from chile pepper; discard. Remove stem and seeds. Place vegetables (except corn), cilantro, brown sugar, and the ¼ teaspoon salt in food processor or blender. Process until pureed; stir in corn.

5. Drain chicken from marinade; discarding marinade. Place chicken on a grill rack directly over medium heat. Cover and grill for 8 to 10 minutes (170°F), turning once halfway through grilling. Place chicken on a serving platter.

6. In bowl whisk together sour cream, the 1 tablespoon extra virgin olive oil, lime peel, remaining juice, ¼ teaspoon salt, and ¼ teaspoon black pepper. To serve, spoon salsa over chicken. Pass lime sour cream, lime wedges, jalapeños, and cilantro sprigs.

PER SERVING: 328 cal., 16 g fat (4 g sat. fat), 96 mg chol., 579 mg sodium, 10 g carb., 1 g fiber, 37 g pro.

PREP: 40 MINUTES **MARINATE:** 1 HOUR **GRILL:** 19 MINUTES **STAND:** 10 MINUTES **MAKES:** 6 SERVINGS

spicy chicken kabobs with vegetable rice

YOU GET A DOUBLE DOSE OF VEGGIES IN THIS DISH: SPICY CHUNKS OF GRILLED CHICKEN AND VEGETABLES ARE SERVED WITH A SIDE DISH OF BROWN RICE STUDDED WITH ZUCCHINI, SWEET, PEPPER, AND KALE.

2	tablespoons olive oil
4	teaspoons lemon juice
¼	teaspoon crushed red pepper
⅛	teaspoon salt
⅛	teaspoon dried thyme
⅛	teaspoon ground black pepper
1	medium zucchini
1	pound skinless, boneless chicken breast, cut into 1-inch pieces
1	medium red onion, cut into ½-inch wedges
24	red and/or yellow cherry tomatoes Nonstick cooking spray
¾	cup chopped red sweet pepper (1 medium)
2	cloves garlic, minced
4	cups chopped kale
¼	cup reduced-sodium chicken broth
¾	teaspoon Cajun seasoning
1⅓	cups cooked brown rice

1. In a medium bowl whisk together oil, lemon juice, crushed red pepper, salt, thyme, and black pepper; set aside. Cut zucchini in half crosswise. Chop half of the zucchini; cut the remaining zucchini lengthwise into thin slices. Add zucchini slices, chicken, onion, and tomatoes to oil mixture; toss to coat. On twelve 8-inch skewers (see tip, page 30), alternately thread chicken pieces, zucchini slices, onion wedges, and tomatoes, leaving ¼ inch between pieces.

2. For a charcoal or gas grill, place kabobs on the grill rack directly over medium heat. Cover and grill for 8 to 10 minutes or until chicken is no longer pink, turning occasionally.

3. Meanwhile, for vegetable rice, coat a large skillet with cooking spray. Heat skillet over medium heat. Add chopped zucchini, sweet pepper, and garlic. Cook and stir 3 minutes. Add kale, broth, and Cajun seasoning. Simmer, covered, about 5 minutes or until kale is tender. Stir in rice; heat through. Serve kabobs with vegetable rice.

PER SERVING: *300 cal., 10 g fat (2 g sat. fat), 47 mg chol., 264 mg sodium, 33 g carb., 5 g fiber, 22 g pro.*

PREP: 20 MINUTES **GRILL:** 8 MINUTES **MAKES:** 4 SERVINGS

chicken breast paillard with grilled romaine

A PAILLARD IS A THIN, QUICK-COOKING PIECE OF MEAT OR POULTRY.

¼ cup lemon juice
1 tablespoon minced shallots
1 tablespoon Dijon-style mustard
¼ teaspoon sugar
¼ teaspoon salt
½ cup olive oil
¼ cup finely chopped red sweet pepper
1 tablespoon snipped fresh tarragon
4 skinless, boneless chicken breast halves (6 to 7 ounces each)
2 hearts romaine lettuce, halved lengthwise
Nonstick cooking spray
Salt and ground black pepper
Shaved Parmesan cheese

1. For the vinaigrette, in a medium bowl whisk together lemon juice, shallots, mustard, sugar, and the ¼ teaspoon salt. Gradually add oil, whisking until combined. Stir in sweet pepper and tarragon; cover and set aside.

2. For the chicken, place each chicken breast half between two pieces of plastic wrap. Using the flat side of a meat mallet pound chicken lightly to ¼-inch thickness. Discard plastic wrap. Place chicken in a large resealable plastic bag set in a shallow dish. Add half of the vinaigrette; seal bag. Turn to coat the chicken. Marinate in the refrigerator for 30 minutes to 3 hours.

3. Drain chicken from marinade, discarding marinade. For a charcoal or gas grill, place chicken on a greased grill rack directly over medium heat for 12 to 15 minutes (170°F), turning once. Lightly coat cut side of each romaine piece with cooking spray; sprinkle with salt and black pepper. Grill romaine, cut sides down, about 2 minutes or until edges charred (see page 17).

4. To serve, place chicken and romaine, cut side up, on four serving plates. Drizzle with the remaining vinaigrette and top with cheese.

PER SERVING: 413 cal., 24 g fat (4 g sat. fat), 102 mg chol., 526 mg sodium, 5 g carb., 2 g fiber, 43 g pro.

PREP: 25 MINUTES   MARINATE: 30 MINUTES   GRILL: 10 MINUTES   MAKES: 4 SERVINGS

chicken churrascada with grilled corn and paprika butter

IN SPAIN, PORTUGAL, AND LATIN AMERICA, A CHURRASCADA IS WHAT WE WOULD CALL A BARBECUE—A CONVIVIAL PARTY AT WHICH FOOD IS COOKED OUTDOORS OVER AN OPEN FIRE AND ENJOYED WITH FAMILY AND FRIENDS.

1   **cup oak wood chips**
4   **ears fresh sweet corn in husks (see page 15)**
2   **tablespoons orange juice**
2   **tablespoons lime juice**
½   **teaspoon onion powder**
½   **teaspoon garlic powder**
1   **tablespoon olive oil**
1   **tablespoon red wine vinegar**
1   **pound skinless, boneless chicken thighs, halved lengthwise**
    Kosher salt and ground black pepper
½   **teaspoon paprika**
1   **clove garlic**
¼   **cup butter, softened**
    Snipped fresh cilantro (optional)
    Hot cooked rice (optional)

1. Place wood chips in a medium bowl. Cover chips with water; soak for 30 minutes. Meanwhile, place corn in husks in a large bowl; cover with water and soak for 30 minutes. Drain chips and corn; set aside.

2. In a small bowl combine orange juice, lime juice, onion powder, and garlic powder; whisk in oil and vinegar to combine. On four 10- to 12-inch skewers (see tip, page 30), thread chicken, accordion-style. Sprinkle with salt and pepper.

3. For a charcoal or gas grill, add soaked chips according to manufacturer's directions. Place chicken and corn on the grill rack directly over medium heat. Cover and grill for 15 to 20 minutes or until chicken is no longer pink and corn husks are charred; turn chicken and corn occasionally and brush chicken with juice mixture the first half of grilling. Discard remaining juice mixture.

4. Transfer cooked chicken and corn to a platter; set aside. Meanwhile, for paprika butter, on a cutting board mince garlic; sprinkle with the paprika, ¼ teaspoon kosher salt, and ¼ teaspoon pepper; use the flat side of a knife to mash garlic into a paste. In a small bowl combine butter and the mashed garlic; stir to combine.

5. Before serving, remove corn from charred husks. Serve chicken and corn with paprika butter. If desired, stir snipped cilantro into hot cooked rice; serve with chicken and corn.

PER SERVING: *354 cal., 21 g fat (9 g sat. fat), 125 mg chol., 627 mg sodium, 19 g carb., 2 g fiber, 26 g pro.*

PREP: 30 MINUTES   **SOAK:** 30 MINUTES   **GRILL:** 15 MINUTES   **MAKES:** 4 SERVINGS

grilled eggplant and chicken shawarma

IN THE MIDDLE EAST, SHAWARMA REFERS BOTH TO SPIT-COOKED MEAT AND POULTRY—AND THE SANDWICHES MADE WITH THINLY SHAVED SLICES OF IT.

¼ cup olive oil
½ teaspoon finely shredded lemon peel
¼ cup lemon juice
3 cloves garlic, minced
2 teaspoons ground coriander
2 teaspoons paprika
½ teaspoon salt
¼ teaspoon cayenne pepper
¼ teaspoon ground cinnamon
1 pound skinless, boneless chicken breast halves
1 medium eggplant, peeled if desired, and cut in ½-inch slices (see page 273)
4 soft pita bread rounds
½ cup plain Greek yogurt
2 tablespoons tahini (sesame seed paste)
1 tablespoon lemon juice
1 tablespoon snipped fresh mint
2 roma tomatoes, sliced
1 cup thinly sliced cucumber

1. In a small bowl combine oil, the ¼ cup lemon juice, garlic, coriander, paprika, salt, cayenne pepper, and cinnamon. Transfer 2 tablespoons of the marinade to a small bowl; cover and chill until needed.

2. Place chicken in a large resealable plastic bag set in a shallow dish. Add marinade to bag; seal bag. Turn to coat chicken. Marinate in the refrigerator 1 to 8 hours, turning bag occasionally. Drain chicken from marinade, discarding marinade. Brush eggplant with reserved marinade.

3. For a gas or charcoal grill, place chicken and eggplant slices on the rack of a grill directly over medium heat. Cover and grill chicken 12 to 15 minutes or until no longer pink (170°F). Grill eggplant slices 8 to 10 minutes or until tender and lightly browned. Add pita bread to the grill the last 1 to 2 minutes or until lightly toasted, turning once.

4. For the lemon tahini sauce, in a small bowl combine reserved marinade, yogurt, tahini, lemon peel, 1 tablespoon lemon juice, and the mint. When cool enough to handle, slice chicken and chop eggplant.

5. Top pita bread with chicken, eggplant, tomatoes, and cucumber. Serve with lemon tahini sauce.

PER SERVING: *546 cal., 23 g fat (4 g sat. fat), 76 mg chol., 765 mg sodium, 51 g carb., 7 g fiber, 36 g pro.*

PREP: 30 MINUTES **MARINATE:** 1 HOUR **GRILL:** 12 MINUTES **MAKES:** 4 SERVINGS

tangerine tare–glazed grilled chicken salad

1½ to 2 pounds skinless, boneless chicken breast halves
¼ teaspoon salt
¼ teaspoon ground black pepper
1 recipe Tangerine Tare Glaze and Dressing
10 cups shredded napa cabbage
6 ounces udon (broad white noodles)
1 cup fresh snow pea pods, trimmed and halved
4 to 6 miniature sweet peppers, sliced into rings
2 tangerines or clementines, peeled and sliced crosswise
8 wonton wrappers
1 tablespoon toasted sesame oil
½ teaspoon sesame seeds

1. Sprinkle chicken with salt and black pepper. For a charcoal or gas grill, place chicken on the grill rack directly over medium heat. Cover and grill for 12 to 15 minutes or until no longer pink (170°F), turning once halfway through grilling and brushing with Tangerine Tare Glaze during the last 5 minutes of grilling.

2. Spread cabbage on a large serving platter. Cook udon according to package directions; drain. Rinse with cold water to cool; drain again. In a large bowl combine udon, snow peas, sweet peppers, and tangerines. Add Tangerine Tare Dressing; toss to coat. Spoon udon mixture on top of cabbage.

3. For wonton crisps, preheat oven to 400°F. Cut wonton wrappers into ½-inch-wide strips. In a small bowl combine wonton strips, oil, and sesame seeds; toss to coat. Spread strips on an ungreased baking sheet. Bake for 5 to 6 minutes or until golden and crisp.

4. Slice chicken crosswise. Arrange chicken slices and wonton crisps on top of salad.

TANGERINE TARE GLAZE AND DRESSING In a small saucepan combine ½ teaspoon finely shredded tangerine or clementine peel, ½ cup tangerine or clementine juice, ⅓ cup reduced-sodium soy sauce, ¼ cup coarsely chopped green onions, ¼ cup sweet rice wine (mirin), 2 tablespoons sake or dry white wine, 1 tablespoon sugar, and 1 clove mashed garlic. Bring to boiling, stirring to dissolve sugar; reduce heat. Simmer, uncovered, about 15 minutes or until reduced by half

(about ⅔ cup). Strain mixture; discard solids. Remove half of the mixture for glaze. Whisk 3 tablespoons canola oil and 3 tablespoons rice vinegar into the remaining mixture for dressing.

PER SERVING: *339 cal., 10 g fat (1 g sat. fat), 55 mg chol., 709 mg sodium, 36 g carb., 4 g fiber, 25 g pro.*

PREP: 45 MINUTES   **BAKE:** 5 MINUTES AT 400°F   **GRILL:** 12 MINUTES   **MAKES:** 8 SERVINGS

chicken and grilled escarole salad

12 ounces cooked chicken and apple sausage links, cut in half crosswise

2 shallots, halved

1 medium Jonathan or Rome apple, cored and cut in wedges (see page 270)

2 heads escarole, quartered (8 to 10 ounces each)

3 tablespoons olive oil

3 cups torn butterhead lettuce (1 head)

1 cup fresh pea shoots or other microgreens

2 ounces white cheddar cheese, cubed

¼ cup chopped toasted hazelnuts (see tip, page 77)

2 tablespoons white wine vinegar

2 teaspoons snipped fresh Italian (flat-leaf) parsley

1 clove garlic, minced

¼ teaspoon salt

¼ teaspoon paprika

1. Thread sausage, shallots, and apples on skewers (see tip, page 30). Brush kabobs and cut sides of escarole with 1 tablespoon of the oil.

2. For a charcoal or gas grill, place kabobs on the grill rack directly over medium heat. Cover and grill for 8 minutes, turning once halfway through grilling. Add escarole to grill, cut sides down. Cover and grill 2 to 4 minutes more or until shallots and apples are just tender and escarole is lightly charred.

3. Coarsely chop escarole. Slice shallots. On a serving platter, toss escarole and shallots with lettuce and pea shoots. Top with sausages, apples, cheese, and hazelnuts.

4. In a screw-top jar combine the remaining 2 tablespoons oil, vinegar, parsley, garlic, salt, and paprika. Cover and shake well. Drizzle over salad.

PER SERVING: *449 cal., 31 g fat (8 g sat. fat), 110 mg chol., 940 mg sodium, 26 g carb., 7 g fiber, 23 g pro.*

COOKING APPLES

Certain apple varieties are better for cooking (as opposed to eating fresh) because they hold their shape better when exposed to heat than others do. Both Jonathan and Rome apples fall into this category. Other good cooking apples include Granny Smith, Braeburn, and Golden Delicious.

PREP: 30 MINUTES GRILL: 10 MINUTES MAKES: 4 SERVINGS

greek chicken salad with smoked peaches, pecans, and creamy yogurt dressing

THE TYPE OF WOOD CHIPS OR CHUNKS YOU USE REALLY DOES HAVE AN EFFECT ON THE FLAVOR OF THE FINISHED FOOD. MILDER TASTING MEATS SUCH AS PORK AND CHICKEN ARE BEST COOKED WITH SWEETER WOODS SUCH AS APPLE OR CHERRY. HEARTIER BEEF CAN STAND UP TO HICKORY OR MESQUITE.

¾ cup plain Greek yogurt
2 tablespoons honey
1 tablespoon snipped fresh mint
1 teaspoon finely shredded lemon peel
1 tablespoon lemon juice
2 cloves garlic, minced
½ teaspoon ground coriander
¼ teaspoon salt
¼ teaspoon ground black pepper
1½ pounds skinless, boneless chicken breast halves
2 cups apple or cherry wood chips
2 fresh, ripe peaches, halved and pitted
3 cups coarsely chopped romaine lettuce
3 cups baby spinach leaves
¼ cup crumbled feta cheese
¼ cup dried figs, stemmed and quartered
¼ cup pecan halves, toasted (see tip, page 77)

1. In a small bowl combine yogurt, honey, mint, lemon peel, lemon juice, garlic, coriander, salt, and pepper. Reserve ⅓ cup of the mixture; cover and chill until ready to serve.

2. Place chicken breasts in a large resealable plastic bag set in a large bowl. Add remaining yogurt mixture to the chicken; seal bag. Turn bag to coat chicken with marinade. Marinate in the refrigerator for 2 to 4 hours, turning occasionally. Drain chicken from marinade, discarding marinade.

3. Meanwhile, at least 1 hour before grilling, soak wood chips in enough water to cover. Drain before using.

4. For a charcoal grill, arrange medium-hot coals around a drip pan. Test for medium heat above the pan. Add wood chips to coals. Place chicken breast halves on the grill rack over the drip pan.

Cover and grill 14 to 16 minutes or until an instant-read thermometer inserted in chicken registers 165°F, turning chicken halfway through grilling. Add peach halves, cut sides down, to grill rack over drip pan the last 8 to 10 minutes of grilling or until tender. (For a gas grill, preheat grill. Reduce heat to medium. Adjust for indirect cooking. Grill as directed except add wood chips according to manufacturer's directions.)

5. In a large bowl toss romaine and spinach with reserved yogurt dressing; transfer to a serving platter. Slice chicken and peaches. Serve over lettuce mixture and top with the cheese, figs, and pecans.

PER SERVING: *392 cal., 13 g fat (4 g sat. fat), 122 mg chol., 469 mg sodium, 26 g carb., 5 g fiber, 44 g pro.*

PREP: 25 MINUTES **MARINATE:** 2 HOURS **GRILL:** 14 MINUTES **MAKES:** 4 SERVINGS

grilled strawberry, tomato, and chicken wraps

12 ounces skinless, boneless chicken breast halves
    Salt and ground black pepper
1   small red onion, cut into thin wedges
2   cups fresh strawberries, hulled
1   pint grape or cherry tomatoes
2   tablespoons white balsamic vinegar
2   tablespoons olive oil
1   tablespoon snipped fresh mint
1   teaspoon honey
1   clove garlic, minced
12 butterhead lettuce leaves
¼   cup crumbled feta cheese
¼   cup sliced almonds, toasted (see tip, page 77)

1. Cut chicken into 1½-inch pieces. Sprinkle with salt and pepper. Alternately thread chicken and red onions on skewers (see tip, page 30), leaving ¼-inch space between pieces. Alternately thread strawberries and tomatoes on separate skewers, leaving ¼-inch space between pieces.

2. For a charcoal or gas grill, place chicken kabobs on a grill rack directly over medium heat. Cover and grill 8 to 10 minutes or until chicken is no longer pink, turning kabobs once halfway through grilling. Add strawberry and tomato kabobs to grill rack directly over medium heat. Cover and grill 3 to 5 minutes or until strawberries and tomatoes have softened and are heated through, turning kabobs once halfway through grilling.

3. In a screw-top jar combine vinegar, oil, mint, honey, and garlic. Cover and shake well to combine. Season to taste with salt and pepper.

4. Remove chicken, onions, strawberries, and tomatoes from skewers and place in a large bowl; drizzle with vinaigrette. Serve in lettuce leaves and top with cheese and almonds.

PER SERVING: *284 cal., 14 g fat (3 g sat. fat), 63 mg chol., 356 mg sodium, 18 g carb., 4 g fiber, 22 g pro.*

PREP: 30 MINUTES   **GRILL:** 8 MINUTES   **MAKES:** 4 SERVINGS

poultry sausage, fingerling potato, and leek packets

THIS TASTY PACKET-COOKED SAUSAGE-AND-POTATO COMBO IS PERFECT FOR TAILGATING OR TOTING TO A PICNIC WHERE YOU HAVE ACCESS TO A GRILL. PREP THEM AHEAD IN YOUR KITCHEN, THEN KEEP IN A COOLER UNTIL COOKING TIME.

½ teaspoon fennel seeds, crushed
½ teaspoon sea salt
½ teaspoon paprika
½ teaspoon garlic pepper seasoning
1 12-ounce package fully cooked poultry sausage (chicken and apple, spinach and feta, or Italian-style)
2 leeks
1 pound fingerling potatoes, quartered lengthwise
2 tablespoons olive oil
1 tablespoon snipped fresh sage or thyme or 1 teaspoon dried sage or thyme, crushed

1. For the seasoning, in a small bowl stir together crushed fennel seeds, sea salt, paprika, and garlic pepper seasoning; set aside.

2. For a charcoal or a gas grill, place poultry sausage on the grill rack directly over medium heat. Cover and grill for 5 to 7 minutes or until sausages are browned and heated through, turning once halfway through grilling. Transfer sausages to a cutting board and cool slightly. Cut into ½-inch slices; set aside.

3. Meanwhile, fold four 24×12-inch pieces of foil in half to make a double thickness of foil so each measures 12×12 inches. Cut leeks in half lengthwise and wash thoroughly under cool running water; slice white and green parts of each leek crosswise into ¼-inch pieces. Divide potato wedges and leeks among the pieces of foil, placing vegetables in the center. Drizzle with oil and sprinkle with seasoning mixture. Top with sausage slices. For each packet, bring up opposite edges of foil and seal with a double fold. Fold remaining edges to completely enclose the vegetables, leaving space for steam to build.

4. Place packets on a grill rack directly over medium heat. Cover and grill for about 25 minutes or until potatoes and leeks are tender, turning packets over once halfway through grilling. Carefully open packets and sprinkle with the fresh sage.

PER SERVING: *336 cal., 14 g fat (3 g sat. fat), 60 mg chol., 789 mg sodium, 37 g carb., 4 g fiber, 17 g pro.*

PREP: 25 MINUTES **GRILL:** 30 MINUTES **MAKES:** 4 SERVINGS

chicken salad with creamy tarragon-shallot dressing

IF YOU AREN'T A FAN OF TARRAGON, SUBSTITUTE BASIL INSTEAD.

4	skinless, boneless chicken thighs (about 12 ounces total)
⅛	teaspoon salt
⅛	teaspoon black pepper
8	ounces fresh green beans, trimmed
1	tablespoon olive oil
¼	teaspoon salt
¼	teaspoon ground black pepper
4	ounces fresh mushrooms
6	cups torn Bibb lettuce
4	hard-cooked eggs, peeled and thinly sliced
1	recipe Creamy Tarragon-Shallot Dressing

1. Trim fat from chicken. Sprinkle chicken with the ⅛ teaspoon salt and pepper. For a charcoal grill, place chicken thighs on the grill rack directly over medium coals. Grill, uncovered, for 12 to 15 minutes or until no longer pink (180°F), turning once halfway through grilling. (For a gas grill, preheat grill. Reduce heat to medium. Place chicken thighs on grill rack over heat. Cover and grill as above.) Slice chicken thighs into strips. Set aside.

2. Meanwhile, fill a large saucepan about two-thirds full with water. Bring to boiling. Add green beans; blanch for 3 minutes. Using a slotted spoon, transfer green beans to a large bowl of ice water to cool for 5 minutes; drain. Allow to dry on a paper towel–lined tray. Preheat a grill wok directly over medium heat for 5 minutes. Toss green beans with oil, the ¼ teaspoon salt, and the pepper. Add beans and mushrooms to grill wok. Cover and grill 8 minutes, stirring occasionally, or until tender and lightly charred.

3. To serve, divide torn lettuce among four serving plates. Top with green beans, cooked mushrooms, and eggs. Arrange grilled chicken strips on salads. Drizzle with Creamy Tarragon-Shallot Dressing.

CREAMY TARRAGON-SHALLOT DRESSING In a small bowl whisk together ⅓ cup buttermilk and 2 tablespoons light mayonnaise. Stir in ¼ cup finely chopped shallots, 1 tablespoon snipped fresh tarragon, ⅛ teaspoon salt, and a dash ground black pepper.

PER SERVING: *259 cal., 12 g fat (3 g sat. fat), 287 mg chol., 359 mg sodium, 11 g carb., 3 g fiber, 27 g pro.*

PREP: 20 MINUTES **COOK:** 15 MINUTES **GRILL:** 12 MINUTES **MAKES:** 4 SERVINGS

gingered tuna and pouch-grilled vegetable toss

TUNA IS A RICH-TASTING BUT VERY LEAN FISH AND IT DRIES OUT EASILY IF OVERCOOKED. BE SURE TO TAKE IT OFF THE GRILL WHILE IT IS STILL PINK IN THE CENTER.

4	5 to 6-ounce fresh or frozen tuna steaks, cut 1-inch thick
2	tablespoons vegetable oil
1	tablespoon peeled and grated fresh ginger
1	tablespoon finely shredded lime peel
2	cloves garlic, minced
½	teaspoon salt
½	teaspoon sugar
½	teaspoon ground black pepper
2	tablespoons rice vinegar
1	tablespoon toasted sesame oil
½	teaspoon dry mustard
1	bulb fresh fennel, trimmed, halved, cored, and very thinly sliced (see page 273)
1	head baby bok choy, thinly sliced
1	cup trimmed fresh asparagus, cut into 1-inch pieces
1	medium carrot, coarsely shredded
1	teaspoon vegetable oil
¼	cup toasted sliced almonds (see tip, page 77)

1. Thaw tuna, if frozen; set aside. In a small bowl combine 2 tablespoons vegetable oil, ginger, lime peel, garlic, salt, sugar, and pepper. Set 1 tablespoon of this mixture aside.

2. In a small bowl combine remaining 1 tablespoon ginger mixture, the vinegar, sesame oil, and dry mustard; set aside. Tear off an 18×36-inch piece of heavy-duty foil. Fold in half to make an 18-inch square. Place the fennel, bok choy, asparagus, and carrot in the center of the foil. Drizzle ginger dressing over the vegetables. Bring up two opposite edges of foil and seal with a double fold. Fold remaining edges together to completely enclose vegetables, leaving space for steam to build. Brush tuna with vegetable oil.

3. For a gas or a charcoal grill, place tuna steaks and foil packet on a generously greased rack of a grill directly over medium heat. Cover and grill tuna for 7 to 8 minutes or until fish flakes when tested with a fork and center of fish is still slightly pink, turning tuna and spreading with remaining ginger mixture halfway through grilling. Grill vegetable packet about 10 minutes or until vegetables are tender, turning once.

4. Serve tuna with vegetables and sprinkle with sliced almonds.

PER SERVING: *334 cal., 15 g fat (2 g sat. fat), 55 mg chol., 416 mg sodium, 11 g carb., 4 g fiber, 38 g pro.*

PREP: 20 MINUTES   **GRILL:** 7 MINUTES   **MAKES:** 4 SERVINGS

tuna with grilled cherry vinaigrette and couscous

4 6-ounce fresh or frozen tuna steaks, 1 inch thick
3 cups fresh sweet cherries, pitted (see page 272)
¼ cup red wine vinegar
2 tablespoons honey
1 tablespoon minced shallot
1 tablespoon Dijon-style mustard
½ teaspoon snipped fresh thyme
¼ teaspoon salt
⅛ to ¼ teaspoon cayenne pepper
¼ cup olive oil
1½ cups chicken broth
1 cup couscous
1 cup shredded fresh spinach
¼ cup chopped toasted hazelnuts (see tip, page 77)
2 ounces ricotta salata cheese, crumbled; or Brie cheese, cubed

1. Thaw tuna steaks, if frozen. Thread cherries on skewers. For a gas or charcoal grill, place kabobs on a grill rack directly over medium heat. Cover and grill 5 minutes or until lightly charred, turning once.

2. Remove cherries from skewers. Halve half of the cherries and set aside. In a blender or food processor combine remaining cherries, the vinegar, honey, shallot, mustard, thyme, salt, and cayenne pepper. Cover and blend or process until smooth. With the machine running, add oil in a thin stream until incorporated.

3. Place tuna steaks in a resealable plastic bag set in a shallow dish. Add half of the vinaigrette; seal bag. Turn to coat tuna. Marinate in the refrigerator for 30 to 60 minutes.

4. In a medium saucepan bring broth to boiling. Stir in couscous. Remove saucepan from heat. Cover and let stand 5 minutes. Fluff with a fork. Stir in reserved cherries, spinach, and hazelnuts.

5. For a gas or charcoal grill, place tuna steaks on a greased grill rack directly over medium heat. Cover and grill 8 to 12 minutes or until fish flakes when tested with a fork and center of fish is still slightly pink, turning and brushing with some of the reserved marinade halfway through grilling. Discard marinade.

6. Slice tuna and serve with couscous and remaining vinaigrette. Sprinkle with cheese.

PER SERVING: *675 cal., 22 g fat (5 g sat. fat), 81 mg chol., 802 mg sodium, 66 g carb., 6 g fiber, 52 g pro.*

PREP: 40 MINUTES **MARINATE:** 30 MINUTES **GRILL:** 8 MINUTES **MAKES:** 4 SERVINGS

salmon satay with cucumber-feta salad

1½ pounds fresh or frozen skinless salmon fillet

½ cup bottled white balsamic vinaigrette dressing

3 lemons

1 large seedless cucumber, diced

8 ounces feta cheese, cut into ¼-inch cubes

½ cup chopped red onion (1 medium)

⅓ cup coarsely chopped pitted Kalamata olives

¼ cup olive oil

1 tablespoon snipped fresh mint

1 tablespoon snipped fresh Italian (flat-leaf) parsley

1 tablespoon snipped fresh dillweed

½ teaspoon salt

¼ teaspoon ground black pepper

Fresh dillweed sprigs (optional)

1. Thaw salmon, if frozen. Rinse salmon; pat dry with paper towels. Cut salmon into twelve ½-inch-wide strips. Place salmon strips in a large resealable plastic bag set in a shallow dish. Pour salad dressing over salmon; seal bag. Turn to coat. Marinate in the refrigerator for 45 minutes (no longer). Cut six thin slices from 2 of the lemons. Juice the remaining lemon to get 3 tablespoons lemon juice; set slices and juice aside.

2. For cucumber salad, in a large bowl combine cucumber, cheese, onion, and olives. Add the lemon juice, oil, mint, parsley, 1 tablespoon snipped dillweed, the salt, and pepper; stir gently to combine. Cover and chill until ready to serve.

3. Drain salmon strips from marinade, reserving marinade. Thread two salmon strips, accordion-style, onto each of six 12-inch skewers (see tip, page 30), alternating salmon strips with folded lemon slices.

4. For a charcoal or gas grill, place kabobs on a grill rack directly over medium heat for 6 to 9 minutes or until fish flakes easily when tested with a fork,

turning and brushing once with reserved marinade. Discard remaining marinade. Serve with cucumber salad. If desired, garnish with dillweed sprigs.

PER SERVING: *490 cal., 36 g fat (11 g sat. fat), 96 mg chol., 844 mg sodium, 16 g carb., 3 g fiber, 30 g pro.*

PREP: 30 MINUTES **MARINATE:** 45 MINUTES **GRILL:** 6 MINUTES **MAKES:** 6 SERVINGS

caramelized salmon with citrus salsa

- 6 4-ounce fresh or frozen salmon fillets with skin, about 1 inch thick
- 2 tablespoons sugar
- 2½ teaspoons finely shredded orange peel
- 1 teaspoon salt
- ¼ teaspoon ground black pepper
- 2 oranges, peeled, sectioned, and chopped (see page 272)
- 1 cup chopped fresh pineapple or canned, crushed pineapple
- 2 tablespoons snipped fresh cilantro
- 1 tablespoon finely chopped shallot
- 2 teaspoons finely chopped fresh jalapeño chile peppers (see tip, page 21)
  Mixed salad greens (optional)
  Orange slices (optional)

1. Thaw fish, if frozen. Measure thickness of fillets. In a small bowl stir together sugar, 1½ teaspoons of the orange peel, the salt, and black pepper. Sprinkle sugar mixture evenly over salmon (not on skin side); rub in with your fingers. Place salmon fillets, sugared sides up, in a glass baking dish. Cover dish; marinate in the refrigerator for 8 hours or up to 24 hours.

2. For the citrus salsa, in a small bowl combine the remaining 1 teaspoon orange peel, the oranges, pineapple, cilantro, shallot, and jalapeño. Cover; chill for up to 24 hours.

3. Lift fillets from dish; discard marinade. For a charcoal grill, arrange medium-hot coals around a drip pan. Test for medium heat above the pan. Place fish, skin sides down, on the oiled grill rack over the drip pan. Cover and grill for 7 to 9 minutes per ½-inch thickness of fish or until fish flakes easily when tested with a fork. (For a gas grill, preheat grill. Reduce heat to medium. Adjust for indirect cooking. Place fillets on oiled rack over burner that is off. Grill as above.)

4. To serve, carefully slip a metal spatula between fish and skin, lifting fish up and away from skin. Serve with the citrus salsa and, if desired, mixed greens. If desired, garnish with orange slices.

PER SERVING: *213 cal., 7 g fat (1 g sat. fat), 62 mg chol., 439 mg sodium, 13 g carb., 2 g fiber, 23 g pro.*

PREP: 30 MINUTES **MARINATE:** 8 HOURS **GRILL:** 7 MINUTES **MAKES:** 6 SERVINGS

orange pistachio-stuffed grilled scallops

EACH BITE OF THESE STUFFED SCALLOPS CONTAINS A BURST OF FENNEL, ORANGE, PARSLEY, AND PISTACHIO.

12   large fresh or frozen sea scallops (1 to 1¼ pounds)
1   small fennel bulb (see page 273)
3   fresh oranges
3   tablespoons olive oil
2   tablespoons snipped fresh Italian (flat-leaf) parsley
1   tablespoon finely chopped pistachios
1   tablespoon sherry vinegar or white balsamic vinegar
2   teaspoons honey
    Salt and ground black pepper
4   cups fresh arugula
    Chopped pistachios (optional)

1. Thaw scallops, if frozen. Rinse scallops; pat dry with paper towels. Split scallops horizontally, to, but not through the opposite side.

2. Remove fennel fronds and chop enough for 2 tablespoons. Trim and quarter fennel bulb.

3. Finely shred 1 teaspoon peel from one of the oranges. Working over a bowl to catch any juice, use a sharp knife to peel and section the remaining oranges.

4. For the gremolata, in a small bowl combine fennel fronds, orange peel, 1 tablespoon of the oil, the parsley, and 1 tablespoon pistachios; set aside.

5. For the vinaigrette, in a screw-top jar combine remaining 2 tablespoons oil, 1 tablespoon reserved orange juice, the vinegar, and honey. Cover and shake well to combine. Season to taste with salt and pepper.

6. Stuff scallops with the orange gremolata (as much as needed, reserving the rest). Secure closed with toothpicks, if needed. Lightly brush scallops with additional oil. Sprinkle scallops with salt and pepper. Place scallops in a lightly greased grill pan.

7. For a charcoal or gas grill, place grill pan with scallops on the grill rack directly over medium-high heat. Place fennel directly on grill rack over medium-high heat. Cover and grill 11 to 14 minutes or until fennel is lightly charred and tender and scallops are opaque, turning once halfway through grilling. When cool enough to handle, slice fennel.

8. Place arugula on a serving platter. Top with fennel, orange segments, scallops and sprinkle with any remaining gremolata. Drizzle with vinaigrette and, if desired, top with additional chopped pistachios.

PER SERVING: *275 cal., 12 g fat (2 g sat. fat), 37 mg chol., 291 mg sodium, 21 g carb., 4 g fiber, 21 g pro.*

PREP: 30 MINUTES **GRILL:** 11 MINUTES **MAKES:** 4 SERVINGS

piri piri scallops with spinach-pineapple salad

PIRI PIRI IS A HOT SAUCE MADE FROM RED CHILE PEPPERS USED IN BOTH PORTUGUESE AND AFRICAN COOKING.

16 fresh or frozen sea scallops
½   cup lime juice
2   tablespoons Asian chili sauce
5   cloves garlic, minced
2   teaspoons smoked paprika or regular paprika
½   teaspoon salt
¾   cup olive oil
1   recipe Spinach-Pineapple Salad

1. Thaw scallops, if frozen. Rinse scallops; pat dry with paper towels. Set aside. For piri piri sauce, in a food processor or blender combine lime juice, chili sauce, garlic, paprika, and salt. Cover and pulse with several on/off turns or blend until smooth. With processor or blender running, gradually add oil in a slow, steady stream through the opening in the lid; process or blend until oil is incorporated.

2. Set aside ¼ cup of the piri piri sauce. Place scallops in a resealable plastic bag set in a bowl; pour the remaining piri piri sauce over scallops. Seal bag; turn to coat. Marinate in the refrigerator for 2 to 4 hours, turning bag occasionally.

3. Drain scallops from marinade, discarding marinade. Thread four scallops on each of four skewers (see tip, page 30).

4. For a charcoal or gas grill, place kabobs on a grill rack directly over medium-hot heat. Cover and grill for 6 to 8 minutes or until scallops are opaque, turning once halfway through grilling.

5. Serve scallops with Spinach-Pineapple Salad and drizzle them with the reserved piri piri sauce.

SPINACH-PINEAPPLE SALAD For dressing, in a small jar with a tight-fitting lid, combine ⅓ cup oil, ¼ cup snipped fresh cilantro. 3 tablespoons white wine vinegar, 1 tablespoon chopped green onion, and the reserved piri piri sauce. Cover and shake well to combine. In a large bowl combine 4 cups fresh baby spinach leaves, 1 cup fresh pineapple chunks, ½ cup slivered jicama, and 4 slices crisp-cooked bacon. Add dressing; toss well.

PER SERVING: 467 cal., 33 g fat (5 g sat. fat), 56 mg chol., 557 mg sodium, 14 g carb., 3 g fiber, 29 g pro

PREP: 35 MINUTES **MARINATE:** 2 HOURS **GRILL:** 6 MINUTES **MAKES:** 4 SERVINGS

grilled zucchini or summer squash

WHEN THE ZUCCHINI HARVEST GOES INTO OVERDRIVE—AS IT DOES EVERY YEAR—TURN THE BOUNTY INTO TASTY DISHES RANGING FROM A GORGEOUS VEGGIE TART TO GRILLED ZUCCHINI NACHOS. SEE PAGE 17 FOR ZUCCHINI AND SUMMER SQUASH GRILLING DIRECTIONS.

1. GRILLED ZUCCHINI AND BEEF SANDWICHES Brush oil on one side of four ½-inch-thick slices of sourdough bread. Place oiled side down on waxed paper. Spread slice with flavored Boursin cheese; layer lengthwise slices of grilled summer squash, thinly sliced beef, and slivers of red onion. Spread Boursin cheese on four more slices of bread and place on top of vegetables. Grill sandwiches. Makes 4 sandwiches.

2. GRILLED ZUCCHINI AND SUMMER SQUASH WITH BLUE CHEESE Arrange 18 thick slices of grilled zucchini and summer squash on a large platter. Top with ½ cup pitted Kalamata olives, ½ cup crumbled blue cheese, and 1 tablespoon snipped fresh chives. Season with salt and pepper. Drizzle with ¼ cup balsamic vinaigrette. Let stand 30 minutes before serving. Makes 6 servings.

3. ORZO-GRILLED VEGETABLES SALAD WITH PESTO Cook 1 cup orzo according to package directions; rinse with cold water. Lightly drizzle with oil. In a large bowl combine orzo, 1 cup chopped grilled summer squash, ½ cup grilled sweet red pepper strips, and ½ cup chopped grilled onions. Add ⅓ cup sliced Kalamata olives and ⅓ cup purchased pesto. Toss to combine. Makes 4 servings.

4. GRILLED VEGETABLE TART Roll 1 sheet puff pastry into a 14×10-inch rectangle. Transfer to the back of a greased 15×10-inch baking sheet. Prick with a fork. Place on grill rack directly over medium-low heat. Cover and grill 1 to 2 minutes or until pastry is starting to get firm. Top pastry with pizza sauce, thinly sliced fresh mozzarella cheese, cooked planks of corn on the cob, grilled lengthwise slices zucchini, and cherry tomatoes. Return tart to grill rack. Cover and grill 3 to 5 minutes or until crust is crisp and cheese melts. Makes 4 servings.

5. GRILLED ZUCCHINI ROLLS Place 1 teaspoon softened onion and chive cream cheese about ½ inch from the end of 8 lengthwise slices of grilled zucchini. Top with a few spinach leaves. Roll up and place seam side down, on a plate. Makes 4 servings.

6. GRILLED ZUCCHINI NACHOS Slice 4 small zucchini into ¼-inch slices. Grill zucchini slices. Sprinkle 1 cup shredded Monterey Jack cheese with fresh jalapeños on zucchini slices; cover and grill until cheese melts. Place zucchini on a platter. Top with one 15-ounce can drained and rinsed black beans, fresh salsa, sour cream, guacamole, and snipped fresh cilantro. Makes 4 servings.

Grilled Vegetable Tart

grilled watermelon-shrimp salad

THIS COOL SUMMER SALAD GETS SWEETNESS FROM WATERMELON AND A SPICY KICK FROM CRUSHED RED PEPPER.

1 pound fresh or frozen large shrimp in shells
6 tablespoons olive oil
½ teaspoon kosher salt
¼ cup lemon juice
2 tablespoons honey
1 teaspoon crushed red pepper
1 1½-inch slice seedless watermelon (2¼ to 2½ pounds), quartered
1 5- to 6-ounce package torn mixed salad greens
½ cup crumbled Gorgonzola cheese or other blue cheese (2 ounces)

1. Thaw shrimp, if frozen. Peel and devein shrimp, leaving tails intact (if desired). Rinse shrimp; pat dry with paper towels. Thread shrimp onto four 10- to 12-inch metal or wooden skewers (see tip, page 30), leaving ¼ inch between pieces. Brush shrimp with 2 tablespoons of the oil and sprinkle with ¼ teaspoon of the salt.

2. In a small bowl whisk together the remaining 4 tablespoons oil, the remaining ¼ teaspoon salt, lemon juice, honey, and crushed red pepper. Using a clean brush, brush watermelon with some of the lemon juice mixture.

3. For a charcoal or gas grill, place shrimp kabobs and watermelon on a grill rack directly over medium heat. Cover and grill shrimp 4 to 6 minutes or until opaque, and watermelon 8 to 10 minutes or until warm and grill marks are visible, turning once halfway through grilling.

4. To serve, divide salad greens among four dinner plates. Top with shrimp skewers and watermelon. Whisk the remaining lemon juice mixture until combined; drizzle over salads. Sprinkle with cheese.

PER SERVING: *473 cal., 27 g fat (6 g sat. fat), 183 mg chol., 616 mg sodium, 33 g carb., 2 g fiber, 28 g pro.*

PREP: 30 MINUTES   **GRILL:** 8 MINUTES   **MAKES:** 4 SERVINGS

grilled shrimp panzanella

PANZANELLA IS A CLASSIC ITALIAN BREAD SALAD—A THRIFTY WAY TO USE UP DAY-OLD BREAD BY TOSSING IT WITH RIPE, JUICY TOMATOES. THIS VERSION CALLS FOR GRILLED BREAD, WHICH HAS A NICE TOASTY TASTE AND TEXTURE.

1½ pounds large fresh or frozen shrimp with tails, peeled and deveined
¾ cup olive oil
½ cup white balsamic vinegar or balsamic vinegar
3 tablespoons lemon juice
2 cloves garlic, minced
¾ teaspoon salt
¾ teaspoon ground black pepper
2 large red and/or yellow sweet peppers, halved and seeded
2 medium zucchini, halved lengthwise
1 1-pound loaf ciabatta bread, cut into 1-inch-thick slices
4 roma tomatoes, halved
½ cup coarsely chopped fresh basil (optional)
½ cup coarsely chopped fresh flat-leaf parsley (optional)
½ cup Kalamata olives, pitted and halved (optional)

1. Thaw shrimp, if frozen. In a medium bowl combine oil, vinegar, lemon juice, garlic, salt, and black pepper. Thread shrimp onto six 12-inch wooden skewers (see tip, page 30). Brush shrimp with about 3 tablespoons of the vinaigrette; reserve remaining vinaigrette.

2. For a charcoal or gas grill, grease grill rack. Place kabobs on the grill rack directly over medium heat. Cover and grill for 4 minutes or until shrimp are opaque, turning once. Remove from grill; set aside.

3. Using a clean brush, brush sweet peppers and zucchini with vinaigrette; add to grill. Cover and grill about 8 minutes or until crisp-tender and lightly charred, turning once. Remove from grill; set aside.

4. Brush bread slices and tomatoes with some of the reserved vinaigrette; add to grill. Cover and grill about 2 minutes or until bread is lightly toasted and tomatoes are softened, turning once halfway through grilling.

5. Remove shrimp from skewers and transfer to a very large bowl. Cut sweet peppers, zucchini, and bread into 1-inch pieces; add to bowl. Drizzle with remaining vinaigrette. If desired, add basil, parsley, and olives; toss to combine.

PER SERVING: *331 cal., 18 g fat (3 g sat. fat), 88 mg chol., 761 mg sodium, 29 g carb., 2 g fiber, 14 g pro.*

PREP: 40 MINUTES CHILL: 1 HOUR GRILL: 14 MINUTES MAKES: 10 SERVINGS

grilled tomatillo clams

48 littleneck clams
6 medium fresh tomatillos, husks removed (see page 277)
1 small onion, cut in ½-inch slices
1 fresh jalapeño chile pepper (see tip, page 21)
1 tablespoon honey
3 cloves garlic, minced
1 cup Mexican lager beer
½ teaspoon finely shredded lime peel
2 tablespoons lime juice
1 tablespoon snipped fresh cilantro
4 ounces cooked smoked chorizo sausage, finely chopped (1 cup)
Crusty French bread

1. Place clams in a large bowl. Add enough fresh water to cover clams. Let the clams stand for 20 minutes. After the clams have soaked, remove clams, one at a time from water and scrub under cold running water with a firm brush.

2. Meanwhile, for a gas or charcoal grill, place tomatillos, onion, and jalapeño on the rack of a grill directly over medium heat. Cover and grill 6 to 8 minutes or until tomatillos are softened, onion and jalapeño are tender and all are lightly charred, turning occasionally. When cool enough to handle, stem and seed jalapeño.

3. In a blender or food processor, combine tomatillos, onion, jalapeño, honey, and garlic. Cover and blend or process until almost smooth, with a few visible chunks.

4. In a 12-inch cast-iron skillet combine tomatillo mixture and beer. For a gas or charcoal grill, place skillet on the grill rack directly over medium-high heat. Cover and grill for 5 minutes or until mixture comes to a boil, stirring once. Stir in lime peel, lime juice, and cilantro.

5. Add clams to skillet in a single layer. Cover and grill 8 to 10 minutes more or until clams open. Remove skillet from grill and sprinkle with the sausage. Serve with crusty French bread.

PER SERVING: *275 cal., 9 g fat (3 g sat. fat), 38 mg chol., 807 mg sodium, 38 g carb., 2 g fiber, 19 g pro.*

PREP: 25 MINUTES **GRILL:** 19 MINUTES **STAND:** 20 MINUTES **MAKES:** 6 SERVINGS

Portobello Fajitas, *recipe page 134*

vegetarian

NO ONE WILL MISS THE MEAT IN THESE HEARTY DISHES FEATURING SMOKY,
FLAME-KISSED VEGETABLES, GRAINS, LEGUMES, AND CHEESES.

grilled summer squash with polenta wedges and tomatillo slather

1 cup coarse-ground yellow cornmeal
1 cup cold water
¼ teaspoon salt
½ cup crumbled queso fresco or feta cheese
1 tablespoon snipped fresh oregano
2 tablespoons olive oil
1 medium zucchini, cut lengthwise into ½-inch slices
1 medium summer squash, cut lengthwise into ½-inch slices
Salt and ground black pepper
1 pound tomatillos, husks removed and rinsed (see page 277)
1 medium poblano chile pepper (see tip, page 21)
1 small red onion, cut into ½-inch slices
Lime wedges
Chopped fresh cilantro (optional)

1. In a medium saucepan bring 2½ cups water to boiling. Meanwhile, in a medium bowl stir together cornmeal, the 1 cup cold water, and the ¼ teaspoon salt. Slowly add cornmeal mixture to boiling water, stirring constantly. Cook and stir until mixture returns to boiling. Reduce heat to medium-low. Cook for 25 to 30 minutes or until mixture is very thick and tender, stirring frequently and adjusting heat as needed to maintain a slow boil. Stir in queso fresco and oregano. Pour the polenta into a greased 9-inch pie plate, spreading it into an even layer. Let stand, uncovered, for 30 minutes. Cover and chill at least 1 hour or until firm. Cut into 8 wedges. Brush wedges with 1 tablespoon of the oil; set aside.

2. Brush the zucchini and summer squash, with the remaining 1 tablespoon oil. Sprinkle with salt and black pepper; set aside.

3. For a gas or charcoal grill, place the whole tomatillos, poblano, and onion slices on a grill rack directly over medium heat. Cover and grill 8 to 10 minutes or until softened and lightly charred. Wrap the poblano in foil and let stand 15 minutes. Make the Tomatillo Slather.

4. Place polenta wedges, zucchini, and summer squash on a well-greased grill rack directly over medium heat. Cover and grill zucchini and summer squash 10 minutes or until tender and lightly browned, turning once. Grill polenta 15 to 18 minutes or until polenta is browned and easily releases from the grill rack, turning once halfway through grilling. When cool enough to handle, cut zucchini and summer squash in 1-inch slices.

5. Serve polenta wedges with zucchini, summer squash, and Tomatillo Slather. Serve with lime wedges and, if desired, sprinkle with cilantro.

TOMATILLO SLATHER Stem, seed and peel off skin from the grilled poblano; chop poblano. In a food processor or blender combine the chopped poblano, the grilled tomatillos and onions, and 1 to 2 teaspoons honey. Cover and process or blend until nearly smooth. Season to taste with salt and black pepper.

PER SERVING: *302 cal., 12 g fat (3 g sat. fat), 10 mg chol., 407 mg sodium, 43 g carb., 6 g fiber, 8 g pro.*

PREP: 45 MINUTES STAND: 45 MINUTES CHILL: 1 HOUR GRILL: 15 MINUTES MAKES: 4 SERVINGS

smoky grilled vegetable torte

½ cup olive oil

4 cloves garlic, minced

1 16-ounce tube refrigerated cooked polenta, sliced ½ inch thick

2 medium red, green, and/or yellow sweet peppers, quartered and seeded

2 fresh portobello mushrooms, stems removed

1 large eggplant, bias-sliced ¼ inch thick

1 medium zucchini, bias-sliced ¼ inch thick

1 medium yellow summer squash, bias-sliced ¼ inch thick

Salt and ground black pepper

1½ cups shredded smoked Gouda cheese (6 ounces)

½ cup lightly packed fresh basil leaves

1 cup halved pear, grape, or cherry tomatoes

Fresh basil leaves (optional)

1. In a small saucepan heat oil and garlic over medium heat until fragrant and garlic is translucent but not browned; remove from heat and set aside.

2. Place polenta, sweet peppers, mushrooms, eggplant, zucchini, and summer squash on large baking sheets. Brush polenta and vegetables generously with the garlic oil. Season with salt and black pepper. For a charcoal or gas grill, place polenta slices on a grill rack directly over medium heat. Cover and grill for 8 to 10 minutes or until polenta is lightly browned and heated through, using a metal spatula to carefully turn slices once. Place vegetables on a grill rack directly over medium heat for 4 to 6 minutes or until tender, turning once. Remove from heat and cool slightly; slice mushrooms.

3. In a 9-inch springform pan layer grilled vegetables and polenta, starting with eggplant. Sprinkle some of the cheese and a few basil leaves over each layer. Press to compact the layers. Top with tomatoes, more basil leaves, and the remaining cheese. Place torte in a foil pan or wrap the outside of the pan with a double layer of foil. Place torte on a grill rack directly over medium-low heat. Cover and grill for 15 to 20 minutes or until heated through.

4. Remove torte from grill; cool on a wire rack for at least 15 minutes. Remove outer ring of springform pan. Using a sharp serrated knife, cut into wedges. If desired, garnish with additional basil leaves.

PER SERVING: *283 cal., 20 g fat (6 g sat. fat), 24 mg chol., 476 mg sodium, 19 g carb., 5 g fiber, 9 g pro.*

PREP: 45 MINUTES **GRILL:** 40 MINUTES **STAND:** 15 MINUTES **MAKES:** 8 SERVINGS

grilled eggplant stacks with basil chiffonade

½ cup extra virgin olive oil

½ cup packed fresh basil leaves

1 large eggplant, cut crosswise into ½-inch slices (10 to 12 slices)

½ teaspoon salt

½ teaspoon black pepper

1 19-ounce can cannellini (white kidney) beans, rinsed and drained

4 ounces feta cheese, crumbled

½ teaspoon finely shredded lemon peel

2 tablespoons lemon juice

1 clove garlic, minced
   Salt and ground black pepper

½ cup bottled roasted red sweet peppers, cut into bite-size strips

¼ cup fresh basil leaves

1. For the basil-infused oil, in a blender combine oil and the ½ cup basil leaves. Cover and blend until finely chopped. Transfer to a small saucepan. Cook over medium heat just until bubbles appear around the edges. Remove from heat. Cool to room temperature. Strain oil. Brush eggplant slices with 2 tablespoons of the basil-infused oil. Sprinkle with the ½ teaspoon salt and ½ teaspoon black pepper.

2. For a charcoal or gas grill, place eggplant slices on a grill rack directly over medium-high heat for 8 to 10 minutes or until very tender and lightly charred, turning frequently.

3. In a food processor or blender combine cannellini beans, cheese, lemon peel, lemon juice, 2 tablespoons of the basil-infused oil, and garlic. Cover and process just until combined but still chunky. Season with salt and black pepper.

4. Arrange eggplant slices on serving plates. Top with bean mixture and roasted pepper strips. Drizzle with the remaining 1 tablespoon basil-infused oil.* For basil chiffonade, roll up basil leaves and cut across the roll; sprinkle over eggplant stacks.

*NOTE: Store leftover basil-infused oil in a covered container in the refrigerator for up to 3 days.

PER SERVING: 302 cal., 19 g fat (5 g sat. fat), 20 mg chol., 771 mg sodium, 27 g carb., 10 g fiber, 11 g pro.

PREP: 25 MINUTES **COOL:** 1 HOUR **GRILL:** 8 MINUTES **MAKES:** 5 SERVINGS

smoked lentil hash with squash

YOU CAN USE EITHER BROWN OR YELLOW LENTILS IN THIS WARM SMOKED-LEGUME SALAD. IF YOU USE YELLOW LENTILS, WATCH THEM CAREFULLY AS THEY COOK. THEY TEND TO BREAK DOWN FASTER THAN BROWN LENTILS, THEY NEED TO KEEP THEIR SHAPE FOR SMOKING ON THE GRILL.

1 cup oak or hickory wood chips
½ cup chopped onion (1 medium)
½ cup chopped celery (1 stalk)
3 cloves garlic, minced
5 tablespoons olive oil
1 32-ounce carton vegetable broth
1 pound brown or yellow lentils
1 cup water
½ teaspoon salt
¼ teaspoon ground black pepper
1 medium butternut squash, (about 1½ pounds) peeled, seeded, and cut lengthwise in ½-inch slices
¼ cup red wine vinegar
4 cups watercress or torn green leaf lettuce
½ cup coarsely chopped toasted walnuts (see tip, page 77)
  Fresh flat-leaf parsley leaves

1. Soak wood chips in enough water to cover for at least 1 hour before grilling.

2. In a large saucepan cook onion, celery, and garlic in 1 tablespoon of the oil over medium heat for 6 to 8 minutes or until tender. Add broth, lentils, water, salt, and pepper. Bring to boiling. Reduce heat and simmer, covered, 20 to 25 minutes or until tender.

3. Spread lentils in a 13½×9½×3-inch disposable foil pan. Drain wood chips. For a charcoal grill, sprinkle wood chips over medium coals. Place foil pan and butternut squash slices on a grill rack directly over coals. Cover and grill 8 to 10 minutes, or until squash is tender, turning once halfway through grilling and stirring lentils once. (For a gas grill, add wood chips to the grill according to manufacturer's directions. Cover and grill as above.)

4. When cool enough to handle, chop squash and stir into lentils. In small bowl combine remaining 4 tablespoons oil and the vinegar. On a serving platter, spoon lentil mixture over watercress, sprinkle with walnuts and parsley. Drizzle with oil-vinegar mixture. Serve at room temperature or chilled.

PER SERVING: *496 cal., 19 g fat (2 g sat. fat), 0 g chol., 734 mg sodium, 62 g carb., 26 g fiber, 23 g pro.*

PREP: 25 MINUTES **SOAK:** 1 HOUR **COOK:** 20 MINUTES **GRILL:** 8 MINUTES **MAKES:** 6 SERVINGS

seitan bulgogi

"BULGOGI" MAY MEAN "FIRE MEAT" IN KOREAN, BUT THIS TRADITIONAL GRILLED MARINATED BEEF DISH GOES MEATLESS IN THIS RECIPE WITH GRILLED MARINATED SEITAN SERVED IN CRISP LETTUCE LEAVES. SEITAN IS A PROTEIN-RICH FOOD MADE FROM WHEAT GLUTEN THAT HAS A CHEWY, MEATLIKE TEXTURE—WHICH IS WHY IT IS SOMETIMES CALLED "WHEAT MEAT."

¼ cup reduced-sodium soy sauce
2 tablespoons water
2 tablespoons honey
1 tablespoon rice vinegar
1 tablespoon peeled and grated fresh ginger
3 cloves garlic, minced
1 teaspoon sesame oil
1 pound seitan (wheat gluten), sliced ½ inch thick*
4 heads baby bok choy, halved lengthwise
8 butterhead lettuce leaves
½ cup julienned carrots
2 tablespoons sliced green onions
2 teaspoons toasted sesame seeds (see tip, page 77)

1. For the marinade, in a small bowl combine soy sauce, water, honey, vinegar, ginger, garlic, and oil.

2. Place a large resealable plastic bag in a shallow dish. Add seitan and marinade; seal bag. Turn to coat seitan. Marinate in the refrigerator for 2 to 4 hours. Drain seitan, reserving marinade.

3. For a charcoal or gas grill, place a grill basket on the rack of a grill directly over medium heat. Add seitan to grill basket. Place baby bok choy directly on the grill rack. Cover and grill 4 to 6 minutes or until lightly browned, turning once halfway through grilling and brushing seitan and bok choy with reserved marinade.

4. When cool enough to handle, slice bok choy. Serve seitan and bok choy in lettuce leaves topped with carrots, green onions, and sesame seeds.

* Or use seitan cubes or strips.

PER SERVING: *215 cal., 3 g fat (0 g sat. fat), 0 g chol., 1,144 mg sodium, 21 g carb., 3 g fiber, 28 g pro.*

PREP: 25 MINUTES **MARINATE:** 2 HOURS **GRILL:** 4 MINUTES **MAKES:** 4 SERVINGS

portobello fajitas

2 tablespoons olive oil
¼ teaspoon salt
¼ teaspoon ground black pepper
3 medium portobello mushrooms
1 red and/or yellow sweet pepper, quartered
8 6- to 7-inch flour tortillas
2 medium avocados, halved, seeded, and peeled
¼ cup light mayonnaise
1 teaspoon chili powder
Salsa verde (optional)
Lime wedges (optional)
Fresh cilantro sprigs (optional)

1. In a small bowl combine oil, salt, and black pepper. Brush the portobello mushrooms and sweet pepper with the oil. Stack tortillas and wrap in foil.

2. For a charcoal or gas grill, place portobellos, sweet pepper quarters, and foil packet on a grill directly over medium heat. Cover and grill for 8 to 10 minutes or until tender, turning once halfway through grilling.

3. Slice portobello and sweet pepper into strips. In a medium bowl mash one of the avocados; stir in mayonnaise and chili powder. Season to taste with salt and pepper. Slice remaining avocado. Serve sweet pepper, portobello, and sliced avocado on tortillas. Top with mayonnaise. If desired, serve with salsa verde and garnish with lime wedges and cilantro.

PER SERVING: *479 cal., 30 g fat (3 g sat. fat), 5 mg chol., 401 mg sodium, 40 g carb., 7 g fiber, 10 g pro.*

PREP: 15 MINUTES   **GRILL:** 8 MINUTES   **MAKES:** 4 SERVINGS

grilled tofu teriyaki with spicy spinach udon

1   **18-ounce package firm tofu (fresh bean curd, not silken-style), drained**
    Canola or vegetable oil
½   **cup hoisin sauce**
¼   **cup reduced-sodium soy sauce**
1   **tablespoon peeled and grated fresh ginger**
2   **teaspoons Asian chili-garlic sauce**
2   **7 to 7.5-ounce packages fresh udon noodles (broad white noodles)**
½   **cup vegetable broth**
3   **tablespoons peanut butter**
1   **9- to 10-ounce bag fresh spinach**
½   **teaspoon toasted sesame oil**
⅓   **cup grape tomatoes, halved**
¼   **cup thinly sliced green onions (2)**

1. Line a tray with paper towels. Cut tofu into six ½-inch-thick slices. Arrange tofu on prepared tray. Top with more paper towels; cover with a baking sheet. Evenly weigh down the baking sheet; let stand for 10 minutes. Change paper towels and repeat. Place tofu in a dish and generously coat both sides with canola oil.

2. For teriyaki sauce, in a small bowl whisk together hoisin sauce, 2 tablespoons of the soy sauce, the ginger, and 1 teaspoon of the chili-garlic sauce.

3. For a charcoal or gas grill, generously grease grill rack. Place tofu on a grill rack directly over medium heat. Cover and grill for 3 to 4 minutes or until brown and tofu releases easily from the rack. Turn tofu over. Cover and grill for 3 minutes more. Brush tofu with some of the teriyaki sauce. Turn and brush again. Cover and grill for 3 minutes more, turning once. Transfer tofu to a plate; cover and keep warm. Set aside remaining teriyaki sauce.

4. Meanwhile, fill a 4-quart Dutch oven half full with water; bring to boiling. Add udon noodles; cook for 2 minutes. Drain.

5. In the same Dutch oven whisk together broth, peanut butter, the remaining 2 tablespoons soy sauce, and the remaining 1 teaspoon chili-garlic sauce until smooth. Bring to boiling;

reduce heat to medium. Add noodles, stirring to coat. Stir in spinach; cook for 2 to 3 minutes or until wilted. Remove from heat; stir in oil. Serve with grilled tofu, tomatoes, and green onions. Pass remaining teriyaki sauce.

PER SERVING: *478 cal., 15 g fat (1 g sat. fat), 1 mg chol., 1051 mg sodium, 63 g carb., 6 g fiber, 22 g pro.*

PREP: 20 MINUTES   **GRILL:** 9 MINUTES   **STAND:** 20 MINUTES   **MAKES:** 6 SERVINGS

grilled strawberries

STRAWBERRIES CAN ONLY TAKE A SHORT TURN ON THE GRILL—BUT EVEN A JUST A COUPLE OF MINUTES OVER THE HEAT INTENSIFIES THEIR FLAVOR AND SWEETNESS. (SEE PAGE 14 FOR DIRECTIONS ON GRILLING STRAWBERRIES.)

1. STRAWBERRY–GOAT CHEESE BRUSCHETTA Halve an 8-ounce baguette crosswise, then lengthwise. Brush with 1 tablespoon oil. Place on grill rack directly over medium heat. Cover and grill 1 to 2 minutes or until toasted. Slice one 4-ounce log goat cheese and divide among toasts. Top with 1½ cups sliced grilled strawberries. Top with ½ cup arugula; drizzle with oil. Sprinkle with sea salt, black pepper, and fresh herbs. Makes 4 servings.

2. STRAWBERRY MILK SHAKE In a blender combine ¼ cup whole milk, 1¾ cups good-quality vanilla or strawberry ice cream, ¼ teaspoon vanilla extract, and 2 cups grilled strawberries. Cover and blend until smooth. Pour into 2 serving glasses. If desired, top with sweetened whipped cream. Makes 2 servings.

3. MASCARPONE AND GRILLED STRAWBERRIES SPREAD In a medium mixing bowl beat one 8-ounce carton mascarpone cheese and ¼ cup powdered sugar with an electric mixer on medium speed until smooth. Fold in ½ cup finely chopped grilled strawberries and ¼ teaspoon lemon zest. Serve with crepes, scones, and toast. Makes about 1 cup.

4. GRILLED STRAWBERRY-RHUBARB SAUCE In a blender or food processor combine 2 cups grilled strawberries, 1 cup sliced rhubarb, 1 tablespoon granulated sugar, and 1 teaspoon vanilla extract. Cover and blend until smooth. Transfer to a saucepan; heat until warm. Serve with pancakes or waffles. Makes 1½ cups.

5. GRILLED CAKE WITH STRAWBERRIES AND CREAM In a bowl combine 4 cups grilled strawberries, 3 tablespoons sugar, and 1 teaspoon Grand Mariner or orange juice; let stand 1 hour. Slice one purchased 9.25-ounce pound cake into six ¾-inch slices. Place slices directly on grill rack over medium heat. Cover and grill 2 to 4 minutes or until toasted, turning once. Serve cake with strawberries and sweetened whipped cream. Makes 6 servings.

6. GREENS WITH GRILLED STRAWBERRIES, PECANS, AND FETA Divide 6 cups arugula among 4 salad plates. Divide 1 cup sliced grilled strawberries, ¼ cup toasted pecans (see tip, page 77), and ¼ cup slivered red onions, and ⅓ cup crumbled feta cheese. In a screw-top jar combine ¼ cup lemon juice, ¼ cup oil, 1 teaspoon honey, and ¼ teaspoon salt. Cover and shake well to combine. Drizzle over salads. Makes 4 servings.

Strawberry–Goat Cheese Bruschetta

vegetarian spiedini

HALLOUMI IS A SEMIHARD, BRINED CHEESE POPULAR IN GREECE AND CYPRUS. IT HAS A HIGH MELTING POINT, WHICH MAKES IT IDEAL FOR GRILLING OR FRYING, AS IT HOLDS ITS SHAPE BEAUTIFULLY.

2 tablespoons balsamic vinegar
4 tablespoons olive oil
1 teaspoon Dijon-style mustard
1 teaspoon honey
4 cloves garlic, minced
¼ teaspoon ground black pepper
⅛ teaspoon salt
1 18-ounce package extra-firm tofu (fresh bean curd), drained, patted dry and cut into 1½-inch cubes
1 small zucchini, sliced ½-inch thick (5 ounces)
1 small red onion, cut into 1-inch wedges
4 ¾-inch-thick slices crusty Italian bread
1 cup cherry tomatoes
  Nonstick cooking spray
4 ounces halloumi cheese, cut horizontally into 4 slices
1 recipe Arugula-Mint Pesto Sauce

1. For the marinade, in a small screw-top jar combine vinegar, 2 tablespoons of the oil, mustard, honey, 2 cloves of the garlic, pepper, and salt. Cover and shake well; set aside.

2. Place tofu, zucchini, and red onion in a large resealable plastic bag set in a shallow dish. Pour marinade over tofu and vegetables; seal bag. Turn bag to coat tofu and vegetables. Marinate in the refrigerator for 30 minutes to 4 hours. Drain tofu and vegetables from marinade, discarding marinade.

3. In a small bowl stir together the remaining 2 tablespoons oil and the remaining 2 cloves garlic. Brush bread slices with oil mixture.

4. Thread tofu, zucchini, onion, and cherry tomatoes on eight 10- to 12-inch skewers (see tip, page 30) leaving ¼-inch space between items. Lightly coat with cooking spray.

5. For a charcoal or gas grill, place vegetable skewers on the rack of a grill directly over medium heat. Cover and grill 6 minutes or until tofu is lightly browned and vegetables are crisp-tender, turning occasionally. Remove from grill; keep warm. Add bread and cheese slices to grill. Cover and grill 1 to 2 minutes or until bread is toasted and cheese is lightly charred and warmed through, turning once halfway through grilling. Serve bread, cheese, and vegetable kabobs with Arugula-Mint Pesto Sauce.

ARUGULA-MINT PESTO SAUCE In a blender or food processor combine 1 cup lightly packed arugula, ½ cup lightly packed fresh mint leaves, ½ cup oil, 2 tablespoons lightly toasted pine nuts (see tip, page 77), 1 tablespoon lime juice, and 2 cloves sliced garlic. Cover; blend or process until smooth, scraping down sides as needed. Add ¼ cup finely shredded Parmesan cheese. Cover and blend or process just until combined. Season to taste with salt and black pepper.

PER SERVING: *643 cal., 51 g fat (12 g sat. fat), 113 mg chol., 810 mg sodium, 25 g carb., 3 g fiber, 24 g pro.*

PREP: 30 MINUTES **MARINATE:** 30 MINUTES **GRILL:** 7 MINUTES **MAKES:** 4 SERVINGS

grilled southwestern falafels with cilantro tabbouleh

TWO MEATLESS MIDDLE EASTERN FAVORITES COME TOGETHER IN THIS DISH—WITH A DECIDEDLY MEXICAN ACCENT. CORIANDER AND CUMIN FLAVOR THE FALAFEL, WHILE A LIME VINAIGRETTE DRESSES TABBOULEH STUDDED WITH GRILLED JALAPEÑO, CILANTRO, AND CRUNCHY JICAMA AND RADISH.

- ¾ cup bulgur, rinsed and drained
- ¾ cup water
- 2 fresh jalapeño chile peppers (see tip, page 21)
- ½ cup chopped jicama
- ⅔ cup chopped fresh cilantro
- ¼ cup julienned radishes
- ¼ cup finely chopped red onion
- 5 tablespoons olive oil
- 3 tablespoons lime juice
- 2 tablespoons water
- ¾ teaspoon salt
- 1 large tomato, chopped
- 1 15- to 16-ounce can chickpeas (garbanzo beans), rinsed and drained
- 2 tablespoons all-purpose flour
- 3 cloves garlic, halved
- 1 teaspoon ground coriander
- ½ teaspoon ground cumin
- ⅛ teaspoon ground black pepper
- 4 tablespoons Mexican crema or sour cream (optional)
  Lime wedges

1. In a medium saucepan, bring the bulgur and ¾ cup water to boiling; reduce heat. Cover and simmer about 5 minutes or until the water is almost absorbed. Remove from heat. Let stand, covered, for 10 minutes. Drain.

2. For a charcoal or gas grill, place whole jalapeños on a grill rack directly over medium heat. Cover and grill for 4 to 6 minutes or until tender and lightly charred. Remove stems and seeds and finely chop jalapeños. Reserve half of the chopped jalapeños.

3. In a large bowl combine bulgur, half of the grilled jalapeños, the jicama, ½ cup of the cilantro, the radishes, and onion.

4. For dressing, in a screw-top jar combine 3 tablespoons of the oil, the lime juice, the 2 tablespoons water, and ¼ teaspoon of the salt. Cover and shake well to combine. Drizzle dressing over bulgur mixture; toss to coat. Cover and chill for 4 to 24 hours. Stir tomato into mixture just before serving.

5. In a food processor combine the beans, reserved jalapeño, remaining cilantro, 1 tablespoon of the oil, remaining ½ teaspoon salt, the flour, garlic, coriander, cumin, and black pepper. Cover and process until finely chopped and mixture holds together, stopping and scraping down sides as needed. Shape into 4 patties. Brush patties with the remaining 1 tablespoon oil.

6. For a charcoal or gas grill, place patties on the greased rack of a grill directly over medium heat. Cover and grill for 6 to 8 minutes or until heated through and lightly browned, turning once halfway through grilling. Top each falafel with 1 tablespoon crema, if desired. Serve with tabbouleh and lime wedges.

PER SERVING: *390 cal., 22 g fat (4 g sat. fat), 13 mg chol., 739 mg sodium, 42 g carb., 11 g fiber, 10 g pro.*

PREP: 45 MINUTES **STAND:** 10 MINUTES **GRILL:** 10 MINUTES **CHILL:** 4 HOURS **MAKES:** 4 SERVINGS

grilled garden club

A CREAMY COMBO OF AVOCADO AND PESTO SERVES AS A SPREAD ON THIS VEGGIE-PACKED GRILLED SANDWICH.

2 medium portobello mushrooms, stems and gills removed
½ medium red onion, sliced
2 small zucchini and/or yellow squash, sliced lengthwise
2 tablespoons olive oil
  Salt and ground black pepper
1 avocado, halved, seeded, peeled, and chopped (see page 272)
2 tablespoons prepared or homemade pesto (see tip, right)
1 16-ounce ciabatta bread, cut horizontally in three layers
1 8-ounce ball fresh mozzarella, sliced
½ 12-ounce jar bottled roasted red peppers, drained (1 cup)
2 cups fresh spinach leaves

1. Brush mushrooms, onion, and squash with oil; sprinkle with salt and black pepper. For a charcoal or gas grill, place vegetables on a rack directly over medium heat. Cover and grill for, 10 to 12 minutes for mushrooms and onion and 5 to 6 minutes for squash, turning vegetables once halfway through grilling. Meanwhile, mash avocado in a small bowl; stir in pesto.

2. Spread avocado-pesto on cut surfaces of top and bottom slices of ciabatta. Thickly slice mushrooms. To assemble, on bottom bread slice, layer half the mozzarella, mushrooms, onions, squash, center bread slice, remaining mozzarella, roasted red peppers, spinach, then ciabatta top. Press together and wrap in foil. Place on a grill rack directly over medium heat. Cover and grill for 15 minutes or until heated through, turning twice. Slice to serve.

PER SERVING: *615 cal., 30 g fat (11 g sat. fat), 47 mg chol., 889 mg sodium, 65 g carb., 7 g fiber, 24 g pro.*

PRESTO PESTO

Store-bought pesto is convenient, but homemade is so much better: In a blender or food processor combine ⅓ cup olive oil, 2 cups firmly packed basil leaves, ½ cup grated Parmesan cheese, 3 cloves peeled and quartered garlic, and ¼ teaspoon salt. Blend or process until nearly smooth, stopping and scraping down sides as necessary and adding oil until desired consistency. Add black pepper to taste. Makes about ¾ cup pesto. Store in an airtight container for 1 to 2 days or freeze for up to 3 months.

PREP: 30 MINUTES **GRILL:** 25 MINUTES **MAKES:** 4 SERVINGS

summer squash souvlaki

TOOTHSOME CHUNKS OF GRILLED SUMMER SQUASH STAND IN FOR LAMB IN THIS POPULAR GREEK-STYLE SPECIALTY.

¾ cup coarsely shredded, seeded cucumber
½ cup plain Greek yogurt
2 teaspoons lemon juice
1 teaspoon snipped fresh dillweed
1 clove garlic, minced
¼ teaspoon salt
¼ cup crumbled feta cheese (1 ounce)
1 small zucchini, cut into ¾-inch pieces
1 small yellow summer squash, cut into ¾-inch pieces
1 cup small fresh mushrooms
1 small red onion, cut into thin wedges
1 tablespoon olive oil
½ teaspoon dried oregano, crushed
¼ teaspoon crushed red pepper
4 Greek pita flatbreads
1 medium roma tomato, sliced
   Snipped fresh dillweed and/or crumbled feta cheese (optional)

1. For the tzatziki, in a small bowl combine cucumber, yogurt, lemon juice, 1 teaspoon dillweed, garlic, and salt. Fold in ¼ cup cheese. If desired, cover and chill for up to 2 hours.

2. On four 10- to 12-inch skewers (see tip, page 30) alternately thread zucchini, yellow squash, mushrooms, and onion, leaving ¼ inch between pieces. Brush with oil; sprinkle with oregano and crushed red pepper.

3. For a charcoal or gas grill, place skewers on the rack of a grill directly over medium heat. Cover and grill for 12 to 14 minutes or until vegetables are tender, turning occasionally. Remove from grill. Place flatbreads on grill rack. Cover and grill for 2 to 4 minutes or until heated through and lightly toasted, turning once halfway through grilling.

4. Spread flatbreads with tzatziki. Place the vegetables from one skewer on flatbreads. Top with tomato slices and, if desired, additional dillweed and/or cheese.

PER SERVING: *272 cal., 7 g fat (3 g sat. fat), 10 mg chol., 589 mg sodium, 42 g carb., 3 g fiber, 12 g pro.*

PREP: 30 MINUTES **GRILL:** 14 MINUTES **MAKES:** 4 SERVINGS

Pork-Wasabi Tacos, *recipe page 179*

pizza, burgers & sandwiches

A FLAME-COOKED BURGER MAY BE A STAPLE OF THE GRILL, BUT THE FUN DOESN'T HAVE TO STOP THERE. THESE HANDHELD MAIN DISHES—FROM A CLASSIC BEEF BURGER TO A VIETNAMESE BANH MI TO PIZZAS WITH A DIZZYING ARRAY OF TOPPINGS—MAKE FOR CASUAL, RELAXED DINING.

herbed pork burgers and grilled tomato orzo salad

3 slices prosciutto, halved crosswise
1½ pounds ground pork
¼ cup snipped mixed fresh herbs (such as oregano, basil, Italian [flat-leaf] parsley, rosemary, and/or thyme)
3 cloves garlic, minced
½ teaspoon salt
½ teaspoon ground black pepper
1½ cups grape or cherry tomatoes
⅓ cup mayonnaise
¾ teaspoon finely shredded lemon peel
1½ teaspoons snipped fresh rosemary
¼ cup lemon juice
2½ cups fresh spinach
6 ounces orzo pasta, cooked according to package directions
1 cup canned chickpeas (garbanzo beans), rinsed and drained
¼ cup crumbled feta cheese
2 tablespoons olive oil
1 tablespoon toasted pine nuts (see tip, page 77)
½ teaspoon salt
⅛ teaspoon ground black pepper
6 ciabatta rolls, split
3 roma tomatoes, sliced

1. Preheat oven to 400°F. Place prosciutto on a lightly greased baking sheet. Bake for 5 to 8 minutes or until crisp. Remove from baking sheet; set aside.

2. In a large bowl combine pork, snipped herbs, garlic, the ½ teaspoon salt and ½ teaspoon pepper; mix well. Shape into six ¾-inch patties. Thread grape tomatoes on skewers (see tip, page 30).

3. For a charcoal or gas grill, place patties and tomato kabobs on a grill rack directly over medium heat. Cover and grill patties for 14 to 18 minutes or until done (160°F), turning once halfway through grilling. Grill tomato skewers 2 to 4 minutes or until lightly charred, turning once. Place rolls, cut sides down, on grill rack for 1 to 2 minutes or until lightly toasted.

4. For the lemon-rosemary mayonnaise, in a small bowl combine mayonnaise, lemon peel, 1 teaspoon of the rosemary, and 1 tablespoon of the lemon juice; set aside.

5. Shred 1 cup of the spinach. In a medium bowl combine the shredded spinach, grilled tomatoes, orzo, chickpeas, cheese, remaining 2 tablespoons lemon juice, the oil, pine nuts, the ½ teaspoon salt, and the ⅛ teaspoon pepper. Toss to combine.

6. Spread roll bottoms with lemon-rosemary mayonnaise. Top with patties, prosciutto crisps, remaining 1½ cups spinach leaves, tomato slices, and roll tops.

PER SERVING: *744 cal., 42 g fat (12 g sat. fat), 96 mg chol., 1106 mg sodium, 57 g carb., 6 g fiber, 33 g pro.*

PREP: 30 MINUTES **GRILL:** 15 MINUTES **MAKES:** 6 SERVINGS

classic cheeseburgers with grilled romaine & onions

1¼ pounds ground beef chuck
    Kosher or sea salt and ground black
    pepper
1   large red onion, cut into ½-inch-thick
    slices
2   tablespoons olive oil
6   ounces sharp cheddar cheese, thinly
    sliced
6   hamburger buns, split
½   small heart romaine lettuce
¼   cup mayonnaise

1. Shape ground beef into six ¾-inch-thick patties. Season with salt and pepper. Brush both sides of onion slices with 1 tablespoon of the oil. For a charcoal or gas grill, place patties and onion slices on the grill rack over medium heat. Cover and grill onion slices for 8 to 10 minutes or until lightly charred and tender, and patties for 12 to 14 minutes or until done (160°F), turning once halfway through grilling. Top patties with cheese the last 1 minute of grilling. Remove patties from grill.

2. Meanwhile, place buns, cut sides down, on grill rack for 1 to 2 minutes or until lightly toasted. Brush romaine heart with remaining 1 tablespoon oil. Grill 3 minutes, until lightly charred turning once halfway through grilling. Remove from grill; separate into leaves. Spread buns with mayonnaise. Serve patties on buns with onions and romaine.

PER SERVING: *506 cal., 32 g fat (13 g sat. fat), 93 mg chol., 724 mg sodium, 26 g carb., 2 g fiber, 28 g pro.*

HEARTY ROMAINE

Romaine lettuce is sturdy enough to stand up to grilling. The charring and smoky flavor, combined with the contrast of the crisp texture with a little bit of wilting is just delicious. For a quick side dish, prepare the romaine hearts for grilling (see page 17), then brush generously with your favorite vinaigrette. Grill, then chop roughly and toss with additional vinaigrette. Sprinkle with shredded Parmesan or crumbled feta or blue cheese and serve.

PREP: 30 MINUTES **GRILL:** 12 MINUTES **MAKES:** 6 SERVINGS

burger with pickled beets and fried egg

2 medium beets
½ cup sugar
½ cup water
½ cup white wine vinegar
3 strips orange peel
2 teaspoons salt
½ teaspoon cracked black pepper
1 pound ground beef chuck
8 ounces ground beef sirloin
½ teaspoon salt
¼ teaspoon ground black pepper
4 kaiser rolls, split
2 teaspoons olive oil
4 eggs
2 ounces soft goat cheese (chèvre)
4 Bibb lettuce leaves

1. In a large saucepan combine the beets and enough water to cover. Bring to boiling; reduce heat. Cook, covered, about 30 minutes or until tender. Drain and let cool slightly. Under running water, rub off the peels. Halve the beets lengthwise and julienne; set aside. In a medium saucepan bring sugar, the ½ cup water, vinegar, orange peel, 2 teaspoons salt, and the cracked pepper to a simmer, stirring to dissolve the sugar. Add the beets, remove from the heat. Let stand for 30 minutes; drain, discarding vinegar mixture.

2. Meanwhile, for burgers, in a medium bowl combine beef chuck and sirloin. Sprinkle with the ½ teaspoon salt and ground pepper; mix well. Shape into four ¾-inch-thick patties.

3. For a charcoal or gas grill, place patties on the grill rack directly over medium heat. Cover and grill for 10 to 12 minutes or until done (160°F), turning once halfway through grilling. Remove patties from grill. Place rolls, cut sides down, on grill rack for 1 to 2 minutes or until lightly toasted.

4. In a large nonstick skillet heat the oil over medium heat. Break eggs into skillet; cook for 2 minutes. Cover skillet; remove from heat. Let eggs stand about 2 minutes or until whites are set and yolks begin to thicken.

5. Spread goat cheese on the cut side of each roll bottom. Serve patties on rolls with lettuce, beets,* and eggs.

* Store any remaining pickled beets in an airtight container in the refrigerator for 1 week. Use them in salads or as a sandwich relish.

PER SERVING: *671 cal., 36 g fat (14 g sat. fat), 310 mg chol., 777 mg sodium, 36 g carb., 2 g fiber, 48 g pro.*

PREP: 30 MINUTES COOK: 30 MINUTES STAND: 30 MINUTES GRILL: 10 MINUTES MAKES: 4 SERVINGS

pork burgers with grilled mango salsa and sweet jerk sauce

IF YOU MUST HAVE FRIES WITH YOUR BURGER, BAKE A BATCH OF SWEET POTATO FRIES—HOMEMADE OR FROZEN—TO GO WITH THIS ISLAND-STYLE PORK BURGER.

1 medium ripe mango, halved, seeded, and peeled (see page 275)
5 green onions, trimmed
1 fresh jalapeño chile pepper (see tip, page 21)
1 teaspoon peeled and grated fresh ginger
2 cloves garlic, minced
½ teaspoon snipped fresh thyme
1 pound ground pork
¼ cup sweet Asian chili sauce
½ teaspoon finely shredded lime peel
1 teaspoon lime juice
1 teaspoon soy sauce
4 teaspoons Jamaican jerk seasoning
4 hamburger buns, split
4 Bibb lettuce leaves

1. For a charcoal or gas grill, place mango, green onions, and jalapeño on the grill rack directly over medium heat for 6 to 8 minutes or until tender and lightly charred, turning once halfway through grilling.

2. When cool enough to handle, chop the mango and place in a small bowl; set aside. Chop the green onions. Stem, halve, seed, and finely chop the jalapeño. In a medium bowl combine the green onions, jalapeño, ginger, garlic, and thyme. Divide the mixture in half. Add half to the mango. Cover and chill until ready to serve.

3. In a large bowl combine the pork and the remaining half of the green onion mixture; mix well. Shape into four ¾-inch-thick patties.

4. For a gas or charcoal grill, place patties on the grill rack directly over medium heat. Cover and grill for 14 to 18 minutes or until done (160°F), turning once halfway through grilling. Place buns, cut sides down, on grill rack for 1 to 2 minutes or until lightly toasted.

5. In a small bowl combine Asian chili sauce, lime peel, lime juice, soy sauce, and jerk seasoning. Spread sauce on cut sides of buns.

6. Place lettuce leaves on bun bottoms. Serve patties on buns with mango salsa.

PER SERVING: *499 cal., 26 g fat (9 g sat. fat), 82 mg chol., 818 mg sodium, 38 g carb., 2 g fiber, 24 g pro.*

PREP: 30 MINUTES **GRILL:** 21 MINUTES **MAKES:** 4 SERVINGS

turkey burgers with grilled pear slaw

QUICK-COOK BACON IN THE MICROWAVE: PLACE A FEW SLICES ON A PAPER TOWEL–LINED PLATE. COVER WITH ANOTHER PAPER TOWEL, THEN COOK ON HIGH FOR 2 TO 3 MINUTES TO DESIRED DONENESS. TRANSFER TO A CLEAN PAPER TOWEL TO DRAIN. BACON WILL CRISP UP AS IT COOLS.

3	firm ripe pears (about 1 pound)
1	pound ground turkey
½	teaspoon snipped fresh thyme
¼	teaspoon salt
¼	teaspoon ground black pepper
4	slices white cheddar cheese (3 ounces)
4	whole grain hamburger buns, split
¼	cup mayonnaise
¼	cup Dijon-style mustard
2	tablespoons pure maple syrup
4	cups shredded red cabbage
1	stalk celery, thinly bias-sliced
2	green onions, chopped
¼	cup dried cranberries
¼	cup chopped pecans, toasted (see tip, page 77)
2	tablespoons lemon juice
	Salt and ground black pepper
1	cup fresh spinach
4	slices bacon, crisp-cooked

1. Halve and core pears. Shred one pear half. In a large bowl combine shredded pear, turkey, thyme, the ¼ teaspoon salt, and the ¼ teaspoon pepper; mix well. Shape into four ¾-inch-thick patties.

2. For a gas or charcoal grill, place remaining pears on a greased grill rack directly over medium heat. Cover and grill 6 to 8 minutes or until tender and lightly browned, turning once halfway through grilling. Remove from grill; set aside. Place patties on grill rack directly over medium heat. Cover and grill 12 minutes or until no longer pink (170°F), turning once halfway through grilling. Top patties with cheese the last 1 minute of grilling. Place buns, cut sides down, on grill rack for 1 to 2 minutes or until lightly toasted.

3. In a small bowl combine mayonnaise, mustard, and maple syrup. Set aside ¼ cup of the mixture.

4. When cool enough to handle, thinly slice pears. For the grilled pear slaw, in a large bowl combine pears, cabbage, celery, green onions, dried cranberries, and pecans. Add remaining mayonnaise mixture and lemon juice; toss to coat. Season to taste with salt and pepper.

5. Spread reserved mayonnaise mixture on cut sides of buns. Serve patties on buns with spinach and bacon. Pass grilled pear slaw.

PER SERVING: *749 cal., 38 g fat (10 g sat. fat), 115 mg chol., 1295 mg sodium, 71 g carb., 14 g fiber, 40 g pro.*

PREP: 35 MINUTES **GRILL:** 13 MINUTES **MAKES:** 4 SERVINGS

turkey burgers with peaches and blueberries

YOU CAN USE ANY KIND OF GROUND TURKEY IN THIS RECIPE—BREAST MEAT ONLY OR A COMBINATION OF WHITE AND DARK MEAT. IF YOU USE GROUND TURKEY BREAST, AVOID OVERCOOKING, WHICH CAN DRY IT OUT.

4   **small peaches (see page 275)**
1   **pound ground turkey**
    Salt and ground black pepper
4   **slices Monterey Jack cheese**
½   **cup blueberries**
¼   **teaspoon chili powder**
4   **thick slices roasted garlic country bread or garlic bread**
    Fresh mint (optional)
    Chili powder (optional)

1. Finely chop one of the peaches. In a large bowl combine chopped peach, the turkey, salt, and pepper. Shape turkey mixture into four ½-inch-thick patties.

2. For a charcoal or gas grill, place patties on the grill rack directly over medium-high heat. Cover and grill for 8 to 10 minutes or until done (165°F), turning once halfway through grilling. Top patties with cheese the last 1 minute of grilling. Place bread, cut sides down, on grill rack for 1 to 2 minutes or until lightly toasted.

3. Meanwhile, coarsely chop the remaining three peaches. In a large skillet combine the peaches, blueberries, and ¼ teaspoon chili powder. Cook over medium heat for 5 to 6 minutes or until heated through and juices are beginning to form, stirring occasionally.

4. Serve patties on bread with some of the peach-blueberry sauce. If desired, top with mint and sprinkle with additional chili powder.

PER SERVING: *464 cal., 25 g fat (10 g sat. fat), 114 mg chol., 614 mg sodium, 28 g carb., 3 g fiber, 31 g pro.*

PREP: 20 MINUTES   **GRILL:** 9 MINUTES   **MAKES:** 4 SERVINGS

chili-glazed salmon burgers

PROCESS THE SALMON IN THE FOOD PROCESSOR WITH ON/OFF TURNS JUST UNTIL IT IS FINELY CHOPPED. OVERWORKING THE FLESH CAN TOUGHEN IT.

2 pounds fresh or frozen skinless, boneless salmon fillets
1 egg, lightly beaten
¼ cup thinly sliced green onions (2)
½ teaspoon salt
½ teaspoon ground black pepper
⅔ cup mayonnaise
2 to 3 tablespoons Asian chili sauce (Sriracha sauce)
1 tablespoon vegetable oil or canola oil
1 tablespoon rice vinegar
1 tablespoon soy sauce
1 teaspoon sugar
1 teaspoon toasted sesame oil
4 cups shredded cabbage with carrot (coleslaw mix)
¼ cup snipped fresh cilantro
  Vegetable oil or canola oil
  Sweet Asian chili sauce
6 sesame seed hamburger buns, split
1 cup thinly sliced seedless cucumber

1. Thaw salmon, if frozen. Rinse salmon; pat dry with paper towels. Cut into 1-inch pieces. Place salmon, half at a time, in a food processor. Cover and process until finely chopped. In a large bowl combine egg, green onions, salt, and pepper. Add chopped salmon; mix gently until combined. Using damp hands, shape mixture into six ½-inch-thick patties. Cover and chill for at least 30 minutes.

2. Meanwhile, in a small bowl combine mayonnaise and 2 to 3 tablespoons Asian chili sauce. Cover and chill until needed.

3. For slaw, in a large bowl whisk together 1 tablespoon vegetable oil, vinegar, soy sauce, sugar, and sesame oil. Add shredded cabbage and carrots and cilantro; toss to coat.

4. Lightly brush both sides of salmon patties with additional vegetable oil.

5. For a charcoal or gas grill, place patties on the rack of a covered grill directly over medium heat. Cover and grill for 6 to 8 minutes or until done (160°F), turning and brushing once with sweet chili sauce halfway through grilling. Place buns, cut sides down, on grill rack for 1 to 2 minutes or until lightly toasted.

6. Spread cut sides of buns with mayonnaise mixture. Serve patties on buns with slaw and cucumber slices.

PER SERVING: *589 cal., 35 g fat (5 g sat. fat), 123 mg chol., 942 mg sodium, 28 g carb., 2 g fiber, 36 g pro.*

PREP: 30 MINUTES **CHILL:** 30 MINUTES **GRILL:** 6 MINUTES **MAKES:** 6 SERVINGS

grilled summer squash and chicken sandwiches with harissa aïoli

HARISSA IS A TUNISIAN HOT CHILI SAUCE TRADITIONALLY MADE WITH ROASTED RED CHILES, GARLIC, CUMIN, CORIANDER, CARAWAY, AND OLIVE OIL. IT'S USED TO FLAVOR COUSCOUS, SOUPS, AND STEWS. HERE, IT LENDS ITS FIRE POWER TO A LIP-TINGLING MAYO.

2   skinless, boneless chicken breast halves (about 1 pound total)
¼   cup olive oil
¼   cup rice vinegar
1   recipe Harissa Spice Rub*
1   red sweet pepper, quartered
1   yellow summer squash, halved lengthwise
1   zucchini, halved lengthwise
⅓   cup mayonnaise
1   to 2 teaspoons Asian chili sauce (Sriracha sauce)
4   potato or other soft sandwich rolls, split

1. Split chicken breast halves horizontally into equal pieces. Place chicken in a large resealable plastic bag set in a shallow dish. In a small bowl whisk together oil, vinegar, and 2 tablespoons of the Harissa Spice Rub. Pour over chicken; seal bag. Turn to coat chicken. Marinate in the refrigerator 2 to 8 hours, turning occasionally. Drain, discarding marinade.

2. For a charcoal or gas grill, place chicken, sweet pepper (skin side down), summer squash and zucchini on the grill rack directly over medium heat. Cover and grill for 8 to 10 minutes or until sweet pepper is blistered and dark, summer squash and zucchini are tender and lightly charred and chicken is no longer pink (170°F), turning chicken, zucchini, and summer squash halfway through grilling (do not turn the sweet pepper). Place rolls, cut sides down, on grill rack for 1 to 2 minutes or until lightly toasted.

3. Immediately wrap sweet pepper in foil. Let stand about 15 minutes or until cool enough to handle. Use a sharp knife to loosen edges of the skins; gently pull off the skin in strips and discard. Cut summer squash and zucchini in half crosswise then slice in half horizontally.

4. For the harissa aïoli, in a small bowl whisk together mayonnaise, Asian chili sauce, and 1 teaspoon Harissa Spice Rub. Spread aïoli on cut sides of rolls. Serve chicken on rolls with sweet pepper, summer squash, and zucchini.

HARISSA SPICE RUB In a medium skillet toast 1 teaspoon cumin seeds, 1 teaspoon coriander seeds, 1 teaspoon fennel seeds, and ½ teaspoon caraway seeds over medium heat 1 to 2 minutes or until fragrant. In a mortar and pestle or spice grinder, crush spices. In a small bowl, combine crushed spices, 2 teaspoons snipped fresh mint, 1 teaspoon packed brown sugar, 2 cloves minced garlic, ½ teaspoon salt, ½ teaspoon crushed red pepper, and ½ teaspoon finely shredded lemon peel.

* Cover and refrigerate remaining Harissa Spice Rub for up to 1 week.

PER SERVING: *538 cal., 32 g fat (5 g sat. fat), 80 mg chol., 753 mg sodium, 31 g carb., 3 g fiber, 30 g pro.*

PREP: 25 MINUTES   MARINATE: 2 HOURS   GRILL: 8 MINUTES   STAND: 15 MINUTES   MAKES: 4 SERVINGS

muenster, cabbage, and apple sandwiches

THESE TOASTY GRILLED SANDWICHES ARE THE PERFECT END TO A FALL AFTERNOON HIKING THROUGH THE WOODS OR RAKING LEAVES IN THE YARD. SERVE WITH CHILLED HARD CIDER.

1 medium onion, halved lengthwise and thinly sliced
¼ cup apple cider vinegar
¼ cup water
1 cup coarsely shredded green cabbage
1 large cooking apple, such as Granny Smith, Rome Beauty, or Jonathan, thinly sliced (see page 270)
1 tablespoon stone-ground mustard
8 slices caraway rye bread
1 cup shredded Muenster cheese (4 ounces)
   Vegetable oil

1. In a medium skillet combine onion, vinegar, and water. Bring just to boiling; reduce heat. Simmer, covered, for 3 minutes. Stir in cabbage; simmer, covered, for 3 minutes. Stir in apple; simmer, covered, 3 minutes more or just until vegetables and apple are tender; drain. Stir in mustard.

2. Layer four of the bread slices with cabbage mixture and cheese. Top with the remaining bread slices. Lightly brush both sides of sandwiches with the oil.

3. For a charcoal or grill, place sandwiches on the lightly greased grill 13×9×2-inch baking pan on sandwiches; weight pan down with a brick or baking potatoes. Grill for about 2 minutes or until bread is light brown. Use hot pads to remove baking pan. Using a spatula, carefully turn over sandwiches. Place weighted pan back on sandwiches; grill about 2 minutes more or until bread is light brown and filling is heated through.

PER SERVING: *296 cal., 11 g fat (6 g sat. fat), 27 mg chol., 606 mg sodium, 39 g carb., 5 g fiber, 12 g pro.*

PREP: 20 MINUTES   **GRILL:** 4 MINUTES   **MAKES:** 4 SERVINGS

prosciutto-wrapped asparagus panini

16 asparagus spears (12 ounces) (see page 270)
8 very thin prosciutto slices (5 ounces)
8 slices marble rye bread
1 tablespoon stone-ground mustard
1 cup lightly packed arugula (optional)
8 thin slices provolone cheese
1 tablespoon bottled balsamic vinaigrette (or 2 teaspoons olive oil combined with 1 teaspoon balsamic vinegar)

1. Snap off and discard woody bases from asparagus. Trim stalks barely longer than the bread slices. For a charcoal or gas grill, place asparagus directly on the grill rack over medium heat. Cover and grill perpendicular to grates for 4 to 5 minutes or until crisp-tender. Transfer asparagus to a bowl of ice water for 30 seconds to cool; drain.

2. Using kitchen scissors, cut each piece of prosciutto in half lengthwise. Starting at the base of an asparagus spear, wrap 1 halved prosciutto piece around the asparagus spear diagonally to the top of the spear.

3. Spread 4 slices of the bread with mustard. Place 4 prosciutto-wrapped asparagus spears horizontally on each mustard-topped bread slice. If desired, top with arugula. Top with 2 slices of cheese. Lightly brush remaining 4 bread slices with balsamic vinaigrette. Place bread, vinaigrette sides down, on top of cheese.

4. For a charcoal or gas grill, place sandwiches on the lightly greased grill rack directly over medium heat. Place a 13×9×2-inch baking pan on the sandwiches; weight pan down with a brick. Grill about 2 minutes or until sandwiches are light brown. Using hot pads, remove baking pan. Using a spatula, carefully turn over sandwiches. Place weighted pan back on sandwich; grill about 2 minutes more or until cheese melts.

PER SERVING: *402 cal., 15 g fat (8 g sat. fat), 54 mg chol., 1713 mg sodium, 39 g carb., 4 g fiber, 29 g pro.*

PREP: 25 MINUTES **GRILL:** 11 MINUTES **MAKES:** 4 SERVINGS

roasted vegetable and fresh mozzarella panini

1 large Vidalia onion, peeled, halved, and sliced ¼ inch thick
1 red sweet pepper, seeded and cut into quarters
1 medium eggplant, peeled and sliced ¼ inch thick (see page 273)
1 large zucchini, trimmed and sliced ¼ inch thick
¼ cup garlic-flavored olive oil
1 1-pound loaf baguette-style French bread
1 recipe Dried Tomato Pesto
½ cup loosely packed fresh basil leaves
8 ounces fresh mozzarella cheese, sliced
1 tablespoon olive oil

1. Drizzle onion, sweet pepper, eggplant, and zucchini with the garlic-flavored oil; turn to coat vegetables. For a charcoal or gas grill, place vegetables directly on the grill rack over medium heat. Cover and grill and zucchini 5 to 6 minutes, sweet pepper for 6 to 8 minutes, onion for 10 minutes, and eggplant 8 to 12 minutes or until vegetables are tender. Remove from grill and cool slightly.

2. Slice the baguette in half lengthwise. Hollow out the centers of bread, reserving bread for another use. Spread cut sides of the baguette with Dried Tomato Pesto. Carefully arrange roasted zucchini in the bottom of the loaf followed by sweet pepper, eggplant, basil leaves, and onion. Arrange mozzarella slices evenly over the vegetables. Add the baguette top. Evenly brush both sides of sandwich with oil.

3. For a charcoal or gas grill, place sandwich on the lightly greased grill rack directly over medium heat. Place a 13×9×2-inch baking pan on the sandwich; weight pan down with a brick. Grill about 5 minutes or until sandwich is light brown. Using hot pads, remove baking pan. Using a spatula, carefully turn over sandwich. Place weighted pan back on sandwich; grill about 3 minutes more or until cheese melts.

4. Using a serrated knife, carefully cut each sandwich crosswise into 4 panini.

DRIED TOMATO PESTO In a food processor or blender combine ½ cup oil-packed dried tomatoes, 3 tablespoons oil, 2 tablespoons coarsely chopped fresh flat-leaf parsley, 2 tablespoons coarsely chopped fresh basil, 2 cloves coarsely chopped garlic, 2 teaspoons lemon juice, ¼ teaspoon salt, and ⅛ teaspoon ground

black pepper. Cover and process or blend until mixture is smooth. Transfer pesto to a small bowl; stir in ⅓ cup finely shredded Parmesan cheese. Makes ⅔ cup.

PER SERVING: 511 cal., 27 g fat (8.6 g sat. fat), 30 mg chol., 718 mg sodium, 49 g carb., 5 g fiber, 15.4 g pro.

PREP: 20 MINUTES **GRILL:** 20 MINUTES **MAKES:** 4 SERVINGS

spicy pork sandwich with grilled peach chutney and quick pickle

- 1 medium peach, halved and pitted (see page 275)
- 1 fresh jalapeño chile pepper (see tip, page 21)
- 6 tablespoons sugar
- 6 tablespoons white wine vinegar
- 1 teaspoon peeled and grated fresh ginger
- ¾ teaspoon kosher salt
- 1 large cucumber
- ¼ cup water
- ½ cup thinly sliced red onion
- 1 1½- to 2-pound boneless pork top loin roast (single loin)
- 1 tablespoon tandoori seasoning blend
- ¼ teaspoon salt
- 6 French rolls or hoagie rolls, split
- 6 slices Swiss cheese

1. For a charcoal or gas grill, place peach and jalapeño on a grill rack directly over medium heat. Cover and grill for 6 to 8 minutes or until lightly charred, turning once. When cool enough to handle, chop the peach. Stem, seed, and chop the jalapeño.

2. For the peach chutney, in a medium saucepan combine peach, jalapeño, 2 tablespoons of the sugar, 2 tablespoons of the vinegar, the ginger, and ¼ teaspoon of the kosher salt. Cook and stir over medium heat for 5 minutes, stirring frequently. Remove from heat; cool. Cover and refrigerate until ready to serve.

3. For the quick pickle, use a vegetable peeler to cut the cucumber into ribbons. In a medium bowl combine remaining 4 tablespoons vinegar, 4 tablespoons sugar, the water, and remaining ½ teaspoon kosher salt. Stir until dissolved. Add cucumber and onion. Cover and chill until ready to serve or up to 24 hours, stirring occasionally. Drain before serving.

4. Sprinkle pork roast with tandoori seasoning blend and salt. Rub in with your fingers. For a charcoal grill, arrange medium-hot coals around a drip pan. Test for medium-low heat above pan. Place meat on a grill rack over drip pan. Cover; grill for 1 to 1½ hours or until a meat thermometer registers 145°F. (For a gas grill, preheat grill. Reduce heat to medium-low. Adjust for indirect cooking. Grill as above, except place meat on a rack in a roasting pan.) Place French rolls, cut sides down, on grill rack directly over medium heat. Grill for 1 to 2 minutes or until lightly toasted.

5. Remove meat from grill; cover with foil and let stand for 15 minutes before slicing. (The meat's temperature will rise 10°F during standing.) Thinly slice pork.

6. Place French rolls on a baking sheet. Broil 4 to 5 inches from heat 1 to 2 minutes or until toasted; set roll tops aside. Top roll bottoms with pork and cheese. Broil 1 to 2 minutes or until cheese melts. Top with the quick pickle, peach chutney, and roll tops.

PER SERVING: *446 cal., 14 g fat (7 g sat. fat), 98 mg chol., 771 mg sodium, 40 g carb., 2 g fiber, 37 g pro.*

PREP: 45 MINUTES **GRILL:** 1 HOUR + 7 MINUTES **STAND:** 15 MINUTES **BROIL:** 2 MINUTES **MAKES:** 6 SERVINGS

catfish bahn mi with grilled radish pickle

WHEN THE FRENCH COLONIZED VIETNAM, THEY BROUGHT WITH THEM BAGUETTES—WHICH THE VIETNAMESE USED TO MAKE A VARIETY OF CRUNCHY, FLAVORFUL SANDWICHES THAT USUALLY FEATURED GRILLED PORK, CILANTRO, AND PICKLED CARROTS. THIS TASTY TWIST CALLS ON GRILLED CATFISH AND PICKLED RADISH INSTEAD.

1¼ pounds fresh or frozen catfish fillets, about ½ inch thick
1 tablespoon barbecue seasoning or chili powder
1 cup radishes, scrubbed and trimmed
2 ½-inch slices red onion
1 tablespoon olive oil
1 loaf baguette-style French bread, split horizontally
½ cup rice vinegar
2 tablespoons sugar
¼ teaspoon salt
1 cup shredded green cabbage
⅓ cup mayonnaise
2 teaspoons Asian chili sauce (Sriracha sauce)
⅓ cup fresh cilantro leaves
1 fresh jalapeño chile pepper, seeded if desired, and thinly sliced (see tip, page 21)

1. Thaw fish if frozen, Rinse fish; pat dry with paper towels. Sprinkle barbecue seasoning over catfish fillets. Rub in with your fingers; set aside.

2. Brush radishes and onion with oil. For a charcoal or gas grill, place a grill tray or grill wok on the grill rack directly over medium heat. Preheat 5 minutes. Add radishes to the grill tray. Place onion on a grill rack. Cover and grill 8 to 10 minutes or until radishes and onion are tender and lightly browned, turning once or twice. Place fish fillets on a greased grill rack directly over medium heat. Grill 4 to 6 minutes per ½-inch thickness or until fish flakes when tested with a fork, turning once. Place bread on grill, cut side down. Grill for 1 to 2 minutes or until lightly toasted.

3. When cool enough to handle, slice radishes and chop onion. In a medium bowl combine vinegar, sugar, and salt. Stir until dissolved. Add radishes, onion, and cabbage. Let stand 15 minutes. Drain before serving; discard liquid.

4. In a small bowl combine mayonnaise and Asian chili sauce. Spread mayonnaise mixture on the cut sides of the baguette. On the bottom half of the baguette, place fish fillets. Top with drained radish mixture, cilantro, and jalapeño. Top with baguette top. Cut crosswise into 4 to 6 portions.

PER SERVING: *537 cal., 21 g fat (4 g sat. fat), 90 mg chol., 1057 mg sodium, 49 g carb., 1 g fiber, 29 g pro.*

PREP: 30 MINUTES   GRILL: 8 MINUTES   STAND: 15 MINUTES   MAKES: 4 SERVINGS

peachy po' boy

THIS SANDWICH OF SWEET PEACHES AND GRILLED SHRIMP TOPPED WITH SALTY, SMOKY BACON COULD EASILY BE MADE WITH NECTARINES INSTEAD.

⅓ cup fresh or frozen medium shrimp (36 to 40)
⅓ cup butter, melted
1 tablespoon lemon juice
1 clove garlic, minced
¼ teaspoon salt
¼ teaspoon ground black pepper
1½ teaspoons Cajun seasoning
6 miniature baguettes or two 8-ounce baguettes, cut into thirds and split lengthwise
1 large fresh jalapeño chile pepper, thinly sliced (see tip, page 21)
3 peaches, halved and sliced (see page 275)
½ cup light mayonnaise
1 teaspoon coarsely ground black pepper
6 slices bacon, crisp-cooked and broken into small pieces
Snipped fresh cilantro
Lemon wedges (optional)

1. Thaw shrimp, if frozen. Peel and devein shrimp. Rinse shrimp; pat dry with paper towels. Set shrimp aside.

2. In a medium bowl stir together butter, lemon juice, garlic, salt, and the ¼ teaspoon ground black pepper. Lightly brush some of the butter mixture on cut sides of bread; set bread aside. Stir 1 teaspoon of the Cajun seasoning into the remaining butter mixture. Add shrimp and jalapeño; toss to coat. Place shrimp mixture in a large grill tray or grill wok.

3. For a charcoal or gas grill, place grill tray on the grill rack directly over medium heat. Cover and grill for 10 to 14 minutes or until shrimp are opaque, tossing occasionally. Place baguettes, cut sides down, on grill rack, for 1 to 2 minutes or until toasted.

4. Sprinkle sliced peaches with the remaining ½ teaspoon Cajun seasoning. Gently fold peaches into hot shrimp mixture. In a small bowl stir together mayonnaise and the 1 teaspoon coarsely ground black pepper. Spread mayonnaise mixture on the cut sides of the baguette tops. Place shrimp mixture on bottom halves. Top with bacon and cilantro. If desired, serve with lemon wedges.

PER SERVING: *554 cal., 23 g fat (9 g sat. fat), 186 mg chol., 1167 mg sodium, 55 g carb., 4 g fiber, 32 g pro.*

PREP: 35 MINUTES GRILL: 10 MINUTES MAKES: 6 SERVINGS

smoked tomato po' boy sandwiches

A HICKORY OR OAK GRILLING PLANK IMPARTS FABULOUS FLAVOR TO THICK SLICES OF JUICY SUMMER TOMATOES IN THIS VEGETARIAN VERSION OF A NEW ORLEANS FAVORITE.

- 1 14×6×¾-inch hickory or oak grilling plank
- 2 medium green and/or firm ripe tomatoes (5 to 6 ounces each), cut into ½-inch slices
- ¼ teaspoon salt
- ¼ teaspoon ground black pepper
- 1 small red onion, cut into ½-inch slices
- ¼ cup mayonnaise
- 1 tablespoon pickle relish
- 1 tablespoon ketchup
- 2 teaspoons capers
- 2 teaspoons Creole mustard or spicy brown mustard
- 2 teaspoons snipped fresh Italian (flat-leaf) parsley
- ½ teaspoon bottled hot pepper sauce
- 4 hoagie buns, split
- 1 cup fresh baby arugula or spinach
- 4 radishes, thinly sliced

1. Place the grill plank in a container of water; weight down the plank and soak it for at least 1 hour.

2. For a charcoal or gas grill, place plank on the rack of a covered grill directly over medium heat. Grill, uncovered, for 3 to 5 minutes or until plank starts to crackle and smoke. Meanwhile, sprinkle tomatoes with salt and black pepper. Turn plank over; place tomato slices on plank. Cover and grill for 10 to 15 minutes or until tomatoes are softened and starting to brown, turning once halfway through grilling. Add onion slices to grill the last 5 to 8 minutes of grilling. Grill until onion is tender, turning once halfway through grilling. Remove tomatoes and onion from grill. Separate onion into rings. Place buns, cut sides down, on grill rack for 1 to 2 minutes or until lightly toasted.

3. For remoulade, in a small bowl combine mayonnaise, relish, ketchup, capers, mustard, parsley, and hot pepper sauce. Spread remoulade on cut sides of buns. Top with arugula, radishes, tomatoes, and onion.

PER SERVING: *425 cal., 14 g fat (2 g sat. fat), 5 mg chol., 951 mg sodium, 66 g carb., 3 g fiber, 12 g pro.*

PREP: 15 MINUTES **SOAK:** 1 HOUR **GRILL:** 10 MINUTES **MAKES:** 4 SERVINGS

Sweet Potato Quesadillas with Cucumber Relish, *recipe on page 170*

sweet potato quesadillas with cucumber relish
pictured on page 168

THE FLAVOR AND NUTRITIONAL CONTENT OF SWEET POTATOES SPURS COOKS TO FIND SURPRISING WAYS TO WORK THEM INTO ALL KINDS OF DISHES. HERE, THEY HELP FILL SUPER-HEALTHY QUESADILLAS PACKED WITH JACK CHEESE, NAVY BEANS, AND BABY SPINACH.

1	15- to 16-ounce can navy beans, rinsed and drained
5	tablespoons snipped fresh cilantro
1	tablespoon lime juice
1	small fresh jalapeño chile pepper, seeded and finely chopped (see tip, page 21)
1	teaspoon ground ancho chile powder
½	cucumber, quartered and sliced
3	to 4 medium radishes, halved and thinly sliced
12	ounces sweet potato, peeled and coarsely chopped
½	teaspoon ground cumin
4	10-inch whole wheat flour tortillas
1½	cups coarsely chopped baby spinach
2	green onions, thinly sliced
¾	cup shredded Monterey Jack cheese (3 ounces)
	Plain Greek yogurt (optional)
	Paprika (optional)

1. In a medium bowl combine beans, ¼ cup of the cilantro, lime juice, jalapeño, and chile powder; set aside. For cucumber relish, in a small bowl combine cucumber, radishes and remaining 1 tablespoon cilantro; set aside.

2. In a medium saucepan cook sweet potatoes, covered, in lightly salted boiling water for 15 minutes or until tender; drain well. Return potatoes to saucepan and coarsely mash; stir in cumin.

3. Spread mashed sweet potatoes over half of each tortilla. Top each with beans, spinach, green onions, and cheese. Fold each tortilla in half over the filling, pressing firmly.

4. For a charcoal or gas grill, place quesadillas directly on the grill rack over medium heat. Cover and grill for 4 minutes, turning once halfway through grilling. To serve, cut quesadillas into wedges and pass cucumber relish and, if desired, Greek yogurt sprinkled with paprika.

PER SERVING: *461 cal., 12 g fat (5 g sat. fat), 19 mg chol., 1167 mg sodium, 67 g carb., 29 g fiber, 23 g pro.*

PREP: 25 MINUTES **GRILL:** 4 MINUTES **MAKES:** 4 SERVINGS

grilled squash and manchego quesadillas with nectarine-tomato salsa

USE EITHER WHITE OR YELLOW CORN TORTILLAS IN THESE CRISP, FRUIT-FILLED QUESADILLAS. MANCHEGO IS A SHARP, BUTTERY SHEEP'S MILK CHEESE FROM SPAIN.

2 medium tomatoes, seeded and chopped
2 ripe, yet firm, nectarines, pitted and chopped
½ cup snipped fresh cilantro
¼ cup finely chopped onion
1 fresh jalapeño chile pepper or serrano chile pepper, stemmed, seeded, and finely chopped (see tip, page 21)
3 tablespoons lime juice
2 to 3 teaspoons bottled green hot pepper sauce
½ teaspoon kosher salt
12 ounces yellow summer squash and/or zucchini
Nonstick cooking spray
¼ teaspoon kosher salt
¼ teaspoon ground black pepper
¼ teaspoon dried oregano, crushed
12 6-inch corn tortillas
3 ounces Manchego or aged white cheddar cheese, shredded (¾ cup)
¼ cup light sour cream
Fresh cilantro sprigs (optional)

1. For salsa, in a medium bowl combine tomatoes, nectarines, cilantro, onion, jalapeño, lime juice, hot pepper sauce, and the ½ teaspoon salt; set aside.

2. Thinly cut the squash lengthwise into slices about ⅓ inch thick. Coat squash slices with cooking spray; sprinkle with the ¼ teaspoon salt, black pepper, and oregano.

3. For a charcoal or gas grill, place squash slices on the grill rack directly over medium heat. Cover and grill for 7 minutes or until crisp-tender, turning once halfway through grilling. Remove from grill; cool slightly. Coarsely chop squash; set aside.

4. Place half of the tortillas on a work surface. Divide the squash among tortillas. Sprinkle with cheese. Top with remaining tortillas, pressing firmly. Coat tortillas with cooking spray.

5. Place filled tortillas on the grill rack directly over medium heat. Cover and grill for 3 to 5 minutes or until golden and crisp, turning once halfway through

grilling. Cut quesadillas into quarters. Serve with salsa, sour cream and, if desired, garnish with cilantro sprigs.

PER SERVING: *213 cal., 7 g fat (2 g sat. fat), 17 mg chol., 383 mg sodium, 32 g carb., 5 g fiber, 8 g pro.*

PREP: 40 MINUTES **GRILL:** 10 MINUTES **MAKES:** 6 SERVINGS

grilled beef and avocado pitas

THESE FRESH SANDWICHES ARE PERFECT FOR A QUICK WEEKNIGHT MEAL. THE MEAT MARINATES FOR TWENTY-FOUR HOURS IN THE REFRIGERATOR. ALL YOU HAVE TO DO FOR FINAL PREP IS GRILL THE MEAT, TOSS WITH VEGGIES AND VINAIGRETTE—AND STUFF INTO A PITA.

12	ounces beef flank steak
½	cup bottled light clear Italian salad dressing
½	teaspoon finely shredded lime peel
¼	cup lime juice
2	tablespoons snipped fresh cilantro
¼	cup finely chopped onion
¼	teaspoon salt
¼	teaspoon ground black pepper
4	cups spring baby salad greens
1	medium red sweet pepper, stemmed, seeded, and cut into bite-size strips
1	medium avocado, halved, seeded, peeled, and thinly sliced (see page 272)
3	whole wheat pita bread rounds, cut in half horizontally

1. Score both sides of steak in a diamond pattern by making shallow diagonal cuts at 1-inch intervals. Place steak in a resealable plastic bag set in a shallow dish.

2. For the vinaigrette, in a screw-top jar combine salad dressing, lime peel, lime juice, and cilantro. Cover and shake well. Pour half of the vinaigrette into a small bowl; add onion. Cover and refrigerate until serving. Pour the remaining vinaigrette over steak; seal bag. Turn to coat steak. Marinate in the refrigerator for 24 hours, turning bag occasionally.

3. Drain steak from the marinade, discarding marinade. Sprinkle with salt and black pepper. For a charcoal or gas grill, place steak on the grill rack directly over medium heat. Cover and grill for 17 to 21 minutes for medium (160°F), turning once halfway through grilling. Thinly slice beef across grain.

4. In a large bowl toss together beef, salad greens, sweet pepper, avocado, and the remaining vinaigrette. To serve, divide filling among pita halves.

PER SERVING: *250 cal., 10 g fat (2 g sat. fat), 37 mg chol., 532 mg sodium, 25 g carb., 5 g fiber, 16 g pro.*

PREP: 20 MINUTES **MARINATE:** 24 HOURS **GRILL:** 17 MINUTES **MAKES:** 6 SERVINGS

grilled turkey gyros

TRADITIONAL GYROS ARE TASTY, BUT HIGH IN FAT, CALORIES, AND SODIUM. THIS VERSION FEATURING FLAVORFUL GROUND TURKEY BREAST PATTIES COMES IN AT UNDER 350 CALORIES AND 10 GRAMS OF FAT PER SERVING.

1	recipe Cucumber-Yogurt Sauce
1	egg, lightly beaten
12	ounces uncooked ground turkey breast
¼	cup finely chopped onion
1	tablespoon fine dry bread crumbs
2	cloves garlic, minced
1	teaspoon ground coriander
½	teaspoon ground cumin
⅛	teaspoon salt
⅛	teaspoon ground black pepper
1	tablespoon olive oil
4	whole-wheat pita bread rounds
1	cup thinly sliced cucumber
1	cup diced tomato
2	tablespoons snipped fresh flat-leaf parsley

1. Prepare Cucumber-Yogurt Sauce. For patties, in a large bowl combine egg, turkey, onion, bread crumbs, garlic, coriander, cumin, salt, and pepper. Shape meat mixture into twelve patties; flatten to about ½-inch thickness. Brush all sides of the patties with oil. Wrap pita bread rounds in foil.

2. For a charcoal or gas grill, place patties and foil-wrapped pita bread on the greased grill rack directly over medium heat. Cover and grill for 6 minutes or until no longer pink (165°F) and pitas are heated through, turning once halfway through grilling.

3. To serve, place three patties on each pita bread round. Top with cucumber slices, tomato, and parsley. Drizzle with Cucumber-Yogurt Sauce. Fold pitas around fillings.

CUCUMBER-YOGURT SAUCE In a small bowl combine ⅓ cup plain fat-free or low-fat yogurt, ¼ cup shredded seeded cucumber, 1 tablespoon tahini (sesame seed paste), 2 cloves minced garlic, and ⅛ teaspoon salt. Cover and chill for at least 20 minutes.

PER SERVING: 332 cal., 9 g fat (1 g sat. fat), 95 mg chol., 560 mg sodium, 37 g carb., 6 g fiber, 31 g pro.

PREP: 20 MINUTES **GRILL:** 6 MINUTES **MAKES:** 4 SERVINGS

grilled jamaican jerk fish wraps

MEATY WHITE FISH SUCH AS FLOUNDER, COD, OR SOLE PROVIDES A NEARLY BLANK SLATE FOR ALL KINDS OF SEASONINGS AND PREPARATIONS, FROM MILD TO INTENSE. USE ANY ONE IN THESE SPICY-SWEET WRAPS.

1   **pound fresh or frozen skinless flounder, cod, or sole fillets**

1½   **teaspoons Jamaican jerk seasoning**

4   **7- to 8-inch whole grain flour tortillas**

2   **cups packaged fresh baby spinach**

¾   **cup chopped seeded tomato**

¾   **cup chopped fresh mango or pineapple (see page 275)**

2   **tablespoons snipped fresh cilantro**

1   **tablespoon finely chopped seeded fresh jalapeño chile pepper (see tip, page 21)**

1   **tablespoon lime juice**

1. Thaw fish, if frozen. Rinse fish; pat dry with paper towels. Sprinkle jerk seasoning over both sides of each fish fillet; rub in with your fingers. Measure thickness of fish.

2. For a charcoal or gas grill, place tortillas on the greased grill rack directly over medium heat. Cover and grill for 1 minute or until bottoms of tortillas have grill marks. Remove from grill; set aside. Place fish on the grill rack directly over medium heat. Cover and grill for 4 to 6 minutes per ½-inch thickness or until fish flakes easily when tested with a fork, turning once halfway through grilling. Remove fish from grill and with a fork coarsely flake the fish.

3. Meanwhile, in a medium bowl toss together spinach, tomato, mango, cilantro, jalapeño, and lime juice.

4. To serve, place tortillas, grill mark sides down, on a flat work surface. Top each tortilla with some of the spinach mixture and flaked fish. Roll up tortilla and cut each in half.

PER SERVING: *254 cal., 4 g fat (1 g sat. fat), 48 mg chol., 509 mg sodium, 23 g carb., 11 g fiber, 29 g pro.*

PREP: 25 MINUTES   **GRILL:** 4 MINUTES   **MAKES:** 4 SERVINGS

grilled vegetable tostadas with quick mole sauce

MENTION "MOLE" AND HOURS STANDING AND STIRRING OVER A HOT STOVE COME TO MIND. THIS SPEEDY VERSION BASED ON BOTTLED BARBECUE SAUCE IS COMPLEX IN ITS FLAVOR ONLY—AND CAN BE MADE IN 30 MINUTES OR LESS.

1	recipe Quick Mole Sauce
4	medium zucchini and/or yellow summer squash, quartered lengthwise
1	medium eggplant, cut in ½-inch slices (see page 273)
1	large red onion, cut in ½-inch slices
2	tablespoons olive oil
¼	teaspoon salt
⅛	teaspoon ground black pepper
16	4- to 6-inch toasted corn tortillas
1	tablespoon olive oil
1	8-ounce carton sour cream
1	cup crumbled queso fresco or feta cheese
	Avocado slices and/or snipped fresh cilantro (optional)

1. Prepare Quick Mole Sauce. Brush zucchini, eggplant, and onion with the 2 tablespoons oil; sprinkle with salt and pepper.

2. For a charcoal or grill, place vegetables on the grill rack directly over medium heat. Cover and grill for 5 to 8 minutes or until tender, turning once halfway through grilling. When cool enough to handle, chop vegetables. Brush both sides of tortillas with oil. Grill directly over medium heat for 1 minute or until warmed, turning once halfway through grilling.

3. To serve, place vegetables on toasted tortillas. Top with cheese and avocado, if desired. Serve with sour cream sprinkled with chili powder and garnished with cilantro, if desired, and Quick Mole Sauce.

QUICK MOLE SAUCE In a large dry skillet toast 2 tablespoons pumpkin seeds and 1 teaspoon sesame seeds over medium heat for 2 to 3 minutes or until toasted. Remove from skillet. In the same skillet cook ½ cup chopped onion and 2 cloves minced garlic in 1 teaspoon hot vegetable oil for 3 minutes or until tender. Stir in 2 to 3 teaspoons chili powder, ½ teaspoon ground cumin, and ¼ teaspoon ground cinnamon. Cook 1 minute or until fragrant. Stir in 1 cup barbecue sauce, ½ ounce bittersweet chocolate, chopped; and, if desired dash of hot pepper sauce. Bring to boiling; reduce heat. Simmer until chocolate is melted. Cool slightly. Transfer onion mixture and toasted seeds to blender or food processor. Cover and blend or process until smooth. Thin with water if needed; cool. Makes 1½ cups.

PER SERVING: *464 cal., 28 g fat (8 g sat. fat), 25 mg chol., 514 mg sodium, 48 g carb., 9 g fiber, 11 g pro.*

PREP: 1 HOUR **COOK:** 10 MINUTES **GRILL:** 5 MINUTES **MAKES:** 4 SERVINGS

pork tacos with spicy watermelon salsa

A SALSA OF WATERMELON AND MILD CHILES MAKES A REFRESHING, SWEET AND SLIGHTLY SPICY ADDITION TO THESE TACOS STUFFED WITH MEATY CHUNKS OF GRILLED COUNTRY-STYLE PORK RIBS.

1½ cups chopped seeded watermelon
1 to 2 fresh banana or Anaheim chile peppers, finely chopped (see tip, page 21)
¼ cup snipped fresh cilantro
½ teaspoon salt
½ teaspoon sugar
½ teaspoon garlic powder
½ teaspoon ground chipotle chile pepper or chili powder
4 boneless pork country-style ribs (about 1¼ pounds)
24 extra-thin or 12 regular corn tortillas

1. For watermelon salsa, in medium bowl combine watermelon, fresh chile pepper, and cilantro; set aside. For rub, in small bowl combine salt, sugar, garlic powder, and ground chipotle chile pepper. Rub onto ribs using fingers.

2. For a gas or charcoal grill, place ribs on the grill rack directly over medium heat. Cover and grill for 10 to 12 minutes or until done (145°F) turning once halfway through grilling. Meanwhile, wrap tortillas in foil. Warm on grill the last 5 minutes of grilling turning once halfway through grilling.

3. Remove ribs; let rest 2 minutes. Slice ribs. Serve in warm tortillas with watermelon salsa.

PER SERVING: *449 cal., 19 g fat (4 g sat. fat), 105 mg chol., 420 mg sodium, 38 g carb., 5 g fiber, 32 g pro.*

PREP: 10 MINUTES   **GRILL:** 10 MINUTES   **MAKES:** 4 SERVINGS

pork-wasabi tacos

THESE CROSS-CULTURAL SANDWICHES COMBINE ASIAN FLAVORS WITH A MEXICAN FOOD CONCEPT—ALL WRAPPED UP IN A MEDITERRANEAN FLATBREAD.

1   1½-pound pork tenderloin, cut into
     1-inch pieces
⅓   cup hoisin sauce
6   flatbreads or flour tortillas
1   to 2 teaspoons prepared wasabi paste
2   tablespoons water
2   tablespoons vegetable oil
½   teaspoon white wine vinegar
½   teaspoon sugar
¼   head napa cabbage, shredded
2   carrots, shredded
½   English cucumber, thinly sliced

1. Thread pork on skewers (see tip, page 30). Brush with hoisin sauce. For a charcoal or gas grill, place kabobs on a grill rack directly over medium heat. Cover and grill for 12 to 14 minutes (160°F), turning once halfway through grilling. Add flatbreads the last 1 minute of grilling, turning once halfway through grilling.

2. Meanwhile, for wasabi oil, in a small bowl whisk together wasabi paste, water, oil, vinegar, and sugar.

3. Serve pork and vegetables in warm flatbreads and drizzle with wasabi oil.

PER SERVING: *447 cal., 13 g fat (5 g sat. fat), 89 mg chol., 470 mg sodium, 50 g carb., 2 g fiber, 31 g pro.*

PREP: 25 MINUTES   **GRILL:** 12 MINUTES   **MAKES:** 6 SERVINGS

steak and herb tacos

THESE TACOS ARE ABOUT AS CLOSE TO AUTHENTIC MEXICAN TACOS AS YOU CAN GET. THE ONLY THING MISSING IS THE MEXICAN GRANDMOTHER STANDING AT THE STOVE PATTING AND COOKING HOMEMADE TORTILLAS. (IF YOU HAVE ONE OF THOSE, LUCKY YOU!) IF NOT, GET THE FRESHEST TORTILLAS YOU CAN FIND.

1 to 1½ pounds lean boneless beef top sirloin steak, 1 inch thick
2 tablespoons snipped fresh marjoram or oregano or 2 teaspoon dried marjoram or oregano, crushed
1 tablespoon chili powder
2 teaspoons garlic powder
¼ teaspoon salt
¼ teaspoon cayenne pepper
1 tablespoon olive oil or vegetable oil
12 6- to 8-inch corn or flour tortillas
2 tomatoes, chopped
1 small onion, chopped
4 to 6 radishes with tops, sliced
½ cup snipped fresh cilantro
8 to 10 ounces queso fresco cheese, crumbled or Monterey Jack cheese, shredded
Lime wedges (optional)

1. Trim fat from steak. In small bowl combine marjoram, chili powder, garlic powder, salt, cayenne pepper, and oil. Spread rub on both sides of steak. Place steak in a large resealable plastic bag set in a shallow bowl; seal bag. Turn to coat steak. Marinate in the refrigerator for 2 to 4 hours.

2. For charcoal or gas grill, place steaks on the grill rack directly over medium heat. Cover and grill for 14 to 18 minutes for medium rare (145°F) or 18 to 22 minutes for medium (160°F), turning once halfway through grilling. Meanwhile, wrap tortillas in foil. Place on grill during the last 10 minutes of grilling, turning occasionally.

3. Slice or coarsely chop steak. Serve in warm tortillas with tomatoes, onion, radishes, cilantro, and cheese. Pass lime wedges, if desired.

PER SERVING: *189 cal., 8 g fat (2 g sat. fat), 18 mg chol., 115 mg sodium, 16 g carb., 2 g fiber, 14 g pro.*

PREP: 25 MINUTES **CHILL:** 2 HOURS **GRILL:** 14 MINUTES **MAKES:** 6 SERVINGS

fish tacos with spicy mango-jicama slaw

MARINATE THE FISH FOR NO MORE THAN 20 MINUTES. AFTER THAT, THE ACID IN LIME JUICE BEGINS TO "COOK" THE FISH. YOU WANT IT TO COOK ON THE GRILL—NOT IN A PLASTIC BAG.

¼ cup canola or vegetable oil
5 tablespoons lime juice
¼ cup snipped fresh cilantro
1 tablespoon ground ancho chile pepper
6 cloves garlic, minced
1¼ to 1½ pounds white fish fillets, such as tilapia or mahi mahi
2 tablespoons mayonnaise or salad dressing
¼ to ½ teaspoon cayenne pepper
¼ teaspoon kosher salt
1 slightly unripe mango, peeled and cut into ¼-inch-thick strips (see page 275)
1 cup shredded cabbage
1 cup jicama, peeled and cut into ¼-inch-thick strips
1 cup red sweet pepper, cut into ¼-inch-thick strips (1 medium)
12 6-inch corn tortillas

1. In a small bowl combine oil, 3 tablespoons of the lime juice, cilantro, ancho chile pepper, and garlic. Place fish in a resealable plastic bag. Pour marinade over fish; seal bag. Turn to coat fish. Marinate in the refrigerator for 15 to 20 minutes. Drain fish from marinade, discarding marinade.

2. For spicy mango-jicama slaw, in a medium bowl combine the remaining 2 tablespoons lime juice, the mayonnaise, cayenne pepper, and salt. Add mango, cabbage, jicama, and sweet pepper; stir well. Season to taste with additional cayenne pepper and salt.

3. For a charcoal or gas grill, place fish on a greased grill rack directly over medium heat. Cover and grill for 8 minutes or until fish flakes easily when tested with a fork, turning once halfway through grilling. Place tortillas on grill rack for about 40 seconds or until warmed, turning once.

4. Using a fork, flake fish into bite-size pieces. Serve fish on warm tortillas with the spicy mango-jicama slaw.

PER SERVING: *531 cal., 24 g fat (3 g sat. fat), 73 mg chol., 304 mg sodium, 49 g carb., 9 g fiber, 34 g pro.*

PREP: 25 MINUTES **MARINATE:** 15 MINUTES **GRILL:** 8 MINUTES **MAKES:** 4 SERVINGS

homemade pizza crusts for grilled pizzas

1 cup warm water (105°F to 110°F)
1 tablespoon honey
1 package active dry yeast
2½ cups all-purpose flour
¼ cup whole wheat or all-purpose flour
¾ teaspoon salt
3 tablespoons olive oil
2 tablespoons all-purpose flour
Olive oil

1. In a medium bowl combine water, honey, and yeast. Let stand about 5 minutes or until mixture is foamy.

2. Meanwhile, in a large bowl stir together 1¾ cups of the all-purpose flour, the whole wheat flour, and salt. Using a wooden spoon, stir in yeast mixture and 3 tablespoons oil. Gradually stir in as much of the remaining ¾ cup all-purpose flour as you can.

3. Turn dough out onto a lightly floured surface. Knead about 5 minutes or until smooth and elastic, adding enough of the remaining ¾ cup all-purpose flour to keep dough from sticking. Shape into a ball. Place in a lightly greased bowl, turning once. Cover; let rise in a warm place until double in size (about 1 hour).

4. Punch dough down. Turn dough out onto a lightly floured surface. Knead for 2 minutes, adding enough of the 2 tablespoons all-purpose flour to keep dough from sticking. Return to the lightly greased bowl. Cover; let rise in a warm place until nearly double in size (about 40 minutes). Punch dough down again. Divide into six portions. Cover; let rest for at least 10 minutes.

5. Invert a large baking sheet; brush the back of the sheet with additional oil. Place dough portions, one at a time, on the prepared baking sheet. Using your hands, spread and press dough into an 8-inch circle.

6. Line another baking sheet with waxed paper or parchment paper. Stack dough rounds on baking sheet, separating rounds with waxed paper or parchment paper. Use immediately, chill for up to 4 hours, or freeze for at least 2 hours* or until very firm. Use as directed in individual grilled pizza recipes.

*NOTE: For longer storage, transfer pizza dough crusts to 2-gallon freezer bags. Seal bags and freeze for up to 1 month. Do not thaw before using.

PER SERVING: *290 cal., 8 g fat (1 g sat. fat), 0 g chol., 293 mg sodium, 49 g carb., 2 g fiber, 7 g pro.*

PREP: 30 MINUTES   **RISE:** 1 HOUR + 40 MINUTES   **STAND:** 10 MINUTES   **MAKES:** 6 SERVINGS

summer garden pizza

1½   cups fresh baby spinach, chopped
1   teaspoon olive oil
     Dash salt
2   to 3 fresh ears corn (with husks) (see page 15)
1   medium eggplant, cut into ½-inch slices
     Olive oil
     Salt and ground black pepper
1   recipe Homemade Pizza Crusts for Grilled Pizzas (see page 184)
6   tablespoons grated Parmesan cheese
6   cloves garlic, thinly sliced
1½   cups chunky tomato sauce
12   ounces bite-size fresh mozzarella cheese balls, drained, thinly sliced, and patted dry with paper towels
6   slices bacon, crisp-cooked, drained, and crumbled
1½   pounds assorted heirloom tomatoes, seeded and chopped
     Small fresh basil leaves
     Ground black pepper
     Sea salt (optional)

1. In a small bowl combine spinach, 1 teaspoon oil, and dash salt; set aside. Peel back corn husks and remove silks. Replace husks around corn and place in a bowl or pan; cover with water. Soak for 1 hour; drain. Tie husks at the top with strips of husks or 100-percent cotton kitchen string. Brush eggplant oil and season with salt and pepper. For a charcoal or gas grill, place corn and eggplant on the grill rack directly over medium heat. Cover and grill eggplant for 8 to 12 minutes or until tender, and corn for 25 to 30 minutes, turning once halfway through grilling. When cool enough to handle, chop eggplant (you should have 1½ cups) and remove husks from corn. Cut corn off the cobs (you should have 1½ cups of kernels).

2. Brush the bottoms of two portions of the Homemade Pizza Crusts for Grilled Pizzas with oil. Place on the grill rack directly over medium-low heat. Cover and grill for 1 to 2 minutes or until dough is puffed in some places and starting to become firm. (If the crust is frozen, grill for 2 to 3 minutes.) Using tongs, carefully turn crust over and transfer to the back of a baking sheet(s). Quickly brush grilled side of crust with additional oil.

3. Sprinkle each crust with 1 tablespoon of the Parmesan cheese and 1 clove of the garlic over crust; top with ¼ cup of the tomato sauce. Add ¼ cup of the spinach mixture, 2 ounces of the mozzarella cheese, ¼ cup of the corn, ¼ cup of the eggplant, and 1 slice of the crumbled bacon. Transfer pizzas from baking sheet to grill rack. Cover and grill for 3 to 5 minutes or until crusts are crisp and cheese melts, rotating pizzas as necessary to prevent burning. Remove pizzas from grill. Repeat with remaining crusts and toppings.

4. To serve, top pizzas with tomatoes, basil, pepper and, if desired, sea salt.

PER SERVING: *642 cal., 28 g fat (12 g sat. fat), 53 mg chol., 942 mg sodium, 70 g carb., 7 g fiber, 26 g pro.*

PREP: 25 MINUTES **GRILL:** 4 MINUTES **MAKES:** 6 SERVINGS

grilled endive, apple, and bacon pizza

SMALL WEDGES OF THIS PIZZA MAKE GREAT APPETIZERS WITH A GLASS OF CHILLED WHITE WINE—OR SERVE INDIVIDUAL PIZZAS AS A MAIN DISH WITH A PEPPERY WATERCRESS SALAD ON THE SIDE.

1 large head Belgian endive, halved lengthwise (6 ounces)
1 medium Granny Smith or Jonathan apple, cored and cut horizontally in ½-inch slices (see page 270)
1 tablespoon olive oil
1 recipe Homemade Pizza Crusts for Grilled Pizzas (page 184)
6 tablespoons olive oil
   Salt and ground black pepper
6 ounces blue cheese, crumbled
6 slices bacon, crisp-cooked and crumbled
6 tablespoons chopped walnuts, toasted (see tip, page 77)
1 tablespoon snipped fresh thyme
6 tablespoons honey (optional)

1. Brush cut sides of endive and apple slices with the 1 tablespoon oil. For a charcoal or gas grill, place endive and apple on a grill rack directly over medium heat. Cover and grill endive 3 to 5 minutes or until lightly charred. Grill apples 5 to 6 minutes or until tender and lightly browned, turning once. When cool enough to handle, chop endive. Cut apple slices into quarters.

2. Brush the bottoms of two portions of the Homemade Pizza Crusts for Grilled Pizzas with oil. Place on the grill rack directly over medium-low heat. Cover and grill for 1 to 2 minutes or until dough is puffed in some places and starting to become firm. (If the crust is frozen, grill for 2 to 3 minutes.) Using tongs, carefully turn crusts over and transfer to the back of a baking sheet(s).

3. Brush 1 tablespoon oil over each crust; sprinkle with salt and pepper and 1 ounce cheese. Top with 2 tablespoons crumbled bacon, 2 tablespoons endive, and 4 to 5 pieces of apple. Transfer pizzas from baking sheets to grill rack. Cover and grill for 3 to 5 minutes or until crust is crisp and cheese melts, rotating crust as necessary to prevent burning. Remove pizzas from grill. Repeat with remaining crusts and toppings.

4. To serve, top each pizza with 1 tablespoon walnuts and ½ teaspoon thyme. If desired, drizzle with 1 tablespoon honey.

PER SERVING: *455 cal., 35 g fat (9 g sat. fat), 30 mg chol., 729 mg sodium, 23 g carb., 3 g fiber, 13 g pro.*

PREP: 40 MINUTES **GRILL:** 10 MINUTES **MAKES:** 6 SERVINGS

grilled artichoke and salami pizza

A BIT DAUNTED BY THE PROCESS OF PREPARING FRESH ARTICHOKES? SEE PAGE 270 FOR STEP-BY-STEP PHOTOS. IT'S REALLY NOT DIFFICULT—AND THE PAYOFF IS WELL WORTH THE PROCESS.

6 fresh artichokes (see page 270)
¼ cup lemon juice
2 tablespoons olive oil
 Salt and ground black pepper
1 recipe Homemade Pizza Crusts for Grilled Pizzas (page 184)
 Olive oil
1 5.2- to 6.5-ounce package semisoft cheese with garlic and fine herbs
6 ounces salami, chopped
2 shallots, thinly sliced
3 cups baby arugula

1. In a large Dutch oven bring a large amount of lightly salted water to boiling. Wash artichokes; trim stems and remove dark outer leaves, leaving the pale green and yellow leaves exposed. Cut through the artichoke crosswise, cutting off the pale green and yellow leaves above the base. Using a spoon, scoop out the choke. Cut each artichoke heart in half lengthwise through the stem. Using a vegetable peeler, trim any rough edges from the outside of the artichoke hearts or stems. Place prepared artichoke hearts in a large bowl containing water and 3 tablespoons lemon juice while preparing the remaining artichokes. Drain and add prepared artichoke hearts to the Dutch oven. Return to a boil. Cover and simmer 10 to 12 minutes or until tender; drain. Toss artichoke hearts with 1 tablespoon of the oil and sprinkle with salt and pepper.

2. For a gas or charcoal grill, place artichoke hearts on the grill rack directly over medium heat. Cover and grill 4 to 6 minutes or until lightly charred, turning once or twice. When cool enough to handle, slice artichoke hearts. Reduce grill to medium-low heat.
3. Brush the bottoms of two Homemade

Pizza Crusts for Grilled Pizzas with oil and place on the grill rack directly over medium-low heat. Cover and grill for 1 to 2 minutes or until dough is puffed in some places and starting to become firm. (If the crust is frozen, grill for 3 to 4 minutes.) Using tongs, carefully turn crusts over and transfer to the back of a baking sheet(s). Quickly brush grilled sides of crusts with additional oil.

4. Spread crusts with cheese; top with 1 ounce salami, 1 sliced artichoke heart, and 1 tablespoon shallot. Transfer pizzas from baking sheet to grill rack. Cover and grill for 3 to 5 minutes more or until crusts are crisp and cheese is melted, rotating crusts as necessary to prevent burning. Remove pizzas from grill. In a medium bowl toss arugula with remaining 1 tablespoon oil and remaining 1 tablespoon lemon juice. Top pizzas with ½ cup arugula each. Repeat with the remaining crusts and toppings.

PER SERVING: *421 cal., 27 g fat (11 g sat. fat), 56 mg chol., 940 mg sodium, 33 g carb., 8 g fiber, 14 g pro.*

PREP: 45 MINUTES **COOK:** 10 MINUTES **GRILL:** 12 MINUTES **MAKES:** 6 SERVINGS

napa valley pizza

THIS PIZZA TOPPED WITH GRILLED GRAPES, KALE, SHALLOTS, BLUE CHEESE, TOASTED HAZELNUTS, AND A DRIZZLE OF HONEY IS ELEGANT FOOD IN A CASUAL FORM—PERFECT FOR EASY ENTERTAINING WHEN YOU WANT TO IMPRESS.

2   cups grapes
     Olive oil
     Salt and ground black pepper
6   cups sliced fresh kale
1   recipe Homemade Pizza Crusts for Grilled Pizzas (page 184)
¾   cup thinly sliced shallots (6 medium)
1½   cups crumbled blue cheese and/or shredded Gruyère or Swiss cheese (6 ounces)
2   tablespoons snipped fresh thyme
6   tablespoons chopped hazelnuts (filberts) (see tip, page 77)
     Honey

1. To grill grapes, lightly coat grapes with oil; season with salt and pepper. For a charcoal or gas grill, place grapes in grill tray or grill wok on the grill rack directly over medium-high heat. Cover and grill for 2 minutes or just until golden grill marks appear, turning occasionally. Cool; slice grapes in half.

2. In a large skillet cook and stir kale in 1 teaspoon oil over medium heat for 8 to 10 minutes or until wilted and tender.

3. Brush the bottoms of two portions of the Homemade Pizza Crusts for Grilled Pizzas with oil. For a charcoal or gas grill, place crusts on the grill rack directly over medium-low heat. Cover and grill for 1 to 2 minutes or until dough is puffed in some places and starting to become firm. (If the crusts are frozen, grill for 2 to 3 minutes.) Using tongs, carefully turn crusts over and transfer to the back of a baking sheet. Quickly brush grilled side of crusts with oil.

4. Sprinkle each crust with ¼ cup of the kale and 2 tablespoons of the shallots; drizzle lightly with additional oil. Transfer pizzas from baking sheet to grill rack. Cover and grill for 3 to 5 minutes or until crusts are crisp, rotating crust as necessary to prevent burning. Top each pizza with ⅓ cup of the grapes, ¼ cup of the cheese, and 1 teaspoon of the thyme. Cover and grill for 1 to 2 minutes or until cheese melts. Remove pizzas from grill. Repeat with remaining crusts and toppings.

5. To serve, sprinkle pizzas with hazelnuts and pepper. Drizzle with honey.

PER SERVING: *590 cal., 28 g fat (9 g sat. fat), 25 mg chol., 780 mg sodium, 72 g carb., 5 g fiber, 17 g pro.*

PREP: 30 MINUTES **COOK:** 8 MINUTES **GRILL:** 7 MINUTES **MAKES:** 6 SERVINGS

primo pesto pizza

PREGRILLING THE CRUSTS FOR JUST A MINUTE OR TWO MAKES THEM STURDY AND EASIER TO TOP.

1 recipe Homemade Pizza Crusts for Grilled Pizzas (see page 184)
   Olive oil
1¼ cups basil pesto, purchased or homemade (page 142)
1½ cups whole-milk ricotta cheese or shredded mozzarella cheese
2 cups thinly sliced yellow summer squash or zucchini
1½ cups thinly sliced red onions
¾ cup oil-packed dried tomatoes, drained and chopped
⅓ cup grated Parmesan cheese
   Fresh oregano leaves
   Crushed red pepper (optional)

1. For a charcoal or gas grill, place two portions of the Homemade Pizza Crusts for Grilled Pizzas on the grill rack directly over medium-low heat. Cover and grill for 1 to 2 minutes or until dough is puffed in some places and starting to become firm. (If the crusts are frozen, grill for 2 to 3 minutes.) Using tongs, carefully turn crusts over and transfer to the back of a baking sheet(s). Quickly brush grilled side of crusts with oil.

2. Spread crusts with about 3 tablespoons of the pesto; top with ¼ cup of the ricotta cheese. Add ⅓ cup of the squash, ¼ cup of the onions, and 2 tablespoons of the dried tomatoes. Sprinkle with about 1 tablespoon of the Parmesan cheese. Transfer pizzas from baking sheet(s) to grill rack. Cover and grill for 3 to 5 minutes more or until crusts are crisp and cheese melts, rotating crusts as necessary to prevent burning. Remove pizzas from grill. Repeat with the remaining crusts and toppings.

3. Before serving, sprinkle pizzas with oregano and, if desired, crushed red pepper.

PER SERVING: *734 cal., 44 g fat (12 g sat. fat), 52 mg chol., 901 mg sodium, 63 g carb., 6 g fiber, 23 g pro.*

PREP: 25 MINUTES **GRILL:** 4 MINUTES **MAKES:** 6 SERVINGS

fresh tomato pizza with oregano and mozzarella

AS GORGEOUS AS IT IS DELICIOUS, THIS EYE-CATCHING FLATBREAD IS A MODEST TWIST ON CLASSIC ITALIAN MARGHERITA PIZZA—WHICH IS SIMPLY TOMATOES, FRESH MOZZARELLA, AND BASIL. THIS VERSION FEATURES OREGANO INSTEAD OF BASIL AND AN OPTIONAL TOPPING OF PROSCIUTTO AND BABY ARUGULA AFTER GRILLING.

2 cups cherry tomatoes
1 tablespoon olive oil
1 sprig fresh oregano
1 clove garlic, sliced
1 tablespoon olive oil
1 1-pound ball fresh pizza dough, at room temperature
8 ounces fresh mozzarella cheese, sliced ¼ inch thick
1 tablespoon olive oil
¼ teaspoon sea salt
1 cup baby arugula (optional)
2 ounces very thinly sliced prosciutto, cut into strips (optional)

1. For the sauce, in a food processor combine cherry tomatoes, 1 tablespoon oil, oregano, and garlic. Process just until tomatoes are coarsely chopped; do not puree. Set aside.

2. Invert a large baking sheet; brush the back of the sheet with oil. Place dough on the prepared baking sheet. Using your hands, spread and press dough into 14×8-inch rectangle.

3. For a charcoal or gas grill, place crust on the grill rack directly over medium-low heat. Cover and grill for 1 to 2 minutes or until dough is puffed in some places and starting to become firm. Using tongs, carefully turn crust over and transfer to the back of a baking sheet. Quickly spread grilled side of crusts with the sauce, leaving a 2-inch border around edges. Top with cheese.

4. Transfer pizza from baking sheet to grill rack. Cover and grill for 3 to 5 minutes or until crust is crisp and cheese melts, rotating crust as necessary to prevent burning. Sprinkle with sea salt. If desired, top with arugula and prosciutto.

PER SERVING: *487 cal., 24 g fat (10 g sat. fat), 40 mg chol., 684 mg sodium, 48 g carb., 3 g fiber, 17 g pro.*

PREP: 20 MINUTES **GRILL:** 4 MINUTES **MAKES:** 4 SERVINGS

grilled potato-leek pizza

1 pound Yukon Gold potatoes
2 tablespoons olive oil
  Salt and ground black pepper
3 small leeks (see page 274)
1 recipe Homemade Pizza Crusts for Grilled Pizzas (page 184)
6 tablespoons olive oil
1 10-ounce carton refrigerated Alfredo pasta sauce
12 ounces Gruyère cheese, shredded
6 ounces Black Forest or honey baked ham, chopped
2 tablespoons snipped fresh chives

1. Scrub potatoes. Cut potatoes into ½-inch slices. Brush slices on both sides with 2 tablespoons oil. Sprinkle with salt and pepper. Trim root ends and green tops of leeks. Rinse leeks thoroughly to remove any grit. Quarter each leek lengthwise; insert a wooden pick crosswise into each leek quarter to hold layers together when grilling.

2. For a gas or charcoal grill, place potato slices and leek quarters on a grill rack directly over medium heat. Cover and grill leeks 8 to 10 minutes or until opaque and lightly charred. Grill potatoes 15 to 20 minutes or until tender and brown, turning occasionally. Remove vegetables from grill as they are done. When cool enough to handle, chop potatoes and leeks.

3. Brush the bottoms of two portions of the Homemade Pizza Crusts for Grilled Pizzas with oil. Place crusts on the grill rack directly over medium-low heat. Cover and grill for 1 to 2 minutes or until dough is puffed in some places and starting to become firm. (If the crust is frozen, grill for 2 to 3 minutes.) Using tongs, carefully turn crust over and transfer to the back of a baking sheet(s).

4. Brush 1 tablespoon oil over each crust. Spread each pizza with 2 to 3 tablespoons Alfredo sauce; top each with ½ cup cheese, ⅓ cup potatoes, ¼ cup leeks, and 1 ounce ham. Transfer pizza from baking sheet(s) to grill rack. Cover and grill for 3 to 5 minutes more or until pizzas are crisp and cheese melts, rotating crusts as necessary to prevent burning. Remove pizzas from grill. Sprinkle with 1 teaspoon chives. Repeat with the remaining crusts and toppings.

PER SERVING: *686 cal., 49 g fat (10 g sat. fat), 104 mg chol., 992 mg sodium, 34 g carb., 3 g fiber, 29 g pro.*

PREP: 45 MINUTES **GRILL:** 19 MINUTES **MAKES:** 6 SERVINGS

morel and asparagus crispy pizza

THE ADDITION OF SEMOLINA FLOUR TO THE CRUST GIVES IT A PLEASING CRUNCHY QUALITY. MAKE THIS EXQUISITE PIZZA IN THE SPRING—WHEN MOREL MUSHROOMS ARE SPROUTING IN THE WOODS AND ASPARAGUS IS AT ITS PEAK.

1 package active dry yeast
1¼ cups warm water (105°F to 115°F)
2 to 2¼ cups all-purpose flour
1½ cups semolina flour
3 tablespoons olive oil
2 teaspoons salt
2 teaspoons sugar
1 tablespoon butter
10 ounces morel mushrooms, cleaned and sliced ½ inch thick
½ cup sliced shallots (4 medium)
¼ cup dry white wine
2 teaspoons snipped fresh thyme
8 ounces thin asparagus, cleaned, trimmed, and cut into 2-inch pieces
2 cups shredded Gruyère cheese (8 ounces)
Cornmeal
Olive oil
Cracked black pepper

1. In a large mixing bowl combine yeast and water. Let stand until yeast is dissolved, about 5 minutes.

2. Add 2 cups of the all-purpose flour, the semolina flour, the 3 tablespoons oil, the salt, and sugar. Beat with an electric mixer on low speed or by hand until combined, scraping sides of bowl. Turn out onto a lightly floured surface. Knead in enough of the remaining all-purpose flour to make a smooth elastic dough (6 to 8 minutes total). Shape dough into a ball. Place dough in a lightly oiled large bowl. Cover; let rise in a warm place until double in size (1 to 1½ hours).

3. Meanwhile, in a large skillet melt butter over medium-high heat. Add mushrooms; cook and stir for 2 to 3 minutes or just until mushrooms begin to soften. Add shallots, wine, and thyme. Cook and stir for 4 to 6 minutes or until shallots are tender. Add asparagus; cook and stir for 2 minutes. Remove from heat.

4. Punch dough down and divide dough in two portions. On a lightly floured surface roll out each portion into an ⅛-inch-thick circle. Brush bottom of crusts lightly with oil. Invert 2 large baking sheets; brush the back of the sheets with additional oil and dust with cornmeal. Place crusts, one at a time, on prepared baking sheets.

5. For a charcoal or gas grill, place crust on the on the grill rack directly over medium-low heat. Cover and grill for 1 to 2 minutes or until dough is puffed in some places and starting to become firm. Using tongs, carefully turn crust over and transfer to the back of a baking sheet. Quickly brush grilled side of crust with additional oil.

6. Top crust with half of the mushroom mixture and half of the cheese; sprinkle with pepper. Transfer pizza from baking sheet to grill rack. Cover and grill for 3 to 5 minutes or until crust is crisp and cheese melts. Repeat with remaining crust and toppings.

PER SERVING: *458 cal., 18 g fat (7 g sat. fat), 35 mg chol., 694 mg sodium, 54 g carb., 3 g fiber, 18 g pro.*

PREP: 30 MINUTES RISE: 1 HOUR GRILL: 4 MINUTES MAKES: 4 SERVINGS

brussels sprouts and spicy fennel sausage pizza

A QUICK HOMEMADE PORK SAUSAGE SPIKED WITH FENNEL SEED AND CRUSHED RED PEPPER GIVES THIS HEARTY FALL PIZZA GREAT FLAVOR.

1	cup warm water (105° to 115°F)
1	teaspoon active dry yeast
2½	to 3 cups bread flour
3	tablespoons olive oil
1½	teaspoons salt
12	ounces ground pork
1	teaspoon fennel seeds
½	teaspoon crushed red pepper
½	teaspoon salt
1	pound fresh Brussels sprouts
2	cups shredded Gruyère cheese (8 ounces)
1	small red onion, thinly sliced and separated into rings
4	cloves garlic, minced
1	tablespoon olive oil

1. For crust, in a small bowl stir together water and yeast. In a large mixing bowl combine 2½ cups of the flour, the 3 tablespoons of the oil, 1½ teaspoons salt, and the yeast mixture. Beat with an electric mixer on low speed until combined. Turn dough out onto a lightly floured work surface. Knead in enough of the remaining dough to make a moderately stiff dough that is smooth and elastic. Shape dough into a ball. Place in a lightly greased bowl, turning once to grease surface of dough. Cover; let rise in a warm place until double in size (about 1 to 2 hours).

2. Meanwhile, for sausage, in a large bowl combine pork, fennel seeds, crushed red pepper, and ½ teaspoon salt. Preheat a large nonstick skillet over medium-high heat. Drop ½-inch pieces of meat mixture into the hot skillet. Cook until meat is no longer pink, stirring occasionally. Remove skillet from heat; drain off fat. Set sausage aside. Meanwhile, trim bottoms from Brussels sprouts and remove any browned outer leaves. Thinly slice Brussels sprouts; set aside.

3. Punch dough down; let rest for 10 minutes. Invert a large baking sheet; brush the back of the sheet with additional oil. Place dough on the prepared baking sheet. Using your hands, spread and press dough into a 12-inch circle.

4. Brush the bottom of the crust with additional oil. For a charcoal or gas grill, place crust on the grill rack directly over medium-low heat. Cover and grill for 1 to 2 minutes or until dough is puffed in some places and starting to become firm. Using tongs, carefully turn crust over and transfer to the back of a baking sheet. Quickly brush grilled side of crust with additional oil.

5. Top crust with cheese, sausage, Brussels sprouts, onion, and garlic. Drizzle with 1 tablespoon oil. Transfer pizza from baking sheet to grill rack. Cover and grill for 3 to 5 minutes or until edges of crust are crisp and cheese melts. Remove from grill.

PER SERVING: 500 cal., 29 g fat (10 g sat. fat), 64 mg chol., 722 mg sodium, 38 g carb., 3 g fiber, 22 g pro.

PREP: 40 MINUTES RISE: 1 HOUR REST: 10 MINUTES GRILL: 4 MINUTES MAKES: 8 SERVINGS

Grilled Spring Onion, Pineapple, and Shrimp Pizzas, *recipe on page 200*

grilled spring onion, pineapple, and shrimp pizzas

pictured on page 199

SPRING ONIONS ARE VERY SIMILAR TO SCALLIONS OR GREEN ONIONS. THEY HAVE A SLIGHTLY LARGER BULB THAN THE MORE SLENDER GREEN ONIONS. THEY MAKE THEIR APPEARANCE BRIEFLY—IN MAY AND JUNE. IF YOU CAN'T FIND THEM, REGULAR GREEN ONIONS WORK PERFECTLY FINE IN THIS RECIPE.

12	ounces fresh or frozen large shrimp in shells
2	tablespoons olive oil
½	teaspoon salt
½	teaspoon crushed red pepper
½	of a peeled, cored pineapple, cut into wedges
6	to 8 ounces red and/or green spring onions or green onions, trimmed
4	3- to 4-ounce pieces garlic-flavored naan or flat bread
1½	cups shredded Manchego cheese (6 ounces)
¼	cup crumbled blue cheese (1 ounce)
8	large basil leaves, thinly sliced
1	tablespoon honey
	Fresh basil leaves (optional)

1. Thaw shrimp, if frozen. Peel and devein shrimp. Rinse shrimp; pat dry with paper towels. Thread shrimp on 4 long metal skewers, leaving a ¼-inch space between shrimp. In a small bowl combine oil, salt, and crushed red pepper. Brush oil mixture over shrimp, pineapple, and green onions.

2. For a charcoal or gas grill, place shrimp, pineapple, and onions directly on grill rack directly over medium-hot heat. Cover and grill for 5 to 8 minutes or until shrimp are opaque and pineapple and onions are nicely charred, turning occasionally. Coarsely chop shrimp, pineapple, and onions.

3. Place naan directly on the grill rack over medium heat. Cover and grill for 1 minute or until lightly toasted. Turn and sprinkle with Manchego cheese and blue cheese. Top with shrimp, pineapple, and onions. Cover and grill for 3 to 4 minutes or until cheese is melted and bottom crusts are toasted. Remove pizzas from grill. Sprinkle with sliced basil and drizzle with honey. If desired, top with additional basil leaves.

PER SERVING: *609 cal., 24 g fat (11 g sat. fat), 151 mg chol., 1415 mg sodium, 65 g carb., 4 g fiber, 33 g pro.*

PREP: 25 MINUTES **GRILL:** 9 MINUTES **MAKES:** 4 SERVINGS

grilled california-style pizza

THIS RECIPE USES ONE PORTION OF THE RECIPE FOR HOMEMADE PIZZA CRUST FOR GRILLED PIZZA (PAGE 184); EACH RECIPE MAKES 6 PORTIONS. HOMEMADE PIZZA DOUGH IS VERY HANDY TO HAVE IN THE FREEZER FOR QUICK MEALS AND SPUR-OF-THE-MOMENT PARTIES.

2 tablespoons olive oil
1 clove garlic, minced
¼ teaspoon crushed red pepper
1 portion recipe Homemade Pizza Crusts for Grilled Pizza (page 184)
1½ cups chopped yellow or red heirloom tomatoes (2 medium)
¾ cup red sweet pepper strips
½ onion, cut into thin slivers
2 ounces semisoft goat cheese or feta cheese, crumbled
8 to 12 Kalamata olives, halved or quartered lengthwise
5 ounces fresh mozzarella cheese, cut into small cubes
Fresh oregano leaves or snipped fresh basil

1. In a small bowl combine oil, garlic, and crushed red pepper. Brush the bottom of one portion of the Homemade Pizza Crusts for Grilled Pizzas with oil mixture. For a charcoal or gas grill, place crust on the grill rack directly over medium-low heat. Cover and grill for 1 to 2 minutes or until dough is puffed in some places and starting to become firm. (If the crust is frozen, grill for 2 to 3 minutes.) Using tongs, carefully turn crust over and transfer to the back of a baking sheet.

2. Top crust with tomatoes, sweet pepper, onion, goat cheese, and olives. Sprinkle with mozzarella cheese. Transfer pizza from baking sheet to grill rack. Cover and grill for 4 to 6 minutes or until crisp and cheese melts, rotating crust as necessary to prevent burning. Remove pizza from grill. Garnish with oregano.

PER SERVING: *698 cal., 31 g fat (10 g sat. fat), 36 mg chol., 1150 mg sodium, 82 g carb., 6 g fiber, 21 g pro.*

PREP: 30 MINUTES **GRILL:** 11 MINUTES **MAKES:** 4 SERVINGS

Grilled Romaine Salad with Tomato and Corn Tumble, *recipe page 215*

salads & sides

KEEP THE MAIN DISH SIMPLE—GRILLED STEAK, CHICKEN, OR FISH—AND MAKE THE MENU SPECIAL WITH ONE OF THESE SURPRISING SIDES.

smoky aubergine salad

MEATY SLICES OF SEASONED AND GRILLED EGGPLANT GIVE HEFT TO THIS HEARTY SIDE SALAD. SERVE IT WITH SOMETHING LIGHT, SUCH AS GRILLED FISH.

6	tablespoons olive oil
¼	cup tahini (sesame seed paste)
¼	cup lemon juice
2	cloves garlic, minced
½	teaspoon bottled hot pepper sauce
	Salt
	Ground black pepper
1	large eggplant, peeled (if desired) and cut into 1-inch slices (see page 273)
2	pita bread rounds
1	teaspoon smoked paprika or ½ teaspoon ground chipotle chile pepper
¼	teaspoon garlic powder
6	cups mixed salad greens
¾	cup fresh mint leaves
¼	cup fresh flat-leaf parsley leaves
1	cup peeled, seeded, and chopped cucumber
⅔	cup canned chickpeas (garbanzo beans), rinsed and drained
¼	cup chopped pistachio nuts (optional)

1. For the tahini dressing, in a small bowl whisk together ¼ cup of the oil, the tahini, lemon juice, garlic, and bottled hot pepper sauce. Season to taste with salt and black pepper. Cover and chill until ready to serve.

2. Brush eggplant and pita bread with the remaining 2 tablespoons oil. Sprinkle with paprika, garlic powder, and additional salt and black pepper.

3. For a charcoal or gas grill, place eggplant slices on the rack of a covered grill directly over medium heat. Grill for 8 to 12 minutes or until very tender and well browned. Remove eggplant from grill. Place pita bread on grill rack. Grill for 2 to 4 minutes or until toasted, turning once halfway through grilling. Cut eggplant into chunks. Cut pita bread into wedges.

4. Line a serving platter with mixed greens; sprinkle with mint and parsley. Arrange eggplant, pita wedges, cucumber, and chickpeas in piles on top of greens. If desired, sprinkle with pistachios. Drizzle with tahini dressing.

PER SERVING: *234 cal., 15 g fat (2 g sat. fat), 235 mg sodium, 22 g carb., 6 g fiber, 6 g pro.*

PREP: 25 MINUTES   **GRILL:** 10 MINUTES   **MAKES:** 8 SERVINGS

grilled panzanella

THIS ITALIAN BREAD SALAD BRIGHTENED BY SWEET PEPPERS AND JUICY RIPE TOMATOES GOES SPLENDIDLY WITH GRILLED STEAK OR ROASTED OR GRILLED CHICKEN.

8 ounces crusty country bread, sliced 1 inch thick

2 medium yellow, red, and/or green sweet peppers, seeded and quartered lengthwise

1 medium red onion, sliced ½ inch thick

4 tablespoons olive oil

3 large tomatoes, cut up

1 medium cucumber, coarsely chopped

3 tablespoons drained capers (optional)

1 tablespoon red wine vinegar

¼ teaspoon salt

¼ teaspoon ground black pepper

1. Brush bread slices, sweet peppers, and onion with 2 tablespoons of the oil. For a charcoal or gas grill, place bread and vegetables on the grill rack directly over medium heat. Cover and grill bread and vegetables, turning once. Allow 2 to 4 minutes for bread or until browned and 10 minutes for onion and sweet peppers or until crisp-tender.

2. Cut bread and sweet peppers into 1-inch pieces. Coarsely chop onion. In a large serving bowl combine bread, sweet peppers, onion, tomatoes, cucumber, and, if desired, capers. Gently toss together.

3. For dressing, in a small bowl whisk together the remaining 2 tablespoons oil, the vinegar, salt, and black pepper. Drizzle over vegetable mixture; toss gently to coat. Let stand at room temperature for 30 minutes before serving.

PER SERVING: *113 cal., 5 g fat (1 g sat. fat), 175 mg sodium, 15 g carb., 2 g fiber, 5 g pro.*

PREP: 20 MINUTES **GRILL:** 10 MINUTES **STAND:** 30 MINUTES **MAKES:** 12 SERVINGS

grilled summer fruits with honey greek yogurt sauce

THERE ARE MORE THAN 300 UNIQUE TYPES OF HONEY AVAILABLE IN THIS COUNTRY ALONE. EACH ONE TASTES LIKE THE FLOWERS FROM WHICH IT WAS MADE, SO WILDFLOWER HONEY HAS FLORAL NOTES—AND ORANGE BLOSSOM HONEY HAS THE FLAVOR AND AROMA OF ORANGES.

8   ¾-inch-thick slices peeled and cored fresh pineapple (see page 276)
1   medium honeydew melon, halved, seeded, peeled, and cut into ¼-inch-thick slices
2   cups halved strawberries
¼   cup granulated sugar
    Nonstick cooking spray
¼   cup fresh basil chiffonade*
1   recipe Honey Greek Yogurt Sauce

1. In a large bowl combine pineapple, honeydew, strawberries, and sugar; toss lightly to combine.

2. For a charcoal or gas grill, place pineapple and honeydew melon on the grill rack directly over medium heat. Cover and grill for 1 to 2 minutes or until fruit is lightly browned, turning once. Place strawberries in a grill basket that has been lightly coated with cooking spray. Place on grill rack directly over medium heat. Cover and grill for 1 to 2 minutes or until heated through, stirring occasionally. Cut pineapple into quarters, if desired.

3. Place fruit on 8 chilled salad plates; sprinkle with basil. Serve salads with Honey Greek Yogurt Sauce.

HONEY GREEK YOGURT SAUCE
In a small bowl combine one 6-ounce carton plain Greek yogurt, plain low-fat yogurt, or sour cream. and 3 tablespoons wildflower honey or other honey. Makes about ¾ cup.

* To make basil chiffonade, stack fresh basil leaves. Starting at a long edge, roll the leaves up. With a sharp knife, slice the roll into thin strips.

PER SERVING: *160 cal., 1 g fat (0 g sat. fat), 1 mg chol., 33 mg sodium, 40 g carb., 3 g fiber, 3 g pro.*

PREP: 20 MINUTES   GRILL: 2 MINUTES   MAKES: 8 SERVINGS

grilled zucchini salad with mozzarella and dill

SERVED WITH SLICES OF GRILLED BREAD, THIS RUSTIC, KNIFE-AND-FORK SALAD OF GRILLED SUMMER SQUASH AND TORN CHUNKS OF FRESH MOZZARELLA IS HEARTY ENOUGH TO MAKE A LIGHT MAIN DISH.

3   medium zucchini and/or yellow squash, sliced lengthwise into ¼-inch planks
3   tablespoons extra virgin olive oil
    Salt and ground black pepper
1   8-ounce fresh mozzarella ball, pulled into large pieces
2   tablespoons coarsely snipped fresh dillweed
¼   teaspoon crushed red pepper
1   tablespoon lemon juice

1. On a baking sheet arrange zucchini in a single layer. Drizzle with 1 tablespoon of the oil and sprinkle with salt and black pepper.

2. For a charcoal or gas grill, place zucchini on grill rack directly over medium heat. Cover and grill for 8 minutes or until tender, turning once halfway through grilling.

3. On a serving platter arrange warm zucchini and mozzarella. Sprinkle with dillweed and crushed red pepper. Drizzle with lemon juice and the remaining 2 tablespoons oil.

PER SERVING: *265 cal., 22 g fat (9 g sat. fat), 40 mg chol., 323 mg sodium, 3 g carb., 1 g fiber, 11 g pro.*

PREP: 10 MINUTES   **GRILL:** 8 MINUTES   **MAKES:** 4 SERVINGS

grilled corn on the cob with chile and lime

SERVED AS SHOWN, THESE TASTY BITES OF MEXICAN-SPICED GRILLED CORN ARE A PERFECT ACCOMPANIMENT TO GRILLED STEAK. SPEARED ON A WOODEN STICK, THEY MAKE A FUN APPETIZER OR SNACK.

6 large ears of corn, husks and silks removed
¼ cup butter, melted
2 tablespoons mayonnaise or salad dressing
2 tablespoons Mexican crema or sour cream
2 teaspoons finely shredded lime peel
2 tablespoons lime juice
1 tablespoon ground ancho chile pepper
½ cup snipped fresh cilantro
   Salt
   Lime wedges (optional)

1. Cut each ear of corn into thirds. In a large pot combine corn pieces and enough water to cover. Let soak for 10 minutes; drain. If desired, insert a wooden crafts stick (see tip, page 30) into one end of each piece of corn.

2. Meanwhile, in an extra-large bowl whisk together butter, mayonnaise, crema, and lime juice; set aside.

3. For a charcoal or gas grill, place corn on the grill rack directly over medium-high heat. Cover and grill for 15 to 20 minutes or until corn is tender, turning every 5 minutes and brushing occasionally with butter mixture during the last 5 minutes of grilling.

4. Add grilled corn to the remaining butter mixture in bowl, turning to coat. Sprinkle corn with ground ancho pepper. Sprinkle with cilantro and lime peel. Season to taste with salt. If desired, serve with lime wedges.

PER SERVING: *215 cal., 14 g fat (6 g sat. fat), 24 mg chol., 231 mg sodium, 24 g carb., 3 g fiber, 4 g pro.*

PREP: 20 MINUTES SOAK: 40 MINUTES GRILL: 15 MINUTES MAKES: 6 SERVINGS

grilled baby veggies with classic pesto sauce

A GRILL WOK PERFORATED WITH HOLES ALLOWS YOU TO GRILL SMALL FOODS (SUCH AS BABY VEGETABLES) WITHOUT FEAR OF LOSING THEM THROUGH THE GRATE.

2	cups packed fresh basil leaves, rinsed
3	tablespoons pine nuts
2	large cloves garlic, peeled
½	cup olive oil
½	cup grated Parmesan cheese (2 ounces)
¾	teaspoon salt
12	baby carrots with tops, trimmed
6	small red shallots, peeled
6	miniature sweet peppers, halved and seeded
2	cups cremini mushrooms
6	baby zucchini and/or yellow summer squash, halved lengthwise
10	to 12 miniature pattypan squash Nonstick cooking spray
12	baby heirloom tomatoes Fresh basil leaves (optional)

1. For the classic pesto sauce, in a food processor combine basil, pine nuts, and garlic; cover and process until finely chopped. With processor running, gradually add oil through feed tube. Process about 1 minute or until smooth. Add cheese and salt; process just until combined.

2. Halve any large carrots lengthwise. Cook carrots in a small amount of boiling water about 5 minutes or just until tender; drain well. Place carrots, shallots, sweet peppers, mushrooms, zucchini, and pattypan squash in a resealable bag set in a large bowl. Add ¼ cup of the sauce to bag; seal bag. Turn to distribute sauce evenly over vegetables.

3. Lightly coat an unheated grill wok with cooking spray. For a charcoal or gas grill, preheat the grill wok on the rack of a covered grill for 1 minute. Add the vegetables to wok. Cover and grill for 25 minutes or until tender, stirring occasionally. Stir tomatoes into vegetable mixture.

4. Place remaining sauce in a small serving bowl. Arrange vegetables on a platter; serve with sauce. If desired, sprinkle vegetables with additional basil leaves.

PER SERVING: *178 cal., 14 g fat (2 g sat. fat), 4 mg chol., 255 mg sodium, 10 g carb., 3 g fiber, 5 g pro.*

PREP: 30 MINUTES   GRILL: 25 MINUTES   MAKES: 10 SERVINGS

plank-smoked portobello mushrooms

A DOUBLE DOSE OF PECAN—IN THE GRILLING-PLANK WOOD AND IN THE NUTS IN THE SAVORY FILLING—GIVE THESE SMOKED MUSHROOMS LUXURIOUS TASTE AND TEXTURE.

1 pecan or cedar grill plank
5 medium portobello mushroom caps
1 tablespoon olive oil
½ cup chopped onion (1 medium)
2 cloves garlic, minced
1 5-ounce package fresh baby spinach
¾ cup coarse soft white bread crumbs (1 slice bread)
½ cup shredded sharp white cheddar cheese (2 ounces)
2 tablespoons chopped pecans
1 tablespoon snipped fresh sage
1 tablespoon spicy brown mustard

1. At least 1 hour before grilling, soak plank in enough water to cover, weighting it to keep it submerged.

2. Remove stems from four of the mushroom caps; chop stems. Chop remaining mushroom cap. Scrape and discard gills from the remaining four mushroom caps.

3. For the filling, in a large skillet heat oil over medium heat; add chopped mushroom and stems, onion, and garlic. Cook and stir about 5 minutes or until vegetables are tender. Add spinach; cook and stir about 2 minutes or until wilted. Remove skillet from heat. Add bread crumbs, cheese, pecans, sage, and mustard; stir until combined. Set aside.

4. For a gas or charcoal grill, place plank on grill rack directly over medium heat for 3 to 5 minutes or until plank begins to crackle and smoke. Meanwhile, grill mushroom caps, stemmed sides up, on grill rack about 3 minutes or until grill marks appear. Place mushroom caps on plank, stemmed sides up. Spoon filling into caps. Cover and grill about 15 minutes or until mushrooms are brown and filling is heated through.

5. Transfer plank with mushrooms to a serving platter.

PER SERVING: *186 cal., 11 g fat (4 g sat. fat), 15 mg chol., 241 mg sodium, 15 g carb., 3 g fiber, 8 g pro.*

PREP: 25 MINUTES **SOAK:** 1 HOUR **GRILL:** 18 MINUTES **MAKES:** 4 SERVINGS

grilled romaine salad with tomato and corn tumble

CORN-ON-THE-COB COOKED ON A GRILL OFFERS A SWEET TASTE OF SUMMER. THE 1-HOUR SOAK IN WATER FIRST ENSURES THAT THE HUSKS AND SILKS WON'T CATCH FIRE DURING COOKING.

2 to 3 ears fresh sweet corn (see page 15)
4 tablespoons extra virgin olive oil
2 tablespoons sherry vinegar or red wine vinegar
1 tablespoon Dijon-style mustard
1 tablespoon snipped garlic chives*
2 hearts of romaine lettuce, halved lengthwise
1 cup grape and/or pear tomatoes (red, yellow, and/or green), quartered
   Sea salt and ground black pepper
¼ cup crumbled ricotta salata or feta cheese (1 ounce)

1. Place corn with husks and silks intact in a large bowl. Add enough cold water to cover. Let soak for 1 hour.

2. Meanwhile, for garlic-chive vinaigrette, in a screw-top jar combine 3 tablespoons of the oil, the vinegar, mustard, and garlic chives. Cover and shake well; set aside.

3. Brush the romaine with the remaining 1 tablespoon oil; set aside. For a charcoal or gas grill, place corn on the grill rack directly over medium heat. Cover and grill for 25 to 30 minutes or until kernels are tender, turning once and rearranging ears occasionally. Grill romaine, cut sides down, directly over medium heat for 2 to 3 minutes or until slightly charred and wilted.

4. Place a romaine heart half on each of 4 salad plates. Remove corn husks and silks from ears. Cut kernels from cobs. In a medium bowl combine corn kernels and tomatoes. Drizzle with some of the vinaigrette; toss to coat. Drizzle romaine with the remaining vinaigrette. Spoon the corn and tomato mixture over romaine halves. Season with salt and pepper. Top with cheese.

* You can substitute 1 tablespoon snipped fresh chives and 1 clove garlic, minced.

PER SERVING: 200 cal., 16 g fat (3 g sat. fat), 6 mg chol., 255 mg sodium, 13 g carb., 3 g fiber, 4 g pro.

PREP: 20 MINUTES   **GRILL:** 27 MINUTES   **SOAK:** 1 HOUR   **MAKES:** 4 SERVINGS

artichokes with tarragon drizzle

THIS SIMPLE BUT BEAUTIFUL SIDE IS JUST THE THING TO SERVE WITH A ROASTED SPRING CHICKEN. IT ALSO MAKES AN ELEGANT APPETIZER.

4 to 5 large whole artichokes or
12 to 15 baby artichokes
(see page 270)
⅔ cup extra virgin olive oil
⅓ cup white wine vinegar
⅓ cup thinly sliced green onions
2 tablespoons snipped fresh tarragon or
2 teaspoons dried tarragon, crushed
2 tablespoons Dijon-style mustard
Sea salt or salt
Ground black pepper
Extra virgin olive oil
2 lemons, each cut into 8 to 10 wedges
Snipped fresh tarragon (optional)

1. Wash large artichokes; trim stems, if desired, and remove loose outer leaves. Snip off the sharp leaf tips. If using baby artichokes, remove outer leaves to reach pale green or yellow leaves on bottom half. Cut darker green portion of leaves off top half of artichoke; discard. Cut off stem and trim any remaining green from base of baby artichokes.

2. In a large pot bring a large amount of lightly salted water to boiling; add artichokes. Return to boiling; reduce heat. Simmer, covered, for 20 to 30 minutes for large artichokes or 10 minutes for baby artichokes or until a leaf pulls out easily.

3. Place artichokes in a large bowl of ice water to cool completely. Drain artichokes upside down on paper towels. Cut artichokes in half from top through stem; using a spoon, scoop out the fibrous cores, leaving the hearts and leaves intact.

4. For tarragon drizzle, in a screw-top jar combine the ⅔ cup oil, vinegar, green onions, 2 tablespoons tarragon, and the mustard. Cover and shake well. Season with salt and pepper.

5. Brush artichoke halves with additional oil. For a charcoal or gas grill, place artichokes, cut sides down, on a grill rack directly over medium heat. Cover and grill for 7 minutes; turn artichokes and grill for 5 to 7 minutes more.

6. On a serving platter place grilled artichokes cut sides up. Shake tarragon drizzle; pour some over artichokes. If desired, sprinkle with additional snipped tarragon. Serve with lemon wedges. Pass the remaining tarragon drizzle.

PER SERVING: *131 cal., 11 g fat (1 g sat. fat), 153 mg sodium, 8 g carb., 4 g fiber, 3 g pro.*

PREP: 25 MINUTES **COOK:** 20 MINUTES **GRILL:** 12 MINUTES **MAKES:** 8 SERVINGS

ratatouille-stuffed portobellos

TRY THIS AS A SIDE WITH A MEATLESS PASTA DISH THAT HAS A SIMPLE CREAM SAUCE AND NOT A LOT OF EXTRA INGREDIENTS. THE MEATINESS OF THE PORTOBELLO MUSHROOMS AND THE FLAVORFUL VEGGIE FILLING WILL ADD INTEREST TO THE PLATE.

6	fresh medium portobello mushrooms
3	tablespoons olive oil
2	cups peeled and chopped eggplant (see page 273)
¾	cup chopped yellow sweet pepper (1 medium)
¾	cup chopped zucchini
½	cup chopped onion (1 medium)
1	clove garlic, minced
½	cup chopped tomato (1 medium)
½	teaspoon dried Italian seasoning, crushed
¼	teaspoon salt
¼	cup crumbled Gorgonzola or finely shredded Parmesan cheese (1 ounce)
2	tablespoons fine dry bread crumbs

1. Remove stems from mushrooms; chop stems. Scrape and discard gills from mushrooms. Brush mushroom caps with 2 tablespoons of the oil; set aside.

2. For filling, in a large skillet heat the remaining 1 tablespoon oil over medium heat. Add chopped mushroom stems, eggplant, sweet pepper, zucchini, onion, and garlic. Cook for 6 to 8 minutes or until tender, stirring occasionally. Add tomato, Italian seasoning, and salt. Cook and stir until vegetables are very tender and liquid has evaporated. Transfer mixture to a medium bowl. Stir in cheese and bread crumbs. Spoon filling into mushroom caps.

3. For a charcoal or gas grill, place mushrooms on the grill rack directly over medium heat. Cover and grill for 10 to 12 minutes or until mushrooms are tender and filling is heated through.

PER SERVING: 118 cal., 7 g fat (2 g sat. fat), 7 mg chol., 215 mg sodium, 11 g carb., 3 g fiber, 5 g pro.

PREP: 20 MINUTES **GRILL:** 10 MINUTES **MAKES:** 6 SERVINGS

balsamic-glazed cauliflower in a coat of parmesan cheese

THIS RECIPE REQUIRES A ROTARY SPIT FOR TURNING THE CAULIFLOWER AS IT COOKS. IF YOUR GRILL DIDN'T COME OUTFITTED WITH A SPIT, YOU CAN ADD ONE TO IT WITHOUT A LOT OF ADDITIONAL EXPENSE.

2   **medium heads fresh cauliflower (2 to 2½ pounds each)**
⅓   **cup olive oil**
⅓   **cup white balsamic vinegar**
2   **teaspoons dried marjoram or oregano, crushed**
½   **teaspoon freshly ground black pepper**
¼   **teaspoon salt**
1   **cup finely shredded Parmesan cheese (4 ounces)**
     Fresh rosemary sprigs (optional)

1. Wash cauliflower heads. Remove leaves and woody stems. Leave heads whole. In a Dutch oven cook one of the cauliflower heads, covered, in a small amount of boiling water for 3 minutes. Remove cauliflower; drain well. Repeat with the remaining cauliflower head. Let cauliflower stand until cool enough to handle.

2. Place one holding fork on the spit rod, tines toward point. Carefully insert rod through the stem end of one whole cauliflower head, pressing tines of holding fork firmly into the cauliflower. Insert rod into the second cauliflower head. Place a second holding fork on rod, tines toward the second cauliflower head; press tines of holding fork firmly into cauliflower. Adjust forks; tighten screws. Test balance, making adjustments as necessary.

3. In a small bowl combine oil, vinegar, marjoram, pepper, and salt. Mix well.

4. For a charcoal grill, attach spit over medium coals; turn on the motor and lower the grill hood. Let the cauliflower rotate for 25 to 30 minutes or until tender, basting frequently with oil mixture. (For a gas grill, preheat grill. Reduce heat to medium. Grill as above.)

5. Carefully remove cauliflower from spit. Brush with the remaining oil mixture; sprinkle with cheese. Serve immediately. If desired, garnish with fresh rosemary.

PER SERVING: *167 cal., 12 g fat (3 g sat. fat), 7 mg chol., 288 mg sodium, 10 g carb., 4 g fiber, 7 g pro.*

PREP: 25 MINUTES   **GRILL:** 25 MINUTES   **MAKES:** 8 SERVINGS

grilled stuffed onions

THE HUMBLE ONION GETS STAR TREATMENT IN THIS SAUSAGE-AND-APPLE-STUFFED SIDE THAT IS PERFECT WITH ROASTED OR GRILLED PORK OR TURKEY.

4 medium sweet onions (9 to 10 ounces each)
8 ounces bulk maple-flavor or sage-flavor bulk pork sausage
½ cup chopped Granny Smith apple (see page 270)
½ cup coarse soft bread crumbs
¼ cup crumbled blue cheese (1 ounce)
1 tablespoon snipped fresh sage
Small sage leaves (optional)
Vegetable oil for frying (optional)

1. Peel onions. Cut a ½-inch slice off the top of each onion. If necessary, cut a very thin slice off the bottom of each onion so it will sit flat. Using a melon baller, scoop out centers of onions, leaving ¼- to ½-inch shells. Chop ¼ cup of the scooped-out onion.

2. For the stuffing, in a large skillet cook sausage and the ¼ cup chopped onion over medium-high heat until meat is brown, using a wooden spoon to break up meat as it cooks. Drain off fat. Add apple; cook for 3 to 4 minutes more or until tender, stirring occasionally. Cool slightly. Stir in bread crumbs, cheese, and snipped sage. Spoon stuffing into onions.

3. Tear off four 12-inch squares of foil. For each packet, place 2 sage leaves in the center of a foil square. Place a stuffed onion on top of sage. Bring up edges of foil and seal to enclose onion, leaving space for steam to build.

4. For a charcoal grill, arrange medium-hot coals around a drip pan. Test for medium heat above pan. Place onion packets on grill rack over drip pan. Cover and grill for 20 minutes. Carefully peel back foil so onions are exposed. Cover and grill for 10 to 15 minutes more or just until onions are tender and lightly browned. (For a gas grill, preheat grill. Reduce heat to medium. Adjust for indirect cooking. Cover and grill as above.)

5. If desired, fry sage leaves in a small amount of hot oil just until crisp. Garnish onions with fried sage leaves.

PER SERVING: *310 cal., 14 g fat (6 g sat. fat), 41 mg chol., 765 mg sodium, 34 g carb., 4 g fiber, 14 g pro.*

PREP: 20 MINUTES **GRILL:** 30 MINUTES **MAKES:** 4 SERVINGS

6 FRESH IDEAS

grilled sweet peppers

OF ALL VEGETABLES, SWEET PEPPERS TAKE TO GRILLING PARTICULARLY WELL. A TOUCH OF SMOKINESS SUITS THEIR NATURAL SWEETNESS. SEE THE RECIPE ON PAGE 157 FOR BASIC INSTRUCTIONS ON GRILLING SWEET PEPPERS.

1. GRILLED RED PEPPER AÏOLI In a blender combine ½ cup chopped grilled sweet red pepper and 2 cloves garlic, cut up. Cover and blend until nearly smooth. Add ⅓ cup mayonnaise; cover and blend until smooth. With the blender running, gradually add 2 tablespoons oil through the opening; blend until smooth. Transfer aïoli to a bowl; season with ⅛ teaspoon salt and black pepper. Serve with scallops, steaks, or chicken. Makes about ½ cup.

2. ANTIPASTO SALAD In a salad bowl combine ½ cup marinated olives, pitted and halved; 4 ounces fresh mozzarella cut into thin strips; 6 slices salami, cut into thin strips; ½ cup chopped grilled green or orange sweet pepper; and 6 pepperoncini salad peppers, chopped. Drizzle with 2 tablespoons bottled Italian vinaigrette. Toss to coat. Makes 4 side-dish servings.

3. GRILLED RED PEPPER HUMMUS In a food processor combine one 15-ounce can chickpeas (garbanzo beans), drained and rinsed; ½ cup chopped grilled sweet red peppers; ⅓ cup tahini paste; 3 tablespoons lemon juice; 4 cloves garlic; ½ chipotle pepper in adobo sauce; 1 teaspoon cumin, ¼ teaspoon salt. Cover and process until smooth. Serve with pita wedges and/or cut up vegetables. Makes 8 appetizer servings.

4. GRILLED YELLOW PEPPER AND RED TOMATO SALAD For dressing, in a screw-top jar combine 2 tablespoons oil, 2 tablespoons white wine vinegar, 2 tablespoon thinly sliced green onions, 2 teaspoons snipped fresh basil, 1 teaspoon sugar, ½ teaspoon Dijon-style mustard, ⅛ teaspoon black pepper. Cover and shake well. Arrange 3 large sliced tomatoes and 3 large grilled yellow peppers, thinly sliced into rings on a spinach-lined platter. Sprinkle with ⅔ cup crumbled Gorgonzola cheese. Drizzle with dressing. Makes 4 side-dish servings.

5. SPINACH AND GRILLED PEPPER DIP Preheat oven to 350°F. In a bowl stir together ½ cup shredded mozzarella cheese, ½ cup plain yogurt, ½ cup mayonnaise, 2 tablespoons Parmesan cheese, and 1 tablespoons flour. Stir in 1 cup loosely packed fresh spinach, chopped; ¾ cup grilled sweet orange or red peppers; and 2 tablespoons sliced green onions. Spread into a 1-quart shallow baking dish. Sprinkle with 2 tablespoons Parmesan cheese. Bake 15 to 20 minutes or until heated through. Serve with sweet pepper strips and/or flatbread. Makes 36 appetizer servings.

6. CREAMY GRILLED PEPPER SOUP In a large saucepan cook and stir 1½ cups chopped sweet onion, ½ cup chopped carrots, and 1 tablespoon minced garlic in 1 tablespoon hot oil until tender. Stir in teaspoon each fresh chopped mint, rosemary, thyme; one 28-ounce can crushed tomatoes, and one 14.5-ounce container reduced-sodium chicken broth. Bring to a boil; reduce heat. Simmer, covered 30 minutes. Stir in 3 grilled sweet red peppers, chopped; ¾ cup milk, 1½ teaspoons honey; and ½ teaspoon black pepper. Puree with an immersion blender. Ladle into bowl and sprinkle with Parmesan cheese. Makes 6 servings.

Spinach and Grilled Pepper Dip

grilled watermelon salad

THIS RECIPE IS A WILD COMBINATION OF FLAVORS AND TEXTURES, STARTING WITH GRILLED WATERMELON (YES, YOU READ THAT RIGHT). AUGMENTING THAT IS QUINOA AND SWEET-SOUR PICKLED RADISHES TOSSED WITH A HONEY-LIME VINAIGRETTE AND TOPPED WITH CREAMY AVOCADO AND SALTY CHEESE. SERVE IT WITH SOMETHING SIMPLE!

2	1-inch-thick slices watermelon
10	cups chopped romaine lettuce
3	cups cooked quinoa
1	recipe Pickled Radishes
1	recipe Honey-Lime Vinaigrette
2	medium avocados, seeded, peeled, and sliced or coarsely chopped
¼	teaspoon chili powder
½	cup crumbled queso fresco or feta cheese (2 ounces)
2	tablespoons snipped fresh cilantro

1. For a charcoal or gas grill, place watermelon on the grill rack directly over medium-high heat. Cover and grill about 4 minutes or until watermelon is lightly charred, turning once halfway through grilling.

2. Spread lettuce on a large serving platter. In a large bowl combine quinoa and Pickled Radishes. Add ⅔ cup of the Honey-Lime Vinaigrette; toss to coat. Spoon quinoa mixture on top of lettuce.

3. Cut each watermelon slice into four wedges. Arrange watermelon wedges and avocados on salad; sprinkle with chili powder. Top with cheese and cilantro. Serve salad with the remaining vinaigrette.

PICKLED RADISHES In a medium bowl combine ½ cup apple cider vinegar, ⅓ cup honey, and 1 teaspoon salt, stirring to dissolve honey and salt. Stir in 1 cup thinly sliced radishes. Cover and let stand at room temperature for 30 minutes to 4 hours. Drain before using.

HONEY-LIME VINAIGRETTE In a screw-top jar combine 1½ teaspoons finely shredded lime peel, 6 tablespoons lime juice, ¼ cup oil, ¼ cup honey, 1½ tablespoons finely chopped shallot, 1½ tablespoons snipped fresh cilantro, and ½ teaspoon salt. Cover and shake well. Chill, covered, for at least 20 minutes (or for up to 3 days). Shake before serving.

PER SERVING: 294 cal., 15 g fat (3 g sat. fat), 5 mg chol., 298 mg sodium, 37 g carb., 6 g fiber, 6 g pro.

PREP: 35 MINUTES **GRILL:** 4 MINUTES **MAKES:** 8 SERVINGS

toasted couscous with grilled mango and zucchini

TOASTING THE COUSCOUS IN A DRY SKILLET BEFORE COOKING DEEPENS ITS NATURALLY NUTTY FLAVOR.

2	cups Israeli (pearl) couscous
1	fresh mango, halved, seeded, and peeled (see page 275)
1	zucchini, sliced into ½-inch slices
1	tablespoon vegetable oil
2½	cups chicken broth
1	tablespoon butter
2	tablespoons fresh Italian (flat-leaf parsley), chopped
½	teaspoon kosher salt

1. In a dry medium saucepan toast couscous over medium-low heat for 8 to 10 minutes or until golden-brown, stirring frequently. Remove from saucepan; set aside.

2. Brush mango and zucchini slices with oil on all sides; season lightly with salt.

3. For a charcoal or gas grill, place mango and zucchini slices on the grill rack directly over medium-high heat. Cover and grill for 5 to 8 minutes or until tender. Cool; cut into ½-inch pieces.

4. In the same medium saucepan bring broth to a boil. Add couscous and stir. Cover; reduce heat to simmer and cook 7 minutes. Add mango, zucchini, butter, parsley, and salt. Cook for about 1 minute or until heated through.

PER SERVING: *243 cal., 5 g fat (1 g sat. fat), 6 mg chol., 619 mg sodium, 44 g carb., 3 g fiber, 6 g pro.*

PREP: 20 MINUTES **COOK:** 23 MINUTES **GRILL:** 5 MINUTES **MAKES:** 6 SERVINGS

southwestern stuffed roasted peppers

SERVE THESE GORGEOUS STUFFED PEPPERS WITH A SIMPLE GRILLED STEAK. PAIRED WITH A LEAFY GREEN SALAD AND SOME BREAD, THEY COULD ALSO BE THE MAIN DISH FOR A LIGHT SUPPER.

4 large red, yellow, and/or orange sweet peppers
1 tablespoon olive oil*
8 ounces fresh peeled and deveined shrimp, chopped; skinless, boneless chicken breasts, cut into bite-size pieces; or bulk pork sausage
½ cup frozen whole kernel corn
½ cup chopped onion (1 medium)
2 cups corn bread stuffing mix
1 cup chicken broth
1 4-ounce can diced green chile peppers, undrained
1 10-ounce container refrigerated Alfredo pasta sauce
1 tablespoon snipped fresh cilantro

1. For a charcoal or gas grill, place sweet peppers on the rack of a covered grill directly over medium-high heat. Grill for 13 to 15 minutes or until charred and very tender, turning occasionally. Wrap grilled peppers in foil. Let stand about 15 minutes or until cool enough to handle.

2. Meanwhile, for the stuffing, in a large skillet heat oil over medium heat. Add shrimp, chicken, and/or sausage; corn; and onion; cook until shrimp is opaque, chicken is no longer pink, and/or sausage is brown, stirring occasionally. Stir in stuffing mix and broth; cook just until broth is absorbed. Remove from heat. Stir in half of the chile peppers.

3. Using a sharp knife, loosen edges of skins from grilled peppers; gently peel off skins in strips and discard. Brush peppers with oil. Cut each pepper in half lengthwise; remove seeds. Spoon stuffing into pepper halves. Return to grill. Grill about 5 minutes more or until heated through.

4. For sauce, in a small saucepan combine Alfredo sauce and the remaining chile peppers. Cook over medium heat until heated through. Spoon sauce over stuffed peppers. Sprinkle with cilantro.

* Omit oil if using sausage.

PER SERVING: 192 cal., 9 g fat (3 g sat. fat), 60 mg chol., 709 mg sodium, 20 g carb., 2 g fiber, 8 g pro.

PREP: 35 MINUTES **GRILL:** 18 MINUTES **MAKES:** 4 SERVINGS

Smoked New York Strip Steaks with Avocado-Horseradish Slather, *recipe page 234*

quick smoke

YOU DON'T NEED TO COOK FOODS FOR HOURS WITH SMOLDERING WOOD TO INFUSE THEM WITH GREAT FLAVOR. MOST OF THESE RECIPES COOK IN 30 MINUTES OR LESS—WITH WOOD CHIPS OR GRILLING PLANKS—FOR A DELICIOUS, SMOKY ACCENT.

rosemary-orange stuffed smoked pork tenderloin

2 cups pecan or alder wood chips
4 ounces pancetta, chopped
½ cup chopped onion (1 medium)
2 cloves garlic, minced
1 small Granny Smith apple
1 tablespoon olive oil
3 oranges (see page 272)
½ teaspoon snipped fresh rosemary
1 12- to 16-ounce pork tenderloin
  Salt and ground black pepper
1 recipe Orange-Apple Relish

1. At least 1 hour before smoke cooking, soak wood chips in enough water to cover. Drain before using.

2. In a large skillet cook pancetta, onion, and garlic over medium heat until pancetta is crisp and onion is tender; drain fat. Drain on paper towels. Transfer to a small bowl.

3. Remove the core from apple. Cut apple crosswise into ½-inch slices; brush with oil. For a charcoal or gas grill, place apple slices on a grill rack directly over medium heat. Cover and grill for 5 to 6 minutes or until apple slices are tender, turning once. Chop apple slices; set aside.

4. To section the orange, use a small sharp knife to cut a thin slice off the end of the orange. Place the orange on a cutting board and cut off the peel from the top to bottom. To remove the sections, use a small sharp knife to cut from the outside to the center of each section on each side of the membrane. The sections will easily pop out of the fruit. Chop the sections. Reserve half of the oranges. Add the other half of the oranges and the rosemary to the pancetta mixture.

5. Trim fat from pork. Split tenderloin lengthwise, cutting from one long side almost to, but not through the other side. Make another lengthwise cut down each side of the meat where it is the thickest. Spread meat open to lay flat. Add pancetta-orange filling, spreading it onto cut sides of the tenderloin. Fold tenderloin back together. Tie with 100-percent cotton kitchen string at 1-inch intervals. Sprinkle with salt and pepper.

6. For a charcoal grill, arrange medium-hot coals around a drip pan. Test for medium heat above the pan. Sprinkle the drained wood chips over the coals. Place pork on the grill rack over drip pan. Cover and grill for 30 to 35 minutes or until an instant-read thermometer inserted into the center reads 145°F. (For a gas grill, preheat grill. Reduce heat to medium. Adjust for indirect cooking. Smoke as directed, except add the drained wood chips according to manufacturer's directions.)

7. Cover pork and let stand 10 minutes before removing kitchen string and slicing. Serve with Orange-Apple Relish.

ORANGE-APPLE RELISH In a small bowl combine reserved oranges, ½ teaspoon snipped fresh rosemary, grilled and chopped apples, 1 tablespoon lemon juice, and 1 tablespoon brown sugar. Cover and chill until ready to serve.

PER SERVING: *298 cal., 13 g fat (4 g sat. fat), 65 mg chol., 346 mg sodium, 22 g carb., 4 g fiber, 24 g pro.*

PREP: 30 MINUTES **SOAK:** 1 HOUR **GRILL:** 30 MINUTES **MAKES:** 4 SERVINGS

smoked duck breast with acorn squash and cherry-apricot compote

WHEN THE WEATHER TURNS COOL IN THE EARLY FALL BUT THE GRILL STILL BECKONS, TRY THIS SMOKY DUCK DISH SERVED WITH GRILLED ACORN SQUASH AND A SWEET AND GINGERY FRUIT COMPOTE.

1   14×6½-inch apple, cherry, or oak grilling plank
½   teaspoon ground coriander
¼   teaspoon salt
¼   teaspoon ground black pepper
⅛   teaspoon ground cinnamon
4   skinless, boneless duck breasts (1½ to 1¾ pounds)*
1   1-pound fresh acorn squash, halved, seeded, and cut in ½-inch slices
1   tablespoon olive oil
    Salt and ground black pepper
1   recipe Cherry-Apricot Compote

1. Place the grill plank in a container of water; weight down the plank and soak it for at least 1 hour.

2. In a small bowl combine coriander, salt, pepper, and cinnamon. Sprinkle evenly over duck breasts, rubbing in with your fingers. Brush squash with oil and sprinkle with additional salt and pepper.

3. For a charcoal or gas grill, place drained grilling plank on the rack of a grill directly over medium heat. Cover and grill 3 to 5 minutes or until plank begins to crackle and smoke. Place duck breasts on the plank. Place squash slices on a grill rack directly over heat. Cover and grill 12 to 15 minutes or until an instant-read thermometer inserted into the center of the duck registers 145°F for medium rare and the squash is tender.

4. Slice duck and serve with squash and Cherry-Apricot Compote.

CHERRY-APRICOT COMPOTE In a medium saucepan combine ⅓ cup apple juice, 1 tablespoon honey, 1 tablespoon lemon juice, and 1 teaspoon peeled and grated fresh ginger; bring to boiling. Add 3 medium apricots, pitted and chopped; and 1 cup fresh sweet cherries, pitted and quartered (see page 272); return to boiling. Reduce heat and simmer, uncovered, 5 to 8 minutes or until softened and liquid has reduced to desired consistency. Let stand and cool to room temperature.

* If you get duck breasts with the skin on, remove the skin and cut it into strips. Cook the strips in a large skillet over medium heat until all the fat is rendered and cracklings are crisp. Remove from the skillet with a slotted spoon and drain on paper towels. Serve with the squash.

PER SERVING: *338 cal., 11 g fat (3 g sat. fat), 131 mg chol., 248 mg sodium, 25 g carb., 3 g fiber, 35 g pro.*

PREP: 25 MINUTES   **SOAK:** 1 HOUR   **COOK:** 6 MINUTES   **GRILL:** 12 MINUTES   **MAKES:** 4 SERVINGS

smoked new york strip steaks with avocado-horseradish slather

2 cups alder or oak wood chips
4 boneless beef top loin steaks, cut 1 inch thick (2 to 2½ pounds total)
2 teaspoons chili powder
¼ teaspoon salt
½ teaspoon ground cumin
¼ teaspoon dry mustard
¼ teaspoon ground black pepper
2 medium avocados, halved and seeded (leave peels on) (see page 272)
  Snipped fresh cilantro
  Finely chopped red onion
1 recipe Acocado-Horseradish Slather

1. At least 1 hour before smoke cooking, soak wood chips in enough water to cover. Drain before using. Trim fat from steaks. In a small bowl combine chili powder, salt, cumin, dry mustard, and black pepper. Sprinkle spice mixture over steaks and rub in with your fingers.

2. For a charcoal grill, arrange medium-hot coals around a drip pan. Test for medium heat above the pan. Sprinkle the drained wood chips over the coals. Place steaks on the grill rack over drip pan. Cover and smoke 16 to 20 minutes for medium rare (145°F) or 20 to 24 minutes for medium (160°F), turning once. Brush the cut sides of avocados with 1 teaspoon lime juice. Add to the grill rack over the drip pan, cut sides up, the last 8 to 10 minutes of grilling or until softened. (For a gas grill, preheat grill. Reduce heat to medium. Adjust for indirect cooking. Smoke as directed, except add drained wood chips according to manufacturer's directions.)

3. Sprinkle steaks with cilantro and onion. Top with Avocado-Horseradish Slather.

AVOCADO-HORSERADISH SLATHER
Scoop flesh out of the smoked avocados and place in a medium bowl. Add 2 tablespoons prepared horseradish, 2 tablespoons lime juice, 3 cloves minced garlic, ¼ teaspoon salt, and ⅛ teaspoon cayenne pepper. Mash with a potato masher or fork until nearly smooth.

PER SERVING: *435 cal., 23 g fat (9 g sat. fat), 75 mg chol., 449 mg sodium, 22 g carb., 5 g fiber, 27 g pro.*

PREP: 20 MINUTES **SOAK:** 1 HOUR **GRILL:** 16 MINUTES **MAKES:** 4 SERVINGS

smoky beets, orange, and ribeye salad

2 cups oak or hickory wood chips
1 pound red and/or golden baby beets or medium beets
2 boneless beef ribeye steaks, cut ¾-inch thick (about 1 pound)
2 teaspoons snipped fresh rosemary
¼ teaspoon salt
¼ teaspoon cracked black pepper
6 sprigs fresh rosemary
2 oranges
3 tablespoons olive oil
2 tablespoons balsamic vinegar
1 teaspoon honey
  Salt and cracked black pepper
6 cups baby arugula
2 ounces goat cheese (chèvre), or ricotta salata crumbled
1 shallot, thinly sliced
¼ cup chopped walnuts, toasted (see tip, page 77)

1. At least 1 hour before smoking, soak wood chips in enough water to cover. Drain before using.

2. Scrub beets. In a medium saucepan cook beets, covered, in a small amount of lightly salted boiling water for 15 to 8 minutes for baby beets (or 30 minutes for medium beets) or just until tender. Drain and cool slightly. Peel or slip skins off beets. Halve baby beets or quarter small beets. Thread beets on skewers (see tip, page 30).

3. Trim fat from steaks. Sprinkle with snipped rosemary, the ¼ teaspoon salt, and the ¼ teaspoon cracked black pepper. Rub in with your fingers.

4. For a charcoal grill, arrange medium-hot coals around a drip pan. Test for medium heat above the pan. Sprinkle the wood chips and rosemary sprigs over the coals. Place steaks and beet skewers on the grill rack over drip pan. Cover and smoke 14 to 16 minutes or until 145°F for medium rare or 16 to 20 minutes or until 160°F for medium, turning once halfway through grilling. Grill beet skewers 14 to 16 minutes or until heated through and lightly charred, turning once. (For a gas grill, preheat grill. Reduce heat to medium. Adjust for indirect cooking. Smoke as directed, except add drained wood chips according to manufacturer's directions.) Let steak stand for 5 minutes. Thinly slice steak diagonally across the grain into bite-size pieces.

5. Meanwhile, using a small sharp knife, remove peel from oranges, working above a bowl to catch any juice. Section oranges; set aside (see page 272).

6. In a small screwtop jar combine oil, vinegar, 1 tablespoon orange juice, and honey. Cover and shake well to combine. Season to taste with salt and cracked black pepper.

7. On a large serving platter toss arugula with dressing to coat. Top with beets, reserved orange segments, goat cheese, shallot, walnuts, and sliced steak.

PER SERVING: *456 cal., 30 g fat (9 g sat. fat), 75 mg chol., 449 mg sodium, 22 g carb., 5 g fiber, 27 g pro.*

PREP: 30 MINUTES **SOAK:** 1 HOUR **COOK:** 14 MINUTES **GRILL:** 14 MINUTES **MAKES:** 4 SERVINGS

rack of lamb with smoked herbed potatoes and pomegranate sauce

1 cup oak or hickory wood chips
1 1 to 1½-pound lamb rib roast (8 ribs)
2 tablespoons Dijon-style mustard
3 tablespoons snipped fresh herbs (such as Italian [flat-leaf] parsley, chives, basil, oregano, and/or thyme)
1 tablespoon olive oil
2 cloves garlic, minced
½ teaspoon salt
½ teaspoon ground black pepper
1½ pounds tiny yellow new potatoes
½ cup milk
2 tablespoons butter
1 recipe Pomegranate Sauce

1. At least an hour before smoke cooking, soak wood chips in enough water to cover. Drain before using.

2. Trim fat from meat. In a small bowl stir together mustard, 1 tablespoon of the herbs, the oil, garlic, ¼ teaspoon of the salt, and ¼ teaspoon of the pepper. Brush the mustard mixture on the meat. Thread potatoes on metal skewers.*

3. For a charcoal grill, arrange medium-hot coals around a drip pan. Sprinkle drained wood chips over the coals. Test for medium heat above pan. Place potato kabobs and meat, bone side down, on grill rack over drip pan. Cover and grill 35 to 45 minutes or until potatoes are tender and an instant-read thermometer inserted into the center registers 140°F for medium rare or 155°F for medium. (For a gas grill, preheat grill. Reduce heat to medium. Adjust for indirect cooking. Grill as directed, except add wood chips according to manufacturer's directions.)

4. Cover meat with foil; let stand 15 minutes before carving. Temperature of meat should rise 5°F during standing.

5. In a small saucepan heat milk and butter until butter melts. Remove potatoes from skewers. In a large bowl coarsely smash potatoes. Add milk

mixture, remaining 2 tablespoons herbs, ¼ teaspoon salt, and remaning ¼ teaspoon pepper. Mash just until combined.

6. Serve lamb with smoked herbed potatoes and Pomegranate Sauce.

POMEGRANATE SAUCE In a small saucepan cook 1 tablespoon minced shallot in 1 tablespoon butter over medium heat until soft. Add ¼ cup pomegranate juice, ¼ cup chicken broth, and 1 teaspoon honey. Bring to boiling. Simmer, uncovered, 8 minutes or until reduced by half. Whisk in 1 tablespoon butter in small pieces until incorporated. Season to taste with salt and black pepper.

* Metal skewers conduct heat and will help the potatoes to cook through in the center. If you don't have metal skewers, use wooden skewers that have been soaked in water for at least 30 minutes before using.

PER SERVING: *364 cal., 20 g fat (10 g sat. fat), 65 mg chol., 690 mg sodium, 33 g carb., 4 g fiber, 14 g pro.*

PREP: 30 MINUTES SOAK: 1 HOUR COOK: 12 MINUTES GRILL: 35 MINUTES MAKES: 4 SERVINGS

cajun stuffed chicken breasts with smoked okra, peppers, and onions

2   cups hickory or oak wood chips
6   ounces fresh or frozen shrimp in shells
¾   cup reduced-sodium chicken broth
¼   cup uncooked long-grain rice
¼   cup finely chopped onion
1   fresh jalapeño chile pepper, seeded and minced (see tip, page 21)
3   cloves garlic, minced
1   teaspoon snipped fresh thyme
¼   teaspoon salt
⅛   teaspoon cayenne pepper
1   teaspoon finely shredded lemon peel
4   skinless, boneless chicken breast halves (about 1¾ pounds total)
2   tablespoons olive oil
     Salt and ground black pepper
4   ounces fresh okra pods
1   red sweet pepper, cut into 1-inch pieces
1   small red onion, cut into wedges
1   recipe Cajun Tomato Sauce

1. At least 1 hour before smoke cooking, soak wood chips in enough water to cover. Drain before using.

2. Thaw shrimp, if frozen. Peel and devein shrimp. Chop shrimp; set aside. In a small saucepan stir together broth, rice, onion, jalapeño, garlic, thyme, ¼ teaspoon salt, and cayenne pepper. Bring to boiling; reduce heat. Cover and simmer for 15 minutes or until rice is tender. Remove from heat. Stir in shrimp and lemon peel. Let stand, covered, 10 minutes. Cool slightly.

3. Using a sharp knife, cut a pocket in each chicken breast by cutting horizontally through the thickest portion to, but not through, the opposite side. Spoon shrimp mixture into each pocket. Secure pockets closed with short skewers or wooden toothpicks. Brush chicken with some of the oil and sprinkle with salt and black pepper.

4. Thread okra, sweet pepper, and onion on skewers (see tip, page 30), leaving ¼-inch headspace between pieces. Brush vegetables with remaining oil and sprinkle with salt and black pepper.

5. For a charcoal grill, sprinkle the drained wood chips over medium coals. Place vegetable skewers and chicken on grill rack. Cover and grill for 15 to 18 minutes or until chicken is tender and no longer pink (165°F) and okra is slightly charred, turning chicken once and vegetable skewers occasionally. (For a gas grill, preheat grill. Reduce heat to medium. Add drained wood chips according to manufacturer's directions. Smoke as directed.)

6. To serve, place chicken and vegetables on serving plate. Spoon warm Cajun Tomato Sauce over chicken.

CAJUN TOMATO SAUCE In a small saucepan cook ¼ cup finely chopped onion, ¼ cup finely chopped celery, ¼ cup finely chopped green sweet pepper, and 2 cloves minced garlic in 2 tablespoons hot oil over medium heat for 3 minutes or until softened. Add 1 cup peeled, seeded, and chopped tomatoes. Bring to boiling; reduce heat. Cook and stir for 5 to 10 minutes or until tomatoes have softened and juice out. Stir in 2 tablespoons whipping cream; heat through. Add ½ teaspoon bottled hot pepper sauce, and season to taste with salt and black pepper. Cover and keep warm.

PER SERVING: *504 cal., 22 g fat (5 g sat. fat), 206 mg chol., 795 mg sodium, 21 g carb., 3 g fiber, 54 g pro.*

PREP: 35 MINUTES **SOAK:** 1 HOUR **COOK:** 15 MINUTES **GRILL:** 15 MINUTES **MAKES:** 4 SERVINGS

planked chicken with grilled corn relish

TO LOOSEN THE SKIN ON THE CHICKEN, USE A SMALL SHARP KNIFE TO CUT THE MEMBRANE BETWEEN THE SKIN AND THE FLESH ON THE EDGE OF ONE PIECE. CAREFULLY WORK YOUR FINGERS UNDER THE SKIN TOWARD THE OPPOSITE EDGE OF THE PIECE WITHOUT PULLING THE SKIN COMPLETELY OFF.

2 14×6½-inch oak or hickory grilling planks
2 3- to 3½-pound broiler-fryer chickens, quartered
2 to 4 tablespoons bottled hot pepper sauce
2 to 4 teaspoons cracked black pepper
1 teaspoon salt
6 ears fresh sweet corn, husked
1 recipe Fresh Ranch Dressing
1 recipe Grilled Corn Relish
¾ cup pecan halves, toasted (see tip, page 77) (optional)
   Lemon wedges (optional)

1. Place the grill plank in a container of water; weight down the plank and soak it for at least 1 hour.

2. Loosen skin on chicken. In a small bowl combine hot pepper sauce, black pepper, and salt. Drizzle under skin of chicken. Rub to disperse pepper mixture.

3. For charcoal or gas grill, place planks on a grill rack directly over medium heat until planks begin to crackle and smoke. Place chicken, bone sides down, on planks. Add corn to grill rack. Cover and grill 15 to 20 minutes or until corn is tender, turning two or three times. Remove corn from grill; set aside and keep warm. Cover and grill chicken 35 to 40 minutes longer or until no pink remains (180°F in a thigh).

4. Place Grilled Corn Relish on large platter. Top with chicken, pecans, and drizzle with remaining Fresh Ranch Dressing.

FRESH RANCH DRESSING: In a blender or food processor combine ⅓ cup buttermilk, ½ cup sour cream, 2 tablespoons mayonnaise, 1½ teaspoons lemon juice, 1 tablespoon bottled hot pepper sauce, 1 clove garlic, ¼ teaspoon salt, and ⅛ teaspoon ground black pepper. Cover and blend or process until smooth.

GRILLED CORN RELISH: Cut corn from cobs. In medium bowl combine corn, one 4-ounce jar pimientos, drained; ½ cup sliced green onions, 2 tablespoons oil, 2 tablespoons honey, and 1 tablespoon lemon juice; toss to combine. Add ⅓ cup Fresh Ranch Dressing and toss to combine.

PER SERVING: *664 cal., 44 g fat (13 g sat. fat), 180 mg chol., 745 mg sodium, 20 g carb., 2 g fiber, 46 g pro.*

PREP: 45 MINUTES **SOAK:** 1 HOUR **GRILL:** 50 MINUTES **MAKES:** 8 SERVINGS

grilled pasta salad with chicken, peaches, and cashews

WHEN POUNDING THE CHICKEN BREASTS FLAT WITH THE MEAT MALLET, WORK FROM THE CENTER OF THE BREAST TOWARD THE EDGES FOR THE MOST EVEN THICKNESS.

1 cup apple or oak wood chips
2 skinless, boneless chicken breast halves (about 12 ounces)
1 large red onion, sliced ½ inch thick*
  Olive oil
  Kosher salt and ground black pepper
6 ounces dried angel hair pasta, broken
1 large ripe peach or nectarine, peeled (if desired), pitted, and chopped (see page 275)
½ cup dry roasted cashews
¼ cup snipped fresh cilantro
3 tablespoons olive oil
4 teaspoons balsamic vinegar
1 teaspoon Dijon-style mustard

1. At least 1 hour before smoke cooking, soak wood chips in enough water to cover. Drain soaked wood chips before using.

2. Place a chicken breast half between two sheets of plastic wrap; using the flat side of a meat mallet, lightly pound the chicken to ½-inch thickness. Remove plastic wrap. Repeat with remaining chicken. Lightly brush both sides of onion slices and chicken breast halves with oil; sprinkle with salt and pepper.

3. For a charcoal grill, sprinkle soaked wood chips over medium coals. Place chicken and onion slices on grill rack directly over medium heat. Cover and grill chicken for 5 to 8 minutes or until no longer pink, turning once. Remove chicken from grill. Grill onions for 2 to 5 minutes more or until onions are crisp-tender, turning once. (For a gas grill, preheat grill. Reduce heat to medium. Smoke as directed, except add drained wood chips according to manufacturer's directions.)

4. Cook pasta according to package directions; drain. Rinse pasta with cold water, and drain again.

5. Meanwhile, coarsely shred chicken and chop onion. In an extra-large bowl combine cooked pasta, chicken, onion, peaches, cashews, and cilantro.

6. For dressing, in a small screw-top jar combine the 3 tablespoons oil, vinegar, and mustard. Cover and shake well. Pour dressing over salad and toss to coat. Season with additional salt and pepper. Serve at room temperature or chill until ready to serve.

* To keep the onion slices from breaking apart while they grill, insert a toothpick or wooden skewer horizontally into the side of each onion slice, piercing each ring until end of skewer reaches the center of the slice.

PER SERVING: *336 cal., 16 g fat (3 g sat. fat), 33 mg chol., 145 mg sodium, 30 g carb., 2 g fiber, 19 g pro.*

PREP: 30 MINUTES **SOAK:** 1 HOUR **GRILL:** 7 MINUTES **MAKES:** 6 SERVINGS

apple-and-sage-stuffed smoked trout

IF YOU DON'T CARE FOR THE STRINGS ON CELERY, REMOVE THEM BY RUNNING A VEGETABLE PEELER DOWN THE BACK OF EACH STALK BEFORE SLICING.

1 cup apple or alder wood chips

4 8- to 10-ounce fresh or frozen dressed, boned rainbow trout

½ teaspoon salt

¼ teaspoon cracked black pepper

½ medium Jonathan or Pink Lady apple, cored and thinly sliced (see page 270)

1 stalk celery, thinly sliced

4 teaspoons snipped fresh sage
Nonstick cooking spray

8 ¼-inch slices lemon

1 tablespoon sliced almonds, toasted (see tip, page 77)

1. At least 1 hour before smoke cooking, soak wood chips in enough water to cover. Drain before using.

2. Thaw fish, if frozen. Rinse fish; pat dry with paper towels. Sprinkle the cavity of each fish with salt and pepper. Layer apple and celery slices in the cavity of each fish. Sprinkle with sage. Coat a sheet of heavy-duty foil with cooking spray. Lay fish on foil and top with lemon slices.

3. For a charcoal grill, arrange medium-hot coals around the edge of the grill. Test for medium heat above the center of the grill. Add drained wood chips to coals. Place foil with fish on the grill rack in the center of the grill. Cover; grill for 20 to 25 minutes or until fish flakes easily when tested with a fork. (For a gas grill, preheat grill. Reduce heat to medium. Adjust for indirect cooking. Add wood chips according to manufacturer's directions. Grill as above.)

4. To serve, sprinkle with toasted almonds.

PER SERVING: *345 cal., 15 g fat (3 g sat. fat), 134 mg chol., 416 mg sodium, 5 g carb.,12 g fiber, 46 g pro.*

PREP: 20 MINUTES **SOAK:** 1 HOUR **GRILL:** 20 MINUTES **MAKES:** 4 SERVINGS

smoky sea bass with grilled mango salsa

SEA BASS IS A LOVELY INTRODUCTORY FISH FOR THOSE WHO CLAIM NOT TO LIKE FISH. MOIST, MILD-TASTING, AND BUTTERY-TEXTURED, IT TAKES BEAUTIFULLY TO A VARIETY OF FLAVORS AND PREPARATIONS.

1   14×6½-inch alder or oak grilling plank
2   fresh mangoes (see page 275)
1   tablespoon packed brown sugar
2   tablespoons chopped green onion
1   teaspoon finely shredded lime peel
3   cloves garlic, minced
1   teaspoon peeled and grated fresh ginger
½   of a fresh jalapeño chile pepper, seeded and finely chopped (see tip, page 21)
4   5- to 7-ounce sea bass, halibut, or red snapper fillets, 1-inch thick
    Salt and ground black pepper
2   tablespoons chopped fresh cilantro
1   teaspoon lime juice
1   tablespoon olive oil

1. At least 1 hour before grilling, soak plank in enough water to cover, weighting it to keep it submerged.

2. Using a sharp knife cut each mango lengthwise down both flat sides, keeping the blade about ¼ inch from the seed. Discard seeds. Score mango halves in a crosshatch fashion, making cuts through fruit but not through peel. Sprinkle cut sides of mango halves with brown sugar; rub sugar into mango. For a gas or charcoal grill, place mango, cut sides down, on the grill rack directly over medium heat. Cover and grill for 8 to 10 minutes or until browned, turning once halfway through grilling. Remove and cool while grilling fish.

3. In a small bowl combine green onion, lime peel, garlic, and ginger. Set half of the mixture aside. Add jalapeño to the remaining half. Sprinkle fish with salt and black pepper. Sprinkle tops of fish fillets with jalapeño mixture.

4. For a gas or charcoal grill, place plank on grill rack directly over medium heat for 3 to 5 minutes or until plank begins to crackle and smoke. Place fish on plank. Cover and grill 10 minutes or until fish flakes easily when tested with a fork.

5. Use a spoon to scoop mango from the peels into a medium bowl. Add reserved green onion mixture, cilantro, and lime juice. Serve with fish. If desired, drizzle fish with oil just before serving.

PER SERVING: *218 cal., 3 g fat (13 g sat. fat), 58 mg chol., 245 mg sodium, 20 g carb., 2 g fiber, 27 g pro.*

PREP: 25 MINUTES **SOAK:** 1 HOUR **GRILL:** 18 MINUTES **MAKES:** 4 SERVINGS

planked salmon with grilled pepper relish

1 2-pound fresh or frozen salmon fillet with skin
1 14×6½-inch alder or cedar grill plank
¼ cup reduced-sodium soy sauce
¼ cup balsamic vinegar
3 tablespoons honey
1 tablespoon peeled and grated fresh ginger
½ teaspoon crushed red pepper
3 red, yellow, and/or orange sweet peppers
3 tablespoons thinly sliced fresh basil
2 tablespoons chopped pitted Kalamata olives
2 teaspoons olive oil
2 teaspoons balsamic vinegar
¼ teaspoon salt
¼ teaspoon ground black pepper
¼ cup thinly bias-sliced green onions

1. Thaw fish if frozen. Rinse fish; pat dry with paper towels. Place the grill plank in a container of water; weight down the plank and soak it for at least 1 hour.

2. For marinade, in a small bowl combine soy sauce, the ¼ cup vinegar, honey, ginger, and crushed red pepper. Place salmon in a large resealable plastic bag set in a shallow dish. Pour marinade over salmon; seal bag. Turn bag to coat fish. Marinate in the refrigerator for 1 hour, turning occasionally. Drain salmon from marinade, discarding marinade.

3. For a gas or charcoal grill, place peppers on the grill rack directly over medium heat for 10 to 12 minutes or until blistered and charred, turning occasionally. Wrap peppers in foil, folding edges together to enclose peppers; let stand for 15 minutes. Using a sharp knife, loosen edges of skins; gently pull off skins in strips and discard. Chop peppers into ½-inch pieces; discard stems, seeds, and membranes.

4. While peppers are standing, place plank on the rack of the uncovered grill directly over medium heat for 3 to 5 minutes or until plank begins to crackle and smoke. Place salmon fillet, skin side down, on grill plank. Cover and grill for 18 to 22 minutes or until fish begins to flake when tested with a fork.

5. Meanwhile, for relish, in a medium bowl stir together the chopped peppers, basil, olives, oil, the 2 teaspoons vinegar, salt, and black pepper.

6. Sprinkle salmon with green onions and serve with the sweet pepper relish.

PER SERVING: *196 cal., 9 g fat (1 g sat. fat), 62 mg chol., 197 mg sodium, 5 g carb., 1 g fiber, 23 g pro.*

PREP: 25 MINUTES SOAK: 1 HOUR MARINATE: 1 HOUR GRILL: 18 MINUTES MAKES: 8 SERVINGS

quinoa-stuffed smoked tomatoes

1 cup apple, pecan, or hickory chips
½ cup quinoa, rinsed and drained
1 cup chicken or vegetable broth
1 small zucchini, chopped (1½ cups)
1 teaspoon olive oil
2 tablespoons olive oil
2 tablespoons lemon juice
1 tablespoon snipped fresh herbs (such as chives, oregano, thyme, basil, and/or parsley)
1 teaspoon honey
  Salt and ground black pepper
2 ounces goat cheese (chèvre), crumbled
2 tablespoons pine nuts, toasted (see tip, page 77)
2 tablespoons minced shallots
4 large firm tomatoes or heirloom tomatoes

1. At least 1 hour before smoke cooking, soak wood chips in enough water to cover. Drain before using.

2. In a small saucepan combine quinoa and broth. Bring to boiling. Reduce heat and simmer, covered, for 15 minutes or until liquid is absorbed. Meanwhile, in a medium skillet cook and stir zucchini in 1 teaspoon hot oil over medium heat until tender, about 5 minutes. Remove from heat; set aside.

3. In a screw-top jar combine 2 tablespoons oil, lemon juice, herbs, and honey. Cover and shake well to combine. Season to taste with salt and pepper. Add to quinoa; toss to combine. Stir in zucchini, goat cheese, pine nuts, and shallots.

4. Core tomatoes. Using a melon baller, scoop out tomatoes, leaving ½-inch shells. Place tomatoes in an 8×8×2-inch disposable foil pan. Spoon quinoa filling into tomatoes, mounding the filling on top.

5. For a charcoal grill, arrange medium-hot coals around the outer edge of the grill. Test for medium heat above the center of the grill. Add drained wood chips to the coals. Place foil pan with the tomatoes on a grill rack in the center of the grill. Cover; grill for 18 to 20 minutes or until softened and heated through. (For a gas grill, preheat grill. Reduce heat to medium. Adjust for indirect cooking. Add wood chips according to manufacturer's directions. Grill as above.)

PER SERVING: *282 cal., 17 g fat 41 g sat. fat), 26 mg chol., 449 mg sodium, 26 g carb., 5 g fiber, 9 g pro.*

PREP: 35 MINUTES **SOAK:** 1 HOUR **GRILL:** 18 MINUTES **MAKES:** 4 SERVINGS

Grilled Skillet Peach Pie, *recipe page 259*

desserts

KEEP THE COALS GOING LONG ENOUGH TO INDULGE IN ONE OF THESE FIRE-KISSED TREATS THAT RANGE FROM FRUIT CRISPS AND PIES TO GOOEY BROWNIES TO GRILLED FRUIT SERVED OVER HOMEMADE ICE CREAM.

grilled strawberries with sweet corn shortcakes and limoncello whipped cream

CORNMEAL ADDS A PLEASING CRUNCH TO THESE SHORTCAKES TOPPED WITH SAUCY BALSAMIC VINEGAR-DRESSED GRILLED STRAWBERRIES AND A SPIRITED, LEMONY WHIPPED CREAM.

1	cup all-purpose flour
½	cup yellow cornmeal
¼	cup sugar
½	teaspoon baking powder
¼	teaspoon baking soda
⅛	teaspoon salt
⅓	cup cold butter, cut up
¼	cup buttermilk
¼	cup whole milk
1	pound fresh strawberries, hulled
¼	cup sugar
1	tablespoon white balsamic vinegar
1	recipe Limoncello Whipped Cream
¼	cup chopped toasted hazelnuts (see tip, page 77)

1. Preheat oven to 350°F. For the shortcakes, in a medium bowl stir together flour, cornmeal, ¼ cup sugar, the baking powder, baking soda, and salt. Using a pastry blender, cut in butter until mixture resembles coarse crumbs. Make a well in the center of the mixture. Add buttermilk and milk to flour mixture all at once. Using a fork, stir just until moistened (batter will be thick).

2. Drop dough into 6 mounds on a large ungreased baking sheet. Bake about 15 minutes or until a wooden toothpick inserted near the center comes out clean. Cool shortcakes on a wire rack.

3. For the strawberries, in a medium bowl toss together strawberries and ¼ cup sugar. Thread strawberries on skewers (see tip, page 30). For a gas or charcoal grill, place skewers on a grill rack directly over medium heat. Cover and grill 3 to 5 minutes or until lightly browned, turning once halfway through grilling.

4. When cool enough to handle, slice strawberries. Add back to the bowl. Drizzle vinegar over strawberries. Toss to combine.

5. In serving bowls, split shortcakes with a fork (cakes will be tender); top with strawberries and Limoncello Whipped Cream. Sprinkle with hazelnuts.

LIMONCELLO WHIPPED CREAM
In a medium chilled bowl beat ½ cup whipping cream with an electric mixer on medium to high speed until thickened. Add 1 tablespoon powdered sugar and 1 tablespoon limoncello. Beat until soft peaks form.

PER SERVING: *421 cal., 22 g fat (12 g sat. fat), 56 mg chol., 256 mg sodium, 53 g carb., 3 g fiber, 5 g pro.*

PREP: 30 MINUTES **BAKE:** 15 MINUTES AT 350°F **GRILL:** 3 MINUTES **MAKES:** 6 SERVINGS

grilled berry crumble

GRILLED IN A FOIL PAN, THIS JUICY FRUIT CRUMBLE IS PERFECT FOR CAMPOUTS AND PICNICS. AFTER THE CRUMBLE IS CONSUMED (AND THERE WON'T BE A BITE LEFT!), THE PAN CAN SIMPLY BE RINSED AND RECYCLED.

3	cups fresh or frozen blueberries
2	cups fresh or frozen strawberries
½	cup granulated sugar
2	tablespoons all-purpose flour
½	cup quick-cooking rolled oats
½	cup packed brown sugar
¼	cup all-purpose flour
¼	teaspoon ground nutmeg
¼	teaspoon ground cinnamon
¼	cup butter
	Whipped cream (see page 258) (optional)
	Fresh strawberries, cut up (optional)

1. In a medium saucepan combine blueberries, 2 cups strawberries, granulated sugar, and the 2 tablespoons flour. Cook and stir over medium heat until mixture is thickened and bubbly. Transfer fruit mixture to an 8×8×2-inch metal or disposable foil baking pan; set aside.

2. For topping, in a medium bowl combine oats, brown sugar, the ¼ cup flour, nutmeg, and cinnamon. Using a pastry blender, cut in butter until mixture resembles coarse crumbs. Sprinkle topping over fruit filling. Cover pan tightly with foil.

3. For a charcoal or gas grill, place pan on a rack of an uncovered grill directly over medium heat for 20 to 25 minutes or until topping is set.

4. Serve warm. If desired, serve with whipped cream and additional strawberries.

PER SERVING: *313 cal., 9 g fat (5 g sat. fat), 20 mg chol., 61 mg sodium, 60 g carb., 4 g fiber, 3 g pro.*

PREP: 20 MINUTES **GRILL:** 20 MINUTES **MAKES:** 6 SERVINGS

cast-iron mixed berry crisp

A CROWN OF CRUSHED ITALIAN MACAROONS MIXED WITH BUTTER, BROWN SUGAR, AND ALMONDS GIVE THIS HOMEY CRISP A SPECIAL TOUCH.

3 cups mixed fresh berries (such as blueberries, blackberries, and/or raspberries)
⅓ cup granulated sugar
4 teaspoons quick-cooking tapioca
½ teaspoon ground cinnamon
½ teaspoon ground ginger
½ cup crushed amaretti cookies
¼ cup all-purpose flour
2 tablespoons sliced almonds
2 tablespoons packed brown sugar
¼ cup butter
1 tablespoon butter, softened
   Vanilla ice cream (optional)

1. In a large bowl combine berries, granulated sugar, tapioca, cinnamon, and ginger. Let stand for 15 minutes, stirring occasionally.

2. For the topping, in a medium bowl combine crushed amaretti, flour, almonds, and brown sugar. Using a pastry blender, cut in the ¼ cup butter until mixture resembles coarse crumbs.

3. Generously butter an 8- to 9-inch cast-iron skillet or two individual 10- to 12-ounce cast-iron skillets with the 1 tablespoon softened butter. Fill skillet(s) with berry mixture. Sprinkle with the topping.

4. For a charcoal grill, arrange medium-hot coals around the edges of the grill. Test for medium heat above the center of the grill. Place skillet(s) in center of grill rack (not over the coals). Cover and grill until bubbly and topping is golden brown. Allow about 35 minutes for large skillet or about 20 minutes for small skillets. (For a gas grill, preheat grill. Adjust for indirect cooking. Place skillet[s] on unheated side of grill. Grill as above.)

5. Remove from grill; cool for 30 minutes before serving. If desired, serve warm with ice cream.

PER SERVING: *544 cal., 25 g fat (14 g sat. fat), 70 mg chol., 169 mg sodium, 75 g carb., 5 g fiber, 6 g pro.*

PREP: 25 MINUTES **STAND:** 15 MINUTES **GRILL:** 35 MINUTES **COOL:** 30 MINUTES **MAKES:** 4 SERVINGS

grilled apple crisp with porter-toffee sauce

SIMPLER TO MAKE THAN APPLE PIE, THIS AUTUMNAL DESSERT MAKES AN APPROPRIATE FINISH TO A MEAL FEATURING GRILLED OR ROASTED PORK. DARK BEER IS THE SURPRISE INGREDIENT IN THE SWEET SAUCE THAT TOPS IT OFF.

7	cups peeled and thinly sliced cooking apples (7 medium) (see page 270)
⅓	cup granulated sugar
1	tablespoon quick-cooking tapioca
1	tablespoon lemon juice
1	teaspoon apple pie spice
¼	teaspoon salt
½	cup rolled oats
½	cup packed brown sugar
¼	cup all-purpose flour
¼	cup butter
1	recipe Porter Toffee Sauce
	Ice cream (optional)

1. In a large bowl combine apples, granulated sugar, tapioca, lemon juice, apple pie spice, and salt. Transfer apple mixture to an 8×8×1¾-inch disposable foil pan or metal pan.

2. For topping, in a medium bowl combine oats, brown sugar, and flour. Using a pastry blender, cut in butter until mixture resembles coarse crumbs. Sprinkle oat mixture evenly over apple mixture. Cover pan tightly with foil.

3. For a charcoal grill, arrange medium-hot coals around edge of grill. Test for medium heat over center of grill. Place pan on grill rack in center of grill. Cover and grill for 15 minutes. Uncover pan. Cover grill and grill about 30 minutes more or until apple filling is bubbly. (For a gas grill, preheat grill. Reduce heat to medium. Adjust for indirect cooking. Place pan on grill rack. Grill as directed.)

4. Remove crisp from grill; cool slightly. Serve warm with Porter-Toffee Sauce and, if desired, ice cream.

PORTER TOFFEE SAUCE In a small saucepan combine 1 cup packed brown sugar, ½ cup whipping cream, ½ cup porter beer, and 2 tablespoons light-color corn syrup. Bring to boiling; reduce heat. Simmer, uncovered, about 12 minutes or until sauce is desired consistency. Store leftover sauce, covered, in the refrigerator for up to 1 week. Makes 1⅓ cups.

PER SERVING: *566 cal., 16 g fat (10 g sat. fat), 48 mg chol., 180 mg sodium, 105 g carb., 5 g fiber, 4 g pro.*

PREP: 25 MINUTES **GRILL:** 45 MINUTES **MAKES:** 6 SERVINGS

grilled plum-topped pizza

A SPRINKLING OF CRYSTALLIZED GINGER ADDS A TOUCH OF SWEET HEAT TO THIS SUPER-SIMPLE AND SPEEDY DESSERT PIZZA. MAKE IT WHEN PLUMS ARE IN SEASON—FROM MAY TO OCTOBER.

¼ cup mascarpone cheese
1 tablespoon honey
2 ripe, yet firm, plums, halved lengthwise and pitted
1 12-inch thin crust pizza shell, such as Boboli brand
2 tablespoons sliced almonds, toasted (see tip, page 77)
1 tablespoon chopped crystallized ginger
Honey (optional)

1. In a small bowl combine cheese and the 1 tablespoon honey; set aside.

2. For a charcoal or gas grill, place plum halves, cut sides down, on the grill rack directly over medium heat. Cover and grill for 6 to 8 minutes or until plums are tender and lightly browned. Remove from grill. When cool enough to handle, slice plum halves.

3. Add the pizza shell to grill. Cover and grill about 3 minutes or until bottom is lightly browned. Remove from grill.

4. Spread cheese mixture over browned side of crust. Add plum slices; sprinkle with almonds and ginger. Return pizza to grill. Cover and grill for 2 to 3 minutes more or until bottom is lightly browned and topping is heated through.

5. If desired, drizzle with additional honey before serving. Cut into wedges.

PER SERVING: *166 cal., 6 g fat (3 g sat. fat), 9 mg chol., 211 mg sodium, 24 g carb., 1 g fiber, 6 g pro.*

PREP: 15 MINUTES **GRILL:** 11 MINUTES **MAKES:** 8 SERVINGS

cast-iron plum-polenta cake

⅓ cup all-purpose flour
⅓ cup yellow cornmeal
1 teaspoon baking powder
½ teaspoon finely shredded lemon peel
¼ teaspoon salt
¼ teaspoon freshly grated nutmeg
¼ cup butter, softened
½ cup sugar
½ teaspoon vanilla extract
2 eggs
¼ cup sour cream
1 tablespoon butter, softened
2 cups sliced plums (2 to 3 pitted plums)
1 recipe Whipped Cream (optional)

1. In a small bowl stir together flour, cornmeal, baking powder, lemon peel, salt, and nutmeg. In a medium mixing bowl beat the ¼ cup butter with an electric mixer on medium to high speed for 30 seconds. Add sugar and vanilla; beat until combined. Add eggs, one at a time, beating well after each addition. Add sour cream; beat until combined. Gently stir in cornmeal batter.

2. Butter an 8- to 9-inch cast-iron skillet or two individual 10- to 12-ounce cast-iron skillets with the 1 tablespoon butter. Add plums to skillet(s). Evenly spread batter over plums.

3. For a charcoal grill, arrange medium-hot coals around the edges of the grill. Test for medium heat above the center of the grill. Place skillet(s) in center of grill rack (not over the coals). Cover and grill until a wooden toothpick inserted near the center(s) comes out clean. Allow 25 to 30 minutes for large skillet or about 20 minutes for small skillets. (For a gas grill, preheat grill. Adjust for indirect cooking. Place skillet[s] on unheated side of grill. Grill as above.)

4. Remove from grill; cool for 30 minutes before serving. If desired, serve warm with Whipped Cream.

PER SERVING: *515 cal., 20 g fat (11 g sat. fat), 150 mg chol., 409 mg sodium, 81 g carb., 2 g fiber, 6 g pro.*

WHIPPED CREAM In a medium bowl combine ½ cup whipping cream, 1 tablespoon sour cream, and 1 tablespoon powdered sugar. Beat with an electric mixer or wire whisk until soft peaks form (tips curl).

PREP: 25 MINUTES **GRILL:** 25 MINUTES **COOL:** 30 MINUTES **MAKES:** 4 SERVINGS

grilled skillet peach pie

3½ pounds peaches, peeled, halved, and pitted (see page 275)
1 tablespoon canola oil
½ cup sugar
¼ cup snipped fresh basil
3 tablespoons cornstarch
1 tablespoon lemon juice
1 15-ounce package (2 crusts) rolled refrigerated unbaked piecrust
Nonstick cooking spray
1 egg, lightly beaten
1 tablespoon water
1 tablespoon sugar

1. For a charcoal grill, arrange medium-hot coals on one side of a grill. Test for medium heat above the empty side of the grill. Brush peach halves with oil. Place peach halves, cut sides down, on grill rack directly over coals; grill about 3 minutes or until lightly browned. Remove from heat. (For a gas grill, preheat grill. Reduce heat to medium. Adjust for indirect cooking. Grill as directed.)

2. Cut peach halves into wedges. In a large bowl combine peaches, the ½ cup sugar, basil, cornstarch, and lemon juice.

3. On a lightly floured surface, roll each crust to a 12-inch diameter. Coat a 9½- to 10-inch cast iron skillet with cooking spray. Line the skillet with one of the crusts, the crust should come three-quarters of the way up the sides of the skillet. Transfer peach filling to crust-lined skillet. Using a sharp knife, cut several slits in the center of the second crust to vent steam. Place the second crust over the peach mixture. Tuck any extra dough at the edges between the side of the skillet and the bottom crust. Crimp edge. In a small bowl combine egg and water. Brush the pie with egg mixture; sprinkle with the 1 tablespoon sugar.

4. Place the skillet on the grill rack over the empty side of the grill (or unlit burner of gas grill). Cover and grill for 1½ to 2 hours or until crust is golden and filling is bubbly, rotating once halfway through grilling. Cool on a wire rack for at least 30 minutes. Serve warm.

PER SERVING: *263 cal., 11 g fat (4 g sat. fat), 24 mg chol., 151 mg sodium, 39 g carb., 2 g fiber, 2 g pro.*

PREP: 30 MINUTES   GRILL: 1 HOUR 30 MINUTES   COOL: 30 MINUTES   MAKES: 12 SERVINGS

chocolate-raspberry grillers

KIDS WILL LOVE THESE TOASTY DESSERT SANDWICHES THAT HAVE MELTED CHOCOLATE AND BERRIES IN THE MIDDLE—AND THAT COME WITH A SIDE OF WARM CHOCOLATE GRAVY FOR DIPPING.

8 ½-inch slices challah or Hawaiian sweet bread
2 tablespoons butter, melted
4 ounces semisweet chocolate, finely chopped
1 cup fresh raspberries
1 recipe Warm Chocolate Gravy

1. Brush one side of each bread slice with some of the butter. Place half the bread slices, buttered side down, on a plate. Sprinkle with chocolate and raspberries to within ¼ inch of crusts. Top with remaining bread, buttered sides up.

2. For a gas or charcoal grill, place a cast-iron griddle or skillet on a grill rack directly over medium-low heat for 5 minutes to preheat. Place sandwiches, two at a time, on griddle or skillet. Cover and grill sandwiches 4 to 6 minutes or until chocolate is melted and bread is golden brown, turning once midway through grilling time. Grill remaining sandwiches.

3. Slice in half to serve. Pass Warm Chocolate Gravy for dipping.

WARM CHOCOLATE GRAVY
In a small bowl stir together ¼ cup sugar, 2 tablespoons unsweetened cocoa powder, and 1 tablespoon all-purpose flour; set aside. In a medium saucepan melt 1 tablespoon butter. Stir sugar mixture into melted butter until smooth. Gradually add 1¼ cups milk, stirring constantly. Cook and stir over medium heat until thickened and bubbly; cook and stir for 1 minute. Makes 1¼ cups.

PER SERVING: *217 cal., 8 g fat (5 g sat. fat), 10 mg chol., 180 mg sodium, 34 g carb., 3 g fiber, 4 g pro.*

PREP: 20 MINUTES **GRILL:** 4 MINUTES **MAKES:** 4 SERVINGS

grilled tropical fruit with cinnamon-sugar crisps and dulce de leche

SLIGHTLY GREEN BANANAS WILL HOLD UP TO THE HEAT OF THE GRILL BETTER THAN RIPER ONES. STIR A NIP OF SPICED RUM INTO THE DULCE DE LECHE CARAMEL, IF YOU LIKE.

2 teaspoons sugar
½ teaspoon ground cinnamon
2 8- to 10-inch flour tortillas
1 tablespoon butter, melted
1 tablespoon vegetable oil
2 medium underripe bananas, peeled and halved lengthwise
6 fresh pineapple spears
½ cup dulce de leche
1 tablespoon spiced rum (optional)
1 tablespoon toasted coconut (see tip, page 77)

1. In a small bowl combine sugar and cinnamon. For a gas or charcoal grill, place tortillas on a greased grill rack directly over medium heat. Cover and grill for 2 to 4 minutes or until crisp and brown, turning once halfway through grilling. Remove from grill. Brush both sides of tortillas with butter and sprinkle with cinnamon-sugar mixture. Cut into wedges.

2. Add bananas and pineapple spears to the grill rack cut sides down. Cover and grill for 6 to 10 minutes or until brown and slightly softened, turning once halfway through grilling. Using a spatula, remove fruit from grill; cool. When cool enough to handle, cut fruit in bite-size pieces.

3. Place dulce de leche in a small bowl; if desired, stir in rum. Spread dulce de leche on cinnamon crisps. Top with grilled fruit; sprinkle with coconut.

PER SERVING: *355 cal., 11 g fat (4 g sat. fat), 16 mg chol., 176 mg sodium, 63 g carb., 3 g fiber, 5 g pro.*

PREP: 20 MINUTES GRILL: 8 MINUTES MAKES: 4 SERVINGS

Cast-Iron Brownies, *recipe on page 266*

cast-iron brownies *pictured on page 265*

EAT SOMETHING LIGHT FOR DINNER—THEN MAKE THESE INCREDIBLY INDULGENT BROWNIES. COOKING IN CAST IRON MAKES THE EDGES OF THE BROWNIE DELIGHTFULLY CRISP WHILE THE CENTER STAYS WARM AND GOOEY.

1 tablespoon butter, softened
½ cup butter
3 ounces unsweetened chocolate, coarsely chopped
1 cup sugar
2 eggs
1 teaspoon vanilla
⅔ cup all-purpose flour
¼ teaspoon baking soda
2 medium bananas (unpeeled), halved lengthwise
1 tablespoon butter, melted
  Rocky road ice cream (optional)
  Hot fudge sauce (optional)

1. Generously butter an 8- to 9-inch cast-iron skillet or four individual 10- to 12-ounce cast-iron skillets or casseroles (such as 5-inch skillets) with the 1 tablespoon softened butter; set aside.

2. In a medium saucepan combine the ½ cup butter and the chocolate; cook and stir over low heat until melted and smooth. Remove from heat. Stir in sugar. Add eggs, one at a time, beating with a wooden spoon after each addition just until combined. Stir in vanilla. In a small bowl stir together the flour and baking soda. Add flour mixture to chocolate mixture; stir just until combined. Spread into the prepared skillet(s).

3. For a charcoal grill, arrange medium-hot coals around the edges of the grill. Test for medium heat above the center of the grill. Place skillet(s) in center of grill rack (not over the coals). Cover and grill just until set in center and edges are firm and pull away from sides. Allow 25 to 30 minutes for large skillet or about 20 minutes for small skillets. Meanwhile, brush cut sides of bananas with the

melted butter. For the last 5 minutes of grilling, add bananas to grill rack directly over coals; grill until lightly browned. (For a gas grill, preheat grill. Adjust for indirect cooking. Place skillet[s] on unheated side of grill and later place bananas over heat. Grill as above.) Remove skillet[s] from grill; let stand for 10 minutes.

4. Serve warm topped with grilled banana pieces, and, if desired, ice cream and hot fudge sauce.

PER SERVING: *873 cal., 51 g fat (30 g sat. fat), 197 mg chol., 369 mg sodium, 106 g carb., 7 g fiber, 11 g pro.*

PREP: 20 MINUTES **GRILL:** 25 MINUTES **STAND:** 10 MINUTES **MAKES:** 4 SERVINGS

grilled strawberry-lavender ice cream with white chocolate

THE FLORAL FLAVOR OF LAVENDER AND AROMATIC VANILLA—ITSELF A TYPE OF ORCHID—COMPLEMENT EACH OTHER IN THIS ELEGANT ICE CREAM THAT'S MARBLED AND TOPPED WITH GRILLED STRAWBERRIES.

1½ cups milk
¾ cup sugar
4 egg yolks, lightly beaten
1 tablespoon dried lavender
¼ teaspoon salt
1½ cups whipping cream
1½ teaspoons vanilla
4 cups fresh strawberries, hulled
¼ cup sugar
3 ounces white baking chocolate, chopped

1. In a medium saucepan combine milk, ¾ cup sugar, lavender, and the salt. Stir in egg yolks. Cook and stir over medium heat until mixture just comes to boiling.

2. Quickly place the saucepan in a large bowl of ice water. Stir constantly for 2 to 3 minutes to quickly cool the custard. Pour custard into a bowl. Cover surface with plastic wrap. Chill for at least 4 hours or up to 24 hours. Strain custard through a fine-mesh sieve to remove lavender; discard lavender. Stir in whipping cream and vanilla.

3. In a medium bowl combine strawberries and the ¼ cup sugar. Thread strawberries on skewers (see tip, page 30). For a gas or charcoal grill, place skewers on a grill rack directly over medium heat. Cover and grill 3 to 5 minutes or until lightly browned, turning once halfway through grilling. When cool enough to handle, chop half of the strawberries; set aside. Return remaining strawberries to the reserved bowl and slightly mash or cut up. Cover and refrigerate the strawberries until needed.

4. Freeze mixture in a 2-quart ice cream freezer according to manufacturer's directions. Stir in the chopped strawberries and white chocolate. Ripen up to 4 hours in the freezer. Serve topped with slightly mashed strawberries.

PER SERVING: *309 cal., 19 g fat (11 g sat. fat), 128 mg chol., 100 mg sodium, 33 g carb., 1 g fiber, 4 g pro.*

PREP: 20 MINUTES **CHILL:** 4 TO 24 HOURS **FREEZE:** PER MANUFACTURER'S DIRECTIONS **RIPEN:** UP TO 4 HOURS **MAKES:** 10 SERVINGS

produce guide

BEFORE YOU APPLY SMOKE AND FIRE TO THOSE BEAUTIFUL FRUITS AND VEGETABLES, HERE'S WHAT YOU NEED TO KNOW ABOUT CHOOSING THE BEST YOU CAN BUY, STORING THEM, AND PREPARING THEM FOR COOKING.

apples

The health benefits naturally packed into every apple are certainly the source of the old adage, "An apple a day keeps the doctor away." At about 95 calories a serving, apples are an ample source of antioxidants and fiber (each apple delivers 4 grams of fiber). To get that fiber boost, eat apples with the peels on; two-thirds of the fiber is in the peel. Although this wonder fruit is available everywhere and at all times of the year, their peak season is in the autumn.

1. Cut the skin off with a paring knife.

2. Cut the apple in four wedges.

3. Cut the core out of each piece. Chop or slice as called for in the recipe.

artichokes

Although the spiky, grenadelike appearance of the artichoke makes it look inedible and foreboding, this vegetable is actually easy to prepare and a treat to eat. Two parts of the artichoke are edible—the soft fleshy parts at the base of each leaf and the dense mild heart, which is the very inside base of the artichoke. Artichokes are most commonly boiled or steamed, but you can also braise, bake, or grill them. Enjoy cooked artichoke hot or cold, au naturel or with dipping sauces.

1. Trim stems; remove the dark outer leaves. Cut the artichoke crosswise. Use a spoon to scoop out the inedible choke.

2. Use a vegetable peeler to trim the rough edges.

3. Cut each artichoke in half lengthwise through the stem.

asparagus

One of the true culinary joys of springtime are the slender and juicy spears of asparagus. This fast-growing vegetable (it can grow up to 10 inches in a 24-hour period) grows straight up out of the ground, rising from the soil like a small green missile. It is delicious raw or cooked. You can steam, roast, or sauté it—and it is a favorite for the grill. It is a perennial—it comes back year after year. Its unique fresh flavor and succulent texture complement so many recipes—and it has the highest folic acid content of any vegetable.

1. Snap off the woody base of the asparagus where it bends.

2. Or, simply cut off the woody end with a paring knife.

3. If desired, remove the tough outer skin from the lower part of the spear using a vegetable peeler.

TO KEEP THEM FROM TURNING BROWN, PLACE THE PREPARED ARTICHOKES IN A LARGE BOWL CONTAINING WATER AND LEMON JUICE WHILE PREPARING THE REMAINING ARTICHOKES.

avocados

This tasty fruit native to Central Mexico is commonly called "alligator pear" because of its thin, dark green rubbery skin or "butterfruit" because of its rich, creamy flesh. The flesh can be sliced and eaten raw or mashed into a creamy paste for use in guacamole or sandwich spreads. Use avocados soon after you cut them or they will brown; a little lemon juice sprinkled over the cut fruit helps slow discoloration. Avocados are a good source of fiber, potassium, and vitamins C and K.

1. Cut the avocado in half lengthwise.

2. Twist the avocado to pop open the halves.

3. Insert a spoon underneath the seed and pop it out.

cherries

Dangling from trees like beautiful Chinese lanterns, cherries are one of nature's true delicacies. Available in sour and sweet varieties, there's a cherry for every purpose. Sour cherries are ideal for jams, jellies, syrups, and pies. Sweet cherries can be enjoyed right off the tree and are the cherries most often sold in produce sections. Both types of cherries pack a punch when it comes to antioxidants, beta-carotene, fiber, potassium, magnesium, iron, and vitamins C and E.

1. Pull out the stem.

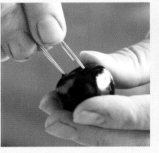

2. Insert a clean paper clip into the cherry. Twist it around the pit to loosen it.

3. Pull out the pit. You can also use a cherry pitter.

citrus fruits

Most citrus fruit is consumed fresh or as juice, but it also adds a healthy zing to vinaigrettes and marinades, steamed vegetables, and meat dishes. Lemons provide zest for pies, cookies, and other lemony baked goods. Limes are a requisite ingredient for many mixed drinks. Tangerines, especially clementines, peel effortlessly and the small sections are just the right size for eating. Grapefruits offer sweet and sour fruit in golden to ruby red colors. All members of the citrus family contain high levels of immune-boosting vitamin C.

1. To section citrus, slice off the top and bottom of the fruit.

2. Slice off the skin and bitter pith.

3. Holding the fruit over a bowl, slide the knife between the membranes. The sections will drop into the bowl.

eggplants

Glossy-skinned eggplant is as beautiful as it is delicious. A close relative of the tomato, it grows in a similar manner, hanging from the vine in the height of summer. When cooked, the flesh becomes tender and develops a rich, complex flavor. Used in Indian, Mediterranean, Middle Eastern, and French cooking, eggplant is a great replacement for meat because of its rich and hearty taste. Its sturdy construction makes it a natural for the grill. Eggplant is the star of dishes such as eggplant Parmesan, ratatouille, and baba ghanoush. It is rich in antioxidants and high in fiber.

1. Cut the top off the eggplant.

2. Use a vegetable peeler to remove the thick skin.

3. Cut eggplant into rounds.

fennel

There are two kinds of fennel: herb fennel, whose ferny leaves and anise-flavor seeds are used as seasonings, and vegetable fennel, whose bulbous base is used as a vegetable. The vegetable fennel is known by several aliases: fennel bulb, Florence fennel, and finocchio. The two kinds share the same botanical name, but only Florence fennel forms the large white bulb at the base of its plant. (Florence fennel has the same type of foliage as herbal fennel but doesn't have the same type of seeds.) For fennel lovers, it's all about the bulb, which has an aniselike flavor.

1. Cut off the stalks; save some of the feathery fronds for garnish, if desired.

2. Remove and discard wilted outer layers. Cut a thin slice from the base of the bulb.

3. Cut the bulb lengthwise into thin slices.

kale

This nutrient-dense member of the cabbage family is the belle of the ball these days. It's showing up sautéed, steamed, roasted in chip form, braised, in salads—and yes, even grilled. The ruffly dark green or purple leaves of kale look rather humble and unassuming, but they are a powerhouse of health benefits that few other vegetables can equal. Like other members of the cabbage family, the flavor of kale—earthy and pleasantly bitter— improves during the cool months.

1. Pull off the leafy part of the rib.

2. Discard the rib.

3. Chop the leaves into the size your recipe calls for.

leeks

Leeks are the regal relative of the onion (Allium) family. Both the leaves and bulb are bigger than that of scallions, but they have a milder onion flavor than scallions or storage onions. They won't overpower a dish in the way that onions might. Leeks are versatile and can be eaten raw (usually chopped up for salads or used as a garnish) as well as cooked. They can be baked, grilled, or sautéed on their own as a side dish or added to roasts, sautés, braises, soups, and stews for flavor. The edible parts of the leek are the white bulb (the part that grows underground) and the lightest green part of the leaves. The dark and fibrous upper part of the leek is discarded. Leeks are a good source of fiber, iron, and vitamins K, C, and A.

1. Trim off the stem and leaf ends of the leek. Cut leeks in half lengthwise, then slice as shown below.

2. Place the sliced leeks in a salad spinner filled with water; swirl the pieces in wtaer to clean. Spin dry.

mangoes

The sweet flavor of mango makes tropical fruit lovers all over the world swoon with delight. This hefty round or oblong fruit is known for two things: its great flavor and its oddly shaped large seed, which to novices can seem to be a cutting conundrum. Mangoes are key ingredients in smoothies, chutneys, and fruit salads. Mango salsa is a refreshing topper for fish dishes. Mango is a good source of vitamin A and fiber. The mango is the national fruit of India, which is also the country that produces the most mangoes.

1. Hold the mango so the "eye" (a small dimple at the base) is looking at you. Cut off the sides of the mango, avoiding the large seed.

2. Slice a checkerboard pattern into the mango, taking care not to slice through the skin.

3. Invert the mango slice so that the dices stand out. Insert the knife next to the skin and slice off the dices.

peaches

There aren't too many things more refreshing than biting into a fresh, tree-ripened peach. First cultivated in China thousands of years ago, the peach traveled across the globe with early explorers and put down roots wherever the climate was ideal. Since then, peached have played starring roles in pies, cobblers, cakes, ice cream, juices, salsas, and jams. They are also terrific grilled, poached, or roasted. Peaches are an excellent source of vitamins A, C, E, and K, as well as antioxidants and dietary fiber.

1. To peel peaches, place in boiling water for 20 seconds, then place into ice water.

2. Remove the loosened skin using a paring knife.

3. Cut in half and remove the pit using your fingers or the tip of a sharp knife.

pears

Pears have enjoyed a long, glamorous history, reaping rave reviews even in ancient times. In *The Odyssey* Homer refers to the pear as a gift of the gods. Succulent and shapely, the pear was also revered for its long storage life, an important trading commodity in the ancient world. A fresh, juicy pear is a special treat, but cooked pears are equally delicious. Pears are also a low-calorie fruit (about 100 calories per medium pear), and are a good source of vitamin C and fiber.

1. Use a paring knife to remove the skin of the pear.

2. Cut the pear in half. Leaving the half intact, use a melon baller to scoop out the seeds.

3. Remove the core by cutting away the stem.

hot peppers

Many foods around the world would be far more ho-hum without the punch provided by hot peppers. All peppers contain the chemical component called capsaicin, which may play a role in killing cancer cells, inflammation relief, increased blood circulation, and helping with sinus infections. The amount of capsaicin determines how hot the pepper is. The heat level of peppers is measured in Scoville Heat Units, and can range from mild (Anaheim) to extremely hot (habanero).

1. Wearing plastic gloves, cut off top of the pepper.

2. Cut pepper in half lengthwise.

3. Remove the membrane and seeds with a paring knife. The seeds contain the most heat, so if you like heat, you can leave them in.

pineapples

Hawaii may be the first place you think of when you see a ripe pineapple, but this sweet, delicious fruit is actually native to the Caribbean and South America. It's a member of the bromeliad family (which is a tropical flower), and the single fruit is actually a series of small fruitlets that have fused together. Pineapple can be consumed fresh or juiced or made into ice cream, yogurt, and baked goods. Pineapple is high in Vitamin C, thiamin, and the trace mineral manganese. One medium pineapple (4 pounds) will yield about 4½ cups peeled and cubed pineapple.

1. Cut off the base and the top of the pineapple.

2. Slice off the rough sides.

3. Cut into large wedges. Slice off the fibrous core on the inside edge of each wedge.

plantains

Often referred to as "cooking bananas," plantains are always intended to be eaten cooked—usually as a side dish, much like a potato. Plantains are a starchier, less sweet variety of common yellow or "dessert bananas." They are very popular in the cooking of Latin America, Africa, and the Caribbean Islands. They are generally used when the skin is still green. If allowed to ripen, they take on a slightly sweet flavor and a soft, spongelike texture.

1. Cut off both ends of the plantain and score lengthwise.

2. Peel back the skin and cut into slices.

tomatillos

Sometimes referred to as the "Mexican tomato," tomatillos are a key ingredient in fresh and cooked Mexican and Central American green sauces. The tomatillo fruit is surrounded by an edible paperlike husk. The husk turns brown and the fruit can be several colors when ripe, including green, yellow, red, or purple. Tomatillos have a high pectin content, which gives them a sticky coating that should be rinsed off before using.

1. Peel back the papery husk. Rinse the tomatillos in water to remove the sticky coating.

selecting fresh vegetables

THESE CHARTS OFFER SPECIFIC GUIDELINES FOR SELECTING AND STORING A VARIETY OF FRESH VEGETABLES. IN GENERAL, CHOOSE VEGETABLES THAT ARE PLUMP, CRISP, BRIGHTLY COLORED, AND HEAVY FOR THEIR SIZE. AVOID ANY THAT ARE BRUISED, SHRIVELED, MOLDY, OR BLEMISHED.

Vegetable	Peak Season	How to Choose	How to Store
Asparagus	Available March through June with peak season in April and May; available year-round in some areas.	Choose crisp, firm, straight stalks with good color and compact, closed tips. If possible, select spears that are the same size for even cooking.	Wrap the bases of fresh asparagus spears in wet paper towels and place in a plastic bag in the refrigerator for up to 3 days.
Beans, green: snap or string	Available April through September; available year-round in some areas.	Select fresh beans that are brightly colored and crisp. Avoid those that are bruised, scarred, or rusty with brown spots or streaks. Bulging, leathery beans are old.	Refrigerate in a covered container for up to 5 days.
Beets	Available year-round with peak season from June through October.	Select small or medium beets; large beets tend to be pithy, tough, and less sweet.	Trim beet greens, leaving 1 to 2 inches of stem. Do not cut the long root. Store unwashed beets in an open container in the refrigerator for up to 1 week.
Bok choy	Available year-round.	Look for firm, white, bulblike bases with deep green leaves. Avoid soft spots on base or wilted, shriveled leaves.	Refrigerate in a plastic bag and use within 3 days.
Broccoli	Available year-round with peak season from October through May.	Look for firm stalks with tightly packed, deep green or purplish green heads. Avoid heads that are light green or yellowing.	Keep unwashed broccoli in a covered container in the refrigerator for up to 4 days.
Brussels sprouts	Available year-round with peak season from August through April.	Pick out the smaller sprouts that are vivid green; they will taste the sweetest. Large ones might be bitter.	Refrigerate in a covered container for up to 2 days.
Cabbage: green, napa, red, or savoy	Available year-round.	The head should feel heavy for its size, and its leaves should be unwithered, brightly colored, and free of brown spots.	Refrigerate in a covered container for up to 5 days.
Carrots	Available year-round.	Select straight, rigid, bright orange carrots without cracks.	Refrigerate in a plastic bag for up to 2 weeks.
Cauliflower	Available year-round.	Look for solid, heavy heads with bright green leaves. Avoid those with brown bruises, yellowed leaves, or speckled appearance.	Refrigerate in a covered container for up to 4 days.
Celery	Available year-round.	Look for crisp ribs that are firm, unwilted, and unblemished.	Refrigerate in a plastic bag or container for up to 2 weeks.
Cucumbers	Available year-round with peak season from late May through early September.	Select firm cucumbers without shriveled or soft spots. Edible wax sometimes is added to prevent moisture loss.	Keep salad cucumbers in refrigerator for up to 10 days. Pickling cucumbers should be picked and used the same day.
Eggplants	Available year-round with peak season from August through September.	Look for plump, glossy eggplants that have fresh-looking, mold-free caps. Skip any that are scarred or bruised.	Refrigerate whole eggplants for up to 2 days.
Fennel	Available October through April; available year-round in some areas.	Look for crisp, clean bulbs without brown spots or blemishes. Tops should be bright green and fresh looking.	Refrigerate, tightly wrapped, for up to 5 days.
Greens, cooking: beet, chard, collard, kale, mustard, turnip	Most available year-round with peak season in winter months; peak season for chard is during the summer months.	Look for crisp or tender leaves that are brightly or richly colored. Avoid wilted or yellowing leaves.	Cut away center stalk of kale leaves. Refrigerate most greens in plastic bag for up to 3 days; refrigerate mustard greens for up to 1 week.
Leeks	Available year-round.	Look for leeks that have clean white ends and fresh green tops.	Refrigerate, tightly wrapped, for up to 5 days.

Vegetable	Peak Season	How to Choose	How to Store
Mushrooms (all varieties)	Available year-round; morel mushrooms available April through June.	Mushrooms should be firm, fresh, plump, and bruise-free. Size is a matter of preference. Avoid spotted or slimy mushrooms.	Store unwashed mushrooms in the refrigerator for up to 2 days. A paper bag or, if packaged, the original packaging lets them breathe so they stay firm longer.
Okra	Available year-round with peak season from May through September.	Look for small, crisp, brightly colored pods without brown spots or blemishes. Avoid shriveled pods.	Refrigerate, tightly wrapped, for up to 3 days.
Onions (all varieties)	Variety determines availability. Some varieties, such as white, red, pearl, and boiling onions, are available year-round. Various sweet onion varieties, such as Vidalia and Walla Walla, are available on and off throughout the year.	Select dry bulb onions that are firm, free from blemishes, and not sprouting. They should have papery outer skins and short necks.	Keep in a cool, dry, well-ventilated place for several weeks.
Peas, pea pods	Peas: Available January through June with peak season from March through May. Pea pods: Available February through August.	Select fresh, crisp, brightly colored peas, snow peas, or sugar snap peas. Avoid shriveled pods or those with brown spots.	Store, tightly wrapped, in the refrigerator for up to 3 days.
Peppers: hot or sweet	Available year-round.	Fresh peppers, whether sweet or hot, should be brightly colored and have a good shape for the variety. Avoid shriveled, bruised, or broken peppers.	Refrigerate in a covered container for up to 5 days.
Potatoes	Available year-round.	Look for clean potatoes that have smooth, unblemished skins. They should be firm and have a shape that is typical for their variety. Avoid those that have green spots or are soft, moldy, or shriveled.	Store for several weeks in a dark, well-ventilated, cool place that is slightly humid but not wet. Do not refrigerate—potatoes tend to get sweet at cold temperatures.
Root vegetables: parsnips, rutabagas, or turnips	Available year-round. Parsnips: Peak season from November through March. Rutabagas: Peak season from September through March. Turnips: Peak season from October through March.	Choose vegetables that are smooth-skinned and heavy for their size. Sometimes parsnips, rutabagas, and turnips are covered with a wax coating to extend storage; cut off this coating before cooking.	Refrigerate for up to 2 weeks.
Spinach	Available year-round.	Leaves should be crisp and free of moisture. Avoid spinach with broken or bruised leaves.	Rinse leaves in cold water and thoroughly dry. Place the leaves in a storage container with a paper towel and refrigerate for up to 3 days.
Squash, winter	Some varieties available year-round with peak season from September through March.	Choose firm squash that are heavy for their size. Avoid those with soft spots.	Store whole squash in a cool, dry place for up to 2 months. Refrigerate cut squash, wrapped in plastic, for up to 4 days.
Sweet potatoes	Available year-round with peak season from October through January.	Choose small to medium smooth-skinned potatoes that are firm and free of soft spots.	Store in a cool, dry, dark place for up to 1 week.
Tomatoes	Available year-round with peak season from June through early September.	Pick well-shaped, plump, fairly firm tomatoes. Ripe tomatoes yield to slight pressure and smell like a tomato.	Store at room temperature for up to 3 days. Do not store tomatoes in the refrigerator because they lose their flavor.
Zucchini, summer squash	Some varieties available year-round with peak season from June through September.	It is almost impossible for tender-skinned zucchini to be blemish-free, but look for small ones that are firm and free of cuts and soft spots.	Refrigerate squash, tightly wrapped, for up to 5 days.

selecting fresh fruits

THESE CHARTS OFFER SPECIFIC GUIDELINES FOR SELECTING AND STORING A VARIETY OF FRESH FRUITS. IN GENERAL, LOOK FOR FRUITS THAT ARE PLUMP, TENDER, AND BRIGHT IN COLOR. FRUITS SHOULD BE HEAVY FOR THEIR SIZE AND FREE FROM MOLD, MILDEW, BRUISES, CUTS, OR OTHER BLEMISHES. SOME FRUITS ARE PICKED AND SHIPPED WHILE STILL FIRM, SO THEY MIGHT NEED ADDITIONAL RIPENING.

Fruit	Peak Season	How to Choose	How to Store
Apples	Available year-round with peak season September through November.	Select firm apples, free from bruises or soft spots. Apples are sold ready for eating. Select variety according to intended use.	Refrigerate for up to 6 weeks; store bulk apples in a cool, moist place. Don't store near foods with strong odors that can be absorbed.
Apricots	Available May through July.	Look for plump, fairly firm apricots with deep yellow or yellowish orange skin.	Ripen firm fruit in a small clean paper bag until it yields to gentle pressure and is golden in color. Refrigerate ripened fruit for up to 2 days.
Avocados	Available year-round.	Avoid bruised fruit with gouges or broken skin. Soft avocados can be used immediately (and are especially good for guacamole).	Ripen firm fruit in a small clean paper bag until it yields to gentle pressure in cradled hands. Store ripened fruit in the refrigerator for up to 3 days.
Bananas	Available year-round.	Choose bananas at any stage of ripeness, from green to yellow.	Ripen at room temperature until they have a bright yellow color. Overripe bananas are brown.
Berries	Blackberries: Available June through August. Blueberries: Available late May through October. Boysenberries: Available late June through early August. Raspberries: Available year-round with peak season from May through September. Strawberries: Available year-round with peak season from April through June.	If picking your own, select berries that separate easily from their stems.	Refrigerate berries in a single layer, loosely covered, for up to 2 days. Rinse just before using.
Cantaloupe	Available year-round with peak season from June through September.	Select cantaloupe that has a delicate, sweet, aromatic scent; look for cream-color netting over rind that is yellowish green or gray. Melon should feel heavy for its size.	Ripen in a small clean paper bag. Refrigerate ripened, whole melon up to 4 days. Refrigerate cut fruit in a covered container or tightly wrapped for up to 2 days.
Carambolas (star fruit)	Available late August through February.	Look for firm, shiny-skinned golden fruit. Some browning on the edge of the fins is natural and does not affect the taste.	Ripen in a small clean paper bag. Refrigerate ripened fruit in a covered container or tightly wrapped up to 1 week.
Cherries	Sweet: Available May through August with peak season in June and July. Tart: Available June through August with peak season in June and July.	Select firm, brightly colored fruit.	Refrigerate in a covered container for 2 to 3 days.
Cranberries	Available October through December with peak season in November.	Fruit is ripe when sold. Avoid soft, shriveled, or bruised cranberries.	Refrigerate for up to 4 weeks or freeze for up to 1 year.
Grapefruit	Available year-round.	Choose fully colored grapefruit with a nicely rounded shape. Juicy grapefruit will be heavy for its size.	Refrigerate for up to 2 weeks.
Grapes	Available year-round.	Look for plump grapes without bruises, soft spots, or mold. Bloom (a frosty white cast) is typical and doesn't affect quality.	Refrigerate in a covered container for up to 1 week.
Honeydew melon	Available year-round with peak season from June through September.	Choose one that is firm and a creamy yellow color with a sweet, aromatic scent. Avoid wet, dented, bruised, or cracked fruit.	Ripen in a small clean paper bag. Refrigerate ripened whole melon up to 4 days. Refrigerate cut fruit in a covered container or tightly wrapped for up to 3 days.

Fruit	Peak Season	How to Choose	How to Store
Kiwifruits	Available year-round.	Choose fruit that is free of wrinkles, bruises, and soft spots.	Ripen firm fruit in a small, celan paper bag until skin yields to gentle pressure. Refrigerate for up to 1 week.
Lemons, limes	Available year-round.	Look for firm, well-shaped fruit with smooth, brightly colored skin. Avoid fruit with shriveled skin.	Refrigerate for up to 2 weeks.
Mangoes	Available April through September with peak season from June through July.	Look for fully colored fruit that smells fruity and feels fairly firm when pressed.	Ripen firm fruit in a small, clean paper bag and refrigerate for up to 5 days.
Oranges	Available year-round.	Choose oranges that are firm and heavy for their size. Brown specks or a slight greenish tinge on the surface of an orange will not affect the eating quality.	Refrigerate for up to 2 weeks.
Papayas	Available year-round.	Choose fruit that is at least half yellow and feels somewhat soft when pressed. The skin should be smooth.	Ripen in a small, clean paper bag until yellow. Refrigerate in a covered container for 1 to 2 days.
Peaches, nectarines	Peaches: Available May through September. Nectarines: Available May through September with peak season in July and August.	Look for fruit with a golden yellow skin and no tinges of green. Ripe fruit should yield slightly to gentle pressure.	Ripen in a small, clean paper bag. Refrigerate ripened fruit for up to 5 days.
Pears	Available year-round.	Skin color is not always an indicator of ripeness because the color of some varieties does not change much as the pears ripen. Look for pears without bruises or cuts. Choose a variety according to intended use.	Ripen in a small, clean paper bag until skin yields to gentle pressure at the stem end. Refrigerate ripened fruit for several days.
Pineapples	Available year-round with peak season from March through July.	Look for a plump pineapple with a sweet, aromatic smell. It should be slightly soft to the touch, heavy for its size, and have deep green leaves. Avoid those with soft spots.	Refrigerate for up to 2 days. Cut pineapple lasts a few more days if placed in a tightly covered container and refrigerated.
Plantains	Available year-round.	Choose undamaged plantains. Slight bruises are acceptable because the skin is tough enough to protect the fruit. Choose plantains at any stage of ripeness, from green to dark brown or black, depending on intended use.	Ripen in a small, clean paper bag. Color will change from green to yellow-brown to black. Black plantains are fully ripe. The starchy fruit must be cooked before eating.
Plums	Available May through October with peak season in June and July.	Find firm, plump, well-shaped fresh plums. Each should give slightly when gently pressed. Bloom (light gray cast) on the skin is natural and doesn't affect quality.	Ripen firm fruit in a small, clean paper bag until skin yields to gentle pressure. Refrigerate ripened fruit for up to 3 days.
Rhubarb	Available February through June with peak season from April through June.	Look for crisp stalks that are firm and tender. Avoid rhubarb that looks wilted or has very thick stalks.	Wrap stalks tightly in plastic wrap and refrigerate for up to 5 days.
Watermelon	Available May through September with peak season from mid-June through late August.	Choose watermelon that has a hard, smooth rind and is heavy for its size. Avoid wet, dented, bruised, or cracked fruit.	Watermelon does not ripen after it is picked. Refrigerate whole melon for up to 4 days. Refrigerate cut fruit in a covered container or tightly wrapped for up to 3 days.

index

Page numbers in italics indicate illustrations

metric information

THE CHARTS ON THIS PAGE PROVIDE A GUIDE FOR CONVERTING MEASUREMENTS FROM THE U.S. CUSTOMARY SYSTEM, WHICH IS USED THROUGHOUT THIS BOOK, TO THE METRIC SYSTEM.

product differences

Most of the ingredients called for in the recipes in this book are available in most countries. However, some are known by different names. Here are some common American ingredients and their possible counterparts:

- Sugar (white) is granulated, fine granulated, or castor sugar.
- Powdered sugar is icing sugar.
- All-purpose flour is enriched, bleached or unbleached white household flour. When self-rising flour is used in place of all-purpose flour in a recipe that calls for leavening, omit the leavening agent (baking soda or baking powder) and salt.
- Light-color corn syrup is golden syrup.
- Cornstarch is cornflour.
- Baking soda is bicarbonate of soda.
- Vanilla or vanilla extract is vanilla essence.
- Green, red, or yellow sweet peppers are capsicums or bell peppers.
- Golden raisins are sultanas.

volume and weight

The United States traditionally uses cup measures for liquid and solid ingredients. The chart below shows the approximate imperial and metric equivalents. If you are accustomed to weighing solid ingredients, the following approximate equivalents will be helpful.

- 1 cup butter, castor sugar, or rice = 8 ounces = ½ pound = 250 grams
- 1 cup flour = 4 ounces = ¼ pound = 125 grams
- 1 cup icing sugar = 5 ounces = 150 grams

Canadian and U.S. volume for a cup measure is 8 fluid ounces (237 ml), but the standard metric equivalent is 250 ml. 1 British imperial cup is 10 fluid ounces.

In Australia, 1 tablespoon equals 20 ml, and there are 4 teaspoons in the Australian tablespoon.

Spoon measures are used for smaller amounts of ingredients. Although the size of the tablespoon varies slightly in different countries, for practical purposes and for recipes in this book, a straight substitution is all that's necessary. Measurements made using cups or spoons always should be level unless stated otherwise.

Common Weight Range Replacements

Imperial / U.S.	Metric
½ ounce	15 g
1 ounce	25 g or 30 g
4 ounces (¼ pound)	115 g or 125 g
8 ounces (½ pound)	225 g or 250 g
16 ounces (1 pound)	450 g or 500 g
1¼ pounds	625 g
1½ pounds	750 g
2 pounds or 2¼ pounds	1,000 g or 1 Kg

Oven Temperature Equivalents

Fahrenheit Setting	Celsius Setting	Gas Setting
300°F	150°C	Gas Mark 2 (very low)
325°F	160°C	Gas Mark 3 (low)
350°F	180°C	Gas Mark 4 (moderate)
375°F	190°C	Gas Mark 5 (moderate)
400°F	200°C	Gas Mark 6 (hot)
425°F	220°C	Gas Mark 7 (hot)
450°F	230°C	Gas Mark 8 (very hot)
475°F	240°C	Gas Mark 9 (very hot)
500°F	260°C	Gas Mark 10 (extremely hot)
Broil	Broil	Grill

*Electric and gas ovens may be calibrated using celsius. However, for an electric oven, increase celsius setting 10 to 20 degrees when cooking above 160°C.
For convection or forced air ovens (gas or electric), lower the temperature setting 25°F/10°C when cooking at all heat levels.

Baking Pan Sizes

Imperial / U.S.	Metric
9×1½-inch round cake pan	22- or 23×4-cm (1.5 L)
9×1½-inch pie plate	22- or 23×4-cm (1 L)
8×8×2-inch square cake pan	20×5-cm (2 L)
9×9×2-inch square cake pan	22- or 23×4.5-cm (2.5 L)
11×7×1½-inch baking pan	28×17×4-cm (2 L)
2-quart rectangular baking pan	30×19×4.5-cm (3 L)
13×9×2-inch baking pan	34×22×4.5-cm (3.5 L)
15×10×1-inch jelly roll pan	40×25×2-cm
9×5×3-inch loaf pan	23×13×8-cm (2 L)
2-quart casserole	2 L

U.S. / Standard Metric Equivalents

⅛ teaspoon = 0.5 ml	
¼ teaspoon = 1 ml	
½ teaspoon = 2 ml	
1 teaspoon = 5 ml	
1 tablespoon = 15 ml	
2 tablespoons = 25 ml	
¼ cup = 2 fluid ounces = 50 ml	
⅓ cup = 3 fluid ounces = 75 ml	
½ cup = 4 fluid ounces = 125 ml	
⅔ cup = 5 fluid ounces = 150 ml	
¾ cup = 6 fluid ounces = 175 ml	
1 cup = 8 fluid ounces = 250 ml	
2 cups = 1 pint = 500 ml	
1 quart = 1 litre	